Effective Retail Security
Protecting the Bottom Line

**A PRACTICAL GUIDE TO RETAIL LOSS
PREVENTION AND SECURITY TECHNIQUES
AND PROCEDURES**

Effective Retail Security
Protecting the Bottom Line

**A PRACTICAL GUIDE TO RETAIL LOSS
PREVENTION AND SECURITY TECHNIQUES
AND PROCEDURES**

DENNY VAN MAANENBERG

BUTTERWORTH
HEINEMANN
AUSTRALIA

Australia
Butterworth–Heinemann, 18 Salmon Street, Port Melbourne, Vic 3207

Singapore
Butterworth–Heinemann, Asia

United Kingdom
Butterworth–Heinemann, Ltd, Oxford

USA
Butterworth–Heinemann, Newton

National Library of Australia Cataloguing-in-Publication entry

Van Maanenberg, Denny.
  Effective retail security: protecting the bottom line.

  ISBN 0 7506 8923 4.

  1. Retail trade — Security measures. 2. Shoplifting —
  Prevention. 3. Employee theft. I. Title.

658.473

Illustrations by Johannes.

Layout and typeset by Editorial Connection.

Printed in Australia by Southwood Press Pty Ltd.

Table of Contents

CASE STUDIES

Foreword

Retail crime is serious crime. It costs the Australian community at least $2 billion each year and ranges from juvenile shop stealing through to sophisticated fraud, professional theft and armed robbery.

Those affected by retail crime include shopkeepers and their staff, shareholders of the larger retailers, consumers, taxpayers and offenders and their families. Government resources in the form of police, courts and correctional facilities are involved in dealing with the consequences of retail crime. In some cases, the level of crime has forced retailers to close their operations. It is therefore important that retailers seriously address the problem and take appropriate steps to protect their livelihood.

The most cost-effective way to tackle retail crime is through prevention. Commonsense protective measures, including staff training, control mechanisms, good systems and disciplines, supported by technology can provide an in-depth defence against criminal activities.

Development of strategies to prevent retail crime requires a good understanding of the potential exposures that exist within the retail environment. It also requires a good understanding of those strategies that have been successful and those that offer a good return on investment.

Effective Retail Security provides an excellent insight into the costs and effects of retail crime. More importantly, it provides a useful guide to retailers who want to improve their bottom line through reducing losses due to crime. I believe that *Effective Retail Security* makes a very positive contribution to the cause of retail loss prevention.

John Frame, APM, BA, DipCrim
Chair
Retailers' Council of Australia Loss Prevention Committee

Dedication

To my father
for his simple and honest values

To Norm
for his gentle and compassionate nature

To Glen
for his unquenchable enthusiasm

Acknowledgments

No publication of any significance is the sole product of any one person and this book is no exception. Researching the contents for this book has required many hours of reading relevant texts, going over old files, verifying concepts, bouncing ideas off industry colleagues and generally making a complete nuisance of myself in the process.

I am grateful for the encouragement and assistance given to me by many professional colleagues and, in particular, I would like to thank Colin Judge and Ray Brown for implanting the idea of this book, Andrew Wilson for his general retailing advice, Michael Day for his levelling influence, and John Rice for his retail loss prevention advice and for the use of some of his ideas. I would also like to thank my New Zealand colleagues Bruce Couper and Trevor Morley for their local advice and Barry Hellberg from the Retail & Wholesale Merchants Association of New Zealand Inc. for his overview of the local retailing scene.

I am also indebted to Michael O'Neill from the National Trauma Clinic for his material on post-traumatic stress.

For the preparation of lists, tables and indexes, formatting, researching and checking grammatical correctness, I cannot forget Jenny Gibbons, Julia McKenzie, Sharon Paull and Therese Ryan for their untiring attention to detail. Special thanks must also go to Helena Klijn, my commissioning editor at Butterworth–Heinemann whose friendly voice was always a great source of encouragement. I would also like to thank two of my brothers. Johannes deserves thanks for his wonderful illustrations. His cartoons bring a touch of humour and he captured the essence of what was required in a delightful manner. For his professional advice on matters relating to retail occupational health and safety issues, my brother Tony deserves my heartfelt appreciation.

But without a doubt, my main supporter in this work has been my wife Jennifer. Her many hours of proof reading the drafts were a great sacrifice and I especially thank her for her patience. There is no doubt a considerable number of friends, work colleagues, professional associates and other people whom I have failed to acknowledge by name, but who have assisted in the production of this work in one way or another. I thank you all for your guidance, helpful criticism, and support. Without a doubt the work has benefited from your input.

Preface

Retailing is probably one of the world's largest industries and perhaps even the oldest. In Australia, for example, figures available from the Australian Bureau of Statistics reveal that the industry employs over one million people. This represents 13.5% of Australia's total employment population. Figures also reveal that in Australia, there are some 172,000 shopfronts with a recorded $108.3 billion turnover (Madden, 1993, pp. 1–2). These figures indicate the size of the retail industry. More than 1 in 10 of our employment population works in retail — certainly a sizeable workforce. It is not surprising then that retail practitioners are expected to acquire the patience of a saint, the logic and rationale of a philosopher and be skilled negotiators and investigators to handle the many facets of human behaviour that the industry encounters.

Retailing is exciting. It is an industry in which high personal goals can be achieved. Retailing supports other major industries such as manufacturing, textiles, primary producers, growers, market gardeners, transportation, marketing, advertising and real estate, and it employs just about every known trade and profession. Retailing is not just about sales. It's about people, about customer service, about market share and about profitability, but the bottom line remains sales, sales and more sales. There is nothing wrong with this philosophy, and it is easy to get excited when listening to the enthusiasm of sales staff relating end-of-day figures, that budgets have been smashed and product is going out the door faster than it can be resupplied. Retailing like this is exciting. It is a different story however when, at the end of the accounting period, stocktakes are finally completed, the figures are in, and suddenly all those sales and the healthy bottom line that had been posted for the period, have been eroded, in some cases drastically, by the most hated word in the retail industry, the ubiquitous 'shrinkage'. It is at this point when managers are sacked, sales supervisors demoted, knee-jerk policy and procedures are implemented, the ancestry of loss prevention managers is questioned and general panic ensues. Somewhere between sales and shrinkage, there lies a huge void, a black hole that retailers tend to shun and rarely wish to acknowledge. To most, it is alien to them. Retailers thrive on positives, motivation and sales. Shrinkage is negative, demotivating and means losses. For retailers, shrinkage is the dark side of retailing.

1 The Question of Retail Loss

CHAPTER OBJECTIVES
1. To examine the fundamentals of retail loss.
2. To acknowledge the three operating principles of retailing.
3. To assess the extent and cause of retail loss.
4. To examine systems for the calculation of loss data.
5. To determine responsibilities for the management of loss.

THE FUNDAMENTALS OF RETAIL LOSS

Maximising profit is fundamental to any retail operation. No prospective retailer, shop owner, stall holder or other trader would set up a retail business with the deliberate intention of making a loss. Certainly there are rules and principles that any business needs to follow to make a profit but, for now, we will consider that maximising profits provides benefits at three main levels:

- retailers;
- retailers' employees; and
- retailers' customers.

Maximising profits allows retailers to obtain a reasonable return for themselves or for their shareholders on their investments. It allows retailers to grow, expand, maintain market profile, improve systems, expand products and improve store appearance. For employees, the maximisation of profits creates more jobs, provides for career paths, promotion, ongoing training, job satisfaction and, in some cases, travel, incentive rewards, peer-group recognition and financial security. For customers, the maximisation of profits provides a greater shopping range, easier shopping, label recognition, generation of greater comfort zones, value for money, and the development of the customer's trust in the retailer's product.

The Three Major Operating Principles

For any business to be successful, it must first lay down operating or business plans. Business and operating plans must follow closely three major operating principles:

- to generate and maximise sales;
- to minimise and control costs; and
- to minimise and control losses.

How can retailers ensure that sales are generated and maximised? How can they minimise and control costs and how can they minimise and control losses? Answers to these questions include providing high profile locations, prime time advertising, popular and quality products, after-sales service, competitive pricing and excellent customer-service philosophies. They include maintaining proficient selling skills, expert merchandising, controlled stock management, functional policy and procedures, control of wages, basic security procedures and managing the correct administrative chain. The retail operating formula is the basis of good retailing. In fact, it is the keystone of the industry. Nevertheless, it is important to understand the operating principles and the precedence each principle has over the other. On occasions, one event may occur which will have a higher degree of priority. The function of this book, however, is not to examine all three basic operating principles, but to focus on the control and administration of losses, why they happen, where they happen, when they happen, how they happen and, most importantly, what to do about them.

THE EXTENT OF RETAIL LOSS

So how much do retailers actually lose? To answer this, we need to look at Australian and overseas research. There have been some excellent publications relating to retail theft in Australia such as Dennis Challinger's book, *Stop Stealing from our Shops: Retail Theft in Australia*. Challinger gives some insight into loss caused by theft and other causes, but admits that, 'The total losses suffered by Australian retailers as a result of criminal activity are not known' (Challinger, 1988, 'Foreword').

In general terms, loss prevention specialists in Australia estimate a 2% loss (calculated at retail value of goods). These industry estimates have generally been proven correct. In 1994, the Australian Institute of Criminology released the results of their 'Crimes Against Business Survey' (Walker, 1994, p. 111). The results indicated a similar figure of approximately 1.97% of gross sales. Based on current retailing figures, retailers throughout Australia could be losing up to $2.17 billion annually (Australian Bureau of Statistics retail trade figures, Jan–Dec 1994).

What does all this mean? Consider the following. The local milkbar has an annual turnover of $150,000. That figure represents the total takings for all goods sold in a financial period prior to any deductions for costs of goods purchased, wages, rent, tax etc. If the milkbar proprietor has an average loss of 2% of the value of annual turnover, the losses would amount to $3,000. If the retailer has a turnover of $850,000, the losses would amount to $17,000. For retailers with sales in excess of $1,000,000, the losses would amount to $20,000 for every million dollars worth of sales. Some might suggest that the 2% average is acceptable, and that 2% of gross is also acceptable, yet when this figure is calculated before outgoings, it then becomes quite apparent that these 'shrinkage' losses can be devastating. The failure to control and minimise losses means a direct loss of profit. Unprofitable retailing simply leads to:

- 'down sizing' (a term that describes a general reduction in operations to reduce expenditure);
- reduction of product range;
- fewer sales;
- an increase in the cost of sales;
- the eventual loss of jobs; and
- forced closure and possible bankruptcy.

The cost of running the business represented about 90% of total sales of $1,000,000, the resulting net profit of $100,000 is reduced by a huge 20% to only $80,000. When viewed in this light, retailers will acknowledge some incentive to begin loss-prevention programs.

Overseas Loss Comparisons

So how do the Australian data compare with the overseas figures. Readers should be cautious with the survey data, as the figures are merely a guide and should only be used for general comparison purposes. Surveys such as these represent only a small fraction of the retail population and often do not reflect each of the retail categories accurately enough to be truly representative. Complete and accurate surveys are rare because, in particular, they are expensive to conduct and the information provided is based only on what retailers are willing to reveal. For a complete and thorough interpretation, readers should refer to the original survey data (see Figure 1.1).

The values shown in Figure 1.1 indicate that Australian retailers are below major international averages in terms of managing financial loss. Even if we take an average of the four Western countries of 1.4%, Australian retailers still appear to fall short of an acceptable figure. Australian retailers lose over $2 billion annually to known and unknown losses. That is nearly $6 million per day.

New Zealand Retail Loss

In New Zealand, the figures are apparently worse. The information from New Zealand has not been included in the above data as they do not result from any valid survey. The information is largely a result of 'guesstimates' from industry sources and, therefore, it would be inappropriate to compare these with the results above. Discussions with representatives of the Retail and Wholesale Merchants Association of New Zealand Inc., suggest that no formal studies have ever been undertaken to determine the actual retail loss figure in New Zealand.

At the time of writing, New Zealand had annual retail sales of about $NZ34 billion. The Merchants Association suggests that $NZ1 million are lost through shop stealing on a daily basis. This amounts to a financial loss of approximately $NZ300 million per year. These figures are estimates based, in part, on police statistical data on known shop theft and employee theft. They also stem from known information collated by loss prevention and security practitioners employed by New Zealand businesses to combat shrinkage losses.

The general theory in New Zealand suggests that some 3–5% of gross annual sales are lost to shrinkage causes. The $NZ300-million loss by shop stealers only equates with approximately 0.9% of gross annual sales. If that 0.9% is attributable to customer dishonesty alone, as indicated by the figures provided by the Merchants Association, then other losses (the remaining 2–4%), caused by administrative and human error, and employee malpractice in New Zealand could amount to a large financial loss of $NZ680 million to $NZ1.2 billion.

The major concern with these estimated figures, whether from the United States, Canada, the United Kingdom, Australia or New Zealand, is that it is difficult to establish if they relate to just financial loss, economic loss or to both. An assumption might need to be made that the given figures relate only to known financial losses. If that assumption is correct, then the value of the unstated economic loss remains quite unknown.

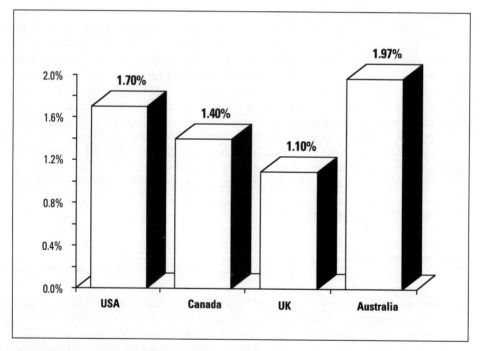

Figure 1.1. Overseas retail loss comparisons

(Source: USA — Berlin, 1994, p. 1; Canada — Berlin, 1994, No. V, p. 1; UK — Braithwaite & Fuller, 1992, p. 4; Australia — Walker, 1994, p. 111.)

THE MAIN CAUSES OF RETAIL LOSS

It is generally accepted that the causes of retail loss can be attributed to one or more of the following:

- human or administrative error;
- customer dishonesty; and
- employee malpractice.

Human and administrative error refers to the simple or complex errors that occur through the natural processes of human behaviour.

Customer dishonesty takes in all shop stealing, price swapping, fraudulent refunding, fraudulent compensation claims and any other deviant behaviour causing a financial or economic loss to the organisation by non-employees.

Employee malpractice includes theft of stock, theft of cash, fraudulent register manipulation and a host of other occurrences that range from simple breaches of company policy to hard-core criminality.

All three areas are discussed in greater detail in later chapters.

The loss figure attributable to each cause is often the basis for debate among loss prevention practitioners and retailers generally. Some assumptions can be made from official police statistical data and loss prevention data supplied by major retail corporations on the number of shop stealers apprehended, the value of recovered property, the number of retail employees charged with offences, the value of stock losses recorded and other data. However, available data is often only as good as the input provided. What is of more concern is that much of the required data on losses is unavailable. Retailers need more empirical information that will provide them with the tools and knowledge necessary to develop prevention strategies.

Retail loss occurs as a result of human or administrative error, customer dishonesty or employee malpractice. The majority of loss identified in any retail operating environment can be attributed to one of these three causes. Some authorities suggest that vendor theft is another major factor in retail loss and should be added as a fourth category. Vendor theft is limited to those non-store employees who enter shops under contract to refill specific display stands with product. Product is wide ranging and includes cosmetic jewellery, sunglasses, supermarket items and any other product sold but not managed or controlled by the store. Often is the case where vendors might short-stock the display or over-invoice the delivery. Certainly, vendor theft is of concern, but to add it as a fourth category, overemphasises its relevance to the retail loss problem.

Distribution of Loss Estimates

To provide some information on loss estimates, three separate sources were reviewed to provide some indicators on the origin, cause and distribution of loss. Challinger (1988) provides some estimates in Retail Theft in Australia. He does warn, however, of generating average figures because these do not take into account the variation between the types of retail stores. (There are some 50 standard (Australian & New Zealand Standard Industrial Classification) retail codes, ranging from supermarkets to recreational retailing, and all are inherently different.) Challinger suggests that

54% of all losses are internal, although he places more emphasis on losses due to customer dishonesty than on the other two elements.

Neill (1981), author of the Australian publication *Modern Retail Risk Management*, blames 75% of all losses on internal influences, human and administrative error and employee malpractice.

Berman and Evans (1986), in their book, *Retail Management — A Strategic Approach*, agree with Neill. They also apportion more than 70% of total losses to internal losses. If all three sets of data are grouped to provide a general figure, the figures suggest that up to 67% of financial losses could be attributable to the deliberate, dishonest, careless or negligent action of retail employees (see Figure 1.2).

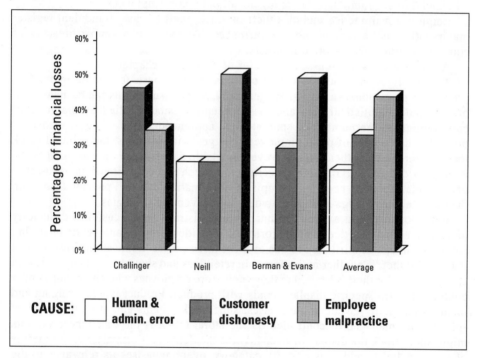

Figure 1.2. Distribution of retail loss estimates

This rather simple application has established that at the very least, between 54% and 75% of all retail loss could be internally related. Although customer dishonesty features significantly in the overall loss figure, it would appear that retailers lose more from internal sources than they do from any customer dishonesty. However, retailers need to be careful in applying these figures to their operating environment because these figures are generic only. They reflect the overall retail scene and do not necessarily apply to each individual retailer. One retailer might have an exceptionally good internal stocktake and an administration system that has virtually eliminated administrative errors. Another retailer may have excellent proactive shop-stealing prevention programs, and another may have minimised opportunities for employee malpractice through a well-developed training and awareness prevention strategy. It could also be that some retailers enjoy low retail loss levels due to the implementation of sound loss prevention principles. These retailers reap the benefits of their initiatives and are at the low end of the retail loss scale.

On the other hand, there are retailers who have virtually no prevention strategies and whose retail loss is affected by all of the loss causes. Some might even record retail losses of 10% or more. It is also common for some retailers to have no idea as to what their retail losses are. They operate on the basis of their known profit (or loss) margins only and do not research, analyse or attempt to increase their profitability through the use of modern stock keeping and accounting control methods.

In summary, using the research figures expressed in Figure 1.2 as a guide, retailers can make some cautious comparisons that internal sources could account for up to 67% of retail loss with external causes accounting for the remaining 33% (see Figure 1.3).

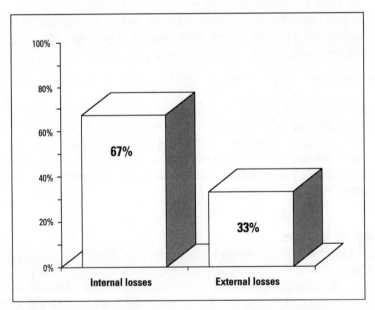

Figure 1.3. Internal and external retail loss comparisons

Once again, it is stressed that these figures may be subjective for the reasons previously stated, and further research is required to obtain more reliable and accurate data applicable to a particular retail operation.

THE TYPES OF RETAIL LOSS

Retailers throughout the industry should be aware that their businesses are subject to major financial loss if the potential for loss remains unchecked. Although this is stating the obvious, retailers need to know what hazards they are facing, what factors have the potential to cause loss and why. This is important in understanding the factors involved in retail losses stemming from human and administrative errors, customer dishonesty and employee malpractice. Losses from these areas need to be scrutinised further and can be categorised into one of two types of retail loss. But first, retail loss itself needs to be defined.

Definition of Retail Loss

Retail loss is defined here as:

> **RETAIL LOSS**
>
> A known or unknown retail loss results from a direct natural disaster, a careless, negligent or criminal action which generates a direct or indirect financial or economic loss for the organisation and which is caused through either internal or external origins and one which is not expected or usually budgeted for.

The key to this definition can be found in the last few words, 'not expected or usually budgeted for'. This definition covers all the various contingencies of retail loss and would include internal or external stock loss, asset loss, information loss and any other loss which has the potential to create financial or economic damage to the organisation generally.

Unexpected Losses

In the pure sense of effective retail security, the loss control management process examines losses that have not been budgeted for. Losses associated with poor seasonal sales figures and mark-downs are not usually within the context of known or unknown retail loss. In essence, the retail loss discussed in this book is generally one caused through carelessness, negligence, criminality or just plain apathy. The loss, therefore, is one which is unexpected, not budgeted for, and generally not covered by insurance.

The following is a list of occurrences that may result in a loss that is unexpected and/or unbudgeted for:

- theft of stock;
- theft of cash;
- theft of company assets;

- theft of staff personal property;
- refund fraud;
- short-changing customers;
- register manipulation;
- false petty-cash claims;
- under-ringing sales for friends and relatives;
- not recording sales;
- staff discount abuse;
- theft of time;
- sabotage of merchandise through product contamination or disruption;
- misuse of telephones; and
- poor performance due to alcohol or drug abuse.

Although this list is not exhaustive, it highlights the fact that the potential for retail loss to occur in any uncontrolled environment is enormous. Many retailers tend to blame shop stealers for all their retail loss woes. However, the opportunities for carelessness, negligence and criminality are far more prevalent for employees than they are for customers. Far more opportunities exist for employees to steal than they do for the shop stealer. The many opportunities that exist for employees as listed above supports this claim.

Naturally Occurring Losses

There often appears some confusion about whether naturally occurring wastage or losses recorded for mark-downs is included in the retail loss figure. Should natural wastage, such as the dumping of expired 'use by date' perishable items (for example, fruit and vegetables), be regarded as a retail loss? Or should the value of the wastage be written off as an operational expense? In most instances, the latter is the case. This type of loss is not really defined as a retail loss because most produce retailers set the selling price of the perishables to include a cost factor covering the cost of wastage. This naturally increases the price of produce for customers. To remain competitive, there is real incentive for produce department managers to manage and keep the costs of wastage to a minimum to maximise the opportunities to sell as much as possible of their available produce.

Let's look at another example. The same rationale would apply to the majority of mark-downs. If, for example, a retail buyer introduces 100 pairs of new shoes as a new line and the cost price is $25.00 for each pair of shoes, the buyer may calculate that for the first two months, 60% of the range will sell at its maximum selling price of $50.00. After that, sales will slow, so the shoes will be marked down to $40.00. After another month, the shoes are further reduced to $30.00 to clear space for additional lines. So, in calculating potential sales, a buyer might use that formula to forecast a profit of $1,900.00:

EXAMPLE

Original selling price:	60 x $50.00 = $3,000.00
1st mark down:	20 x $40.00 = $800.00
2nd mark down:	20 x $30.00 = $600.00
Total sales:	$4,400.00
Less the cost of initial purchase:	100 x $25.00 = $2,500.00
Gross profit	$1,900.00

Thus the calculation would be as follows:

Sales:	$4,400.00
Costs:	$2,500.00
Gross profit:	$1,900.00

The gross profit, of course, would be a lot more if the shoes proved popular and all were sold at $50.00. And this is just the point — if all the shoes were sold at $50.00, the sales would have been $5,000.00 not $4,400.00. You could ask whether the loss of the balance ($600.00) is a retail loss. However, the answer would be 'no', because the selling price included provision for mark-downs.

These two examples would not be defined as a retail loss because both the wastage and the mark-downs were expected and, therefore, budgeted for. It should also be borne in mind that retailing operations can be as different and individual as retailing itself. In this book, the focus remains on retail losses that result from unexpected or unbudgeted sources

Financial and Economic Losses

Financial and economic losses could be regarded as two separate issues, but both need to be understood from a loss-control point of view. By financial loss, a specific dollar amount is referred to. For example, if a burglary committed on a store results in a stock loss of $25,000 (insurance pays all but a $1,000 excess), repairs to damage caused by the burglary equals $2,300 and other incidentals (cost of casual staff, restocking etc.) equal $1,000, the financial loss to the organisation would be $4,300.

Economic loss, on the other hand, could be intangible, yet one that has the potential to do harm on the profitability of the company. An example might be the theft of marketing information which is sold to a competitor and then used to the competitor's advantage generating an economic loss to the victim. The distribution of a seasonal catalogue one week before that of the competitor, showing similar products which are slightly cheaper, effectively denies sales to the competitor. There is no tangible amount of money actually lost, but it ultimately has the potential to create a massive loss in sales and profitability.

The same would apply in the event of an unfair dismissal of an employee. Any resultant adverse publicity might not cause a set dollar loss, but if customers responded to the adverse publicity and stayed away from the retailer in droves, the resulting economic loss would certainly affect the profitability of the organisation.

Known and Unknown Losses

A military strategist knows that to fight and win battles, the enemy must be known. The same rule applies in managing retail loss. The enemy that retailers face is both financial and economic loss. To be able to determine appropriate strategies to deal with retail losses, specific types of loss must be categorised. Research and experience suggests that retailers are generally exposed to two types of losses: known losses and unknown losses.

Known Losses

Examples of known losses may include cash register shortages, known thefts by customers and employees, credit card fraud, burglary, misuse of telephones, instances of armed robbery and losses caused through natural disasters such as fire, flood and earthquake. A known loss can be defined as:

A loss to which a cause can be attributed, one which is identified as it occurs, or is identified shortly after the occurrence.

Unknown Losses

An unknown loss, on the other hand, could be defined as:

> Any discrepancy between the recorded book value of stock (calculated at either cost or retail) and the recorded theoretical levels of stock, calculated through stocktake or audit.

Examples of unknown losses may include stock loss through undetected shop stealing, theft of cash through fraudulent refunding of stock by employees and, of course, simple human and administrative errors such as unrecorded mark-downs and staff discounts.

Comparison of Known and Unknown Losses

Both known and unknown losses have the potential to do great financial damage to a retailing business. The timely discovery of losses aids the recovery and investigative process. In the case of known losses, the value of loss is known almost immediately. The cause of the loss is also identified and therefore proactive measures are more easily put in place than for unknown causes of loss. For example, to prevent burglary, locks are put on doors, all cash is cleared to the bank, and alarm systems are usually installed. This is also largely true for other known loss areas. Controls are put in place to minimise the known loss such as credit card checks, protection against cheque offenders, and fire extinguishers for the possibility of fire.

Because the focus on the prevention of known loss is high, the opportunities for known losses to occur can be largely minimised. This is not necessarily the case for unknown losses, because losses of this nature are exactly that — unknown. There is no direct focus, and therefore loss causes become a lot more difficult to analyse.

Shrinkage

'Shrinkage' is a popular term widely used by the retail community which means 'becomes smaller' or 'becomes of less dimensions'. Thoughts may immediately spring to mind of garments shrinking after a wash and that analogy is not entirely incorrect. Shrinkage in retailing is, typically, a lessening of value. Shrinkage is also known simply as 'stock loss'. However, there is still some confusion about the term: Does shrinkage describe a known or an unknown loss? Does shrinkage extend beyond just the loss of stock calculated at the time of stocktake? Shrinkage certainly includes financial loss, but does it include economic loss?

Experience suggests that the term 'shrinkage' is applied equally to both known and unknown losses. However, how it is specifically used is varied. Shrinkage may or not be applied to loss caused by armed robbery, burglary, unauthorised telephone calls and so on. It would appear that shrinkage is often referred to as any financial loss — but is this correct?

While no real precise definition of the term shrinkage seems to exist, the popular usage of the term will continue to create some confusion. 'Shrinkage' is probably not the most appropriate term to use, partly because it fails to adequately summarise the topic. Given that there is some confusion, retailers need to be more descriptive in highlighting this multi-million dollar problem. Retail shrinkage loss is financial loss and, rather than confuse issues, the terms 'retail loss', 'known loss' and 'unknown loss' will be used in this book.

FORECASTING LOSSES

Forecasting losses is like trying to predict the future. Assumptions can be made as to the likely cause of events based on previous experiences, but the reality is simply that losses are difficult to estimate. Although there have been some attempts to provide a means of forecasting known and unknown loss in a retail environment, there is still no system to ascertain accurate data. Formulae have been designed that relate to the number of known apprehensions, the average value of merchandise stolen, general customer flow and ratio of shop stealers to genuine customers, and previous stocktake loss data. This information, together with statistical variables, is then manipulated to provide an abstract forecast based on known assumptions of known and unknown losses. Although the intentions of these formulae are sound, they tend to be inaccurate due to the vast amount of changeable circumstances for each individual retail operation. All the same, they can form the basis of hypothetical interpretations which can be used as examples in a training environment to show staff the potential for loss (see Figures 1.4 and 1.5).

TYPICAL STORE UNIT	SAMPLE STORE	YOUR STORE
Annual store sales	$1,200,000	
No. sales transactions ($1.2 m sales ÷ $25 av. sales)	48,000	
Percentage of people who will buy when visiting store	60%	
No. people who visit store annually (48,000 ÷ 60%)	80,000	
Percentage of people who will shop steal	1%	
No. shop stealers in store per year (80,000 x 1%)	800	
Av. $ loss per incident (est. to equal av. sale)	$25	
Annual loss to shop stealers (800 x $25)	$20,000	
Shop-stealing losses as a percentage of $1.2 m sales	1.7%	
Shop-stealing losses as a percentage of shrinkage ($28,800 ÷ 2.4%)	69%	

Figure 1.4. Formula for estimating shop stealing

(Reprinted with permission from *Peter Berlin Report on Shrinkage Control*, April 1993a.)

TYPICAL STORE UNIT	SAMPLE STORE	YOUR STORE
Total no. store employees	10	
Av. no. employees in store on any given day (60% of total)	6	
No. employees who will steal on a given day (est. at 5% of total or 1 in every 3 stores)	0.33	
No. theft incidents per year (based on 362 working days = 0.33 x 362)	119	
Av. $ loss per incident (estimated to be 1.5 times that of a shop stealer)	$50	
Annual loss to employee theft	$5,950	
Employee theft losses as a percentage of $1.2 m sales	0.5%	
Employee theft losses as a percentage of shrinkage ($28,800 ÷ 2.4%)	21%	

Figure 1.5. Formula for estimating employee theft

(Reprinted with permission from *Peter Berlin Report on Shrinkage Control*, April 1993a.)

CALCULATION OF RETAIL LOSS THROUGH STOCKTAKES

The main source of data for the calculation of retail loss is through the periodic audit process of stocktakes. Additionally, financial losses caused through burglary, armed robbery, fraudulent credit cards, dishonoured cheques, staff discount abuse and other deliberate or accidental loss which is not recoverable through insurance claims should also be added to the retail loss figure.

Stocktakes are considered necessary by retailers. On the one hand, they provide progressive data on current theoretical and actual stock levels and, therefore, determine the financial progress of the organisation over a given period. On the other hand, they are an expensive cost item in terms of wages and salaries, processing and analysing time and, of course, lost sales due to closure of stores over stocktake periods.

Depending on the retailer, stocktakes may be conducted weekly, monthly, quarterly, half-yearly or annually. The frequency of which stocktakes are conducted is purely a matter of decision. The more frequent the stocktake, the fresher the results. The causes of loss become less evident the longer the period between stocktakes. Retailers generally use either periodic stocktakes or rolling stocktakes.

Periodic Stocktakes

This type of stocktake is usually undertaken monthly, quarterly, half-yearly or annually. More often than not, the store is closed for the stocktaking period. In this sense, it becomes expensive in terms of a labour resource, the temporary cessation of trade and loss of sales and, in some cases, a stock analysis nightmare. The advantages of these stocktakes is that all stock is counted at the one time and results posted fairly quickly. Anomalies such as transposition errors in counting can be checked and adjusted fairly quickly and where major discrepancies are discovered, action plans can be implemented and investigation teams can be tasked to conduct full operational reviews to stem further losses.

Rolling Stocktakes

Another form of stocktake involves a rolling stocktake. This is a stocktake of an entire shop over a period, such as an eight-week period or longer. The process involves counting only, for example, 10% of the total stock items each week. This would need 10 weeks for the counting process to be completed.

This type of stocktake is obviously less expensive in terms of labour required and obviates the need to close the shop. However, the downside is the loss of immediate financial data for the whole store. The availability of complete retail loss data is dependent on the entire shop completing its stocktaking cycle. On some occasions, stock losses may not be readily available. For example, if a periodic stocktake reveals a loss of product bearing a stock-keeping unit number (SKU) as 123456, it could be checked against a corresponding gain which might reveal a similar product or SKU, ie, 123546. In this example, a simple adjustment is needed to correct the original transposition error and the original loss is eliminated. In a rolling stocktake, opportunities for these types of adjustments are diminished.

Stock Accounting Methods

Most retailers use a stocktaking or stock management system based on either the cost method of accounting or the retail method of accounting. When relating retail loss figures, the percentage value (for example, 1.97%), represents a dollar loss and is expressed as a percentage of the gross sales taken over the stocktake period. In either case, the principles are basically the same.

In the simplest form, a stocktake works on the principle of checking what stock is in the shop against what the shop should have. Stock is the sum of all incoming merchandise less sales. The stock in the shop at the close of the stocktaking period is usually referred to as 'actual stock'. This figure is compared against head office figures which also show the amount of stock sent to the store less the value of all sales. This figure is usually referred to as 'theoretical stock'.

The difference between the two is described as either a retail loss (shrinkage) if there is a negative result, or a retail gain (swellage) if there is a positive result. Often, a large retail gain (swellage) is followed by an equally large retail loss (shrinkage). These tend to highlight human and administrative errors in miscalculating cutoff

days or not recording the value of mark-ups rather than theft problems. Figure 1.6 shows a typical sequence of events that have generated a retail loss for one hypothetical trader.

Figure 1.6 follows the history of a particular unit of merchandise through a set stocktaking period. Five events occurred which created retail financial loss:

1. In the first instance, a delivery of stock is not checked, resulting in an immediate discrepancy between theoretical and stock levels. If the discrepancy had been discovered and an investigation revealed a cause, the shortage may have been rectified.

2. A ticketing error, although no physical loss of stock has occurred, does create a dollar loss in the value of actual stock levels.

3. As the stocktake period progresses, a staff member either accidentally or deliberately under-rings a unit by $5.00 causing a dollar loss in the actual stock level.

4. A shop stealer then steals a unit. This of course becomes an unknown loss, because it was not seen.

5. The theft adds to our discrepancies and the actual loss total. Finally, a dishonest staff member fraudulently refunds one unit on the register. This action has an equalling negative effect by negatively refunding. The cash equivalent has been taken out of the till, thereby generating a negative sale which in turn has increased the theoretical stock levels by one unit. Naturally, the physical return of the unit did not take place, thereby creating another discrepancy.

100 UNITS AT $10.00 SELLING PRICE WITH A RETAIL VALUE OF $1,000.00			THEORETICAL STOCK LEVELS		ACTUAL STOCKLEVELS		
ACTIVITY	**Sales**	**Mark-down**	**Units**	**Value ($)**	**Units**	**Value ($)**	**Gain ($) (Loss)**
Delivery of 100 units Paperwork not checked: 1 unit short			100	1000	99	$990	(10)
Ticketing error: 5 units at $9.00				1000	99	$985	(5)
Sales: 5 units at $9.00	$45		95	955	94	$940	
Sales: 60 units at $10.00	$600		35	355	34	$340	
Mark-downs: 10 units to $8.00		$20	35	335	34	$320	
Sales: 10 units at $8.00	$80		25	255	24	$240	
Under-ringing: 1 unit at $5.00	$5		24	250	23	$230	(5)
Breakage: 1 unit write-off		$10	23	240	22	$220	
Theft, unknown: 1 unit (shop stealer)			23	240	21	$210	(10)
Soiled, mark-down: 5 units at $8.00		$10	23	230	21	$200	
Sales: 10 units at $10.00	$100		13	130	11	$100	
Staff refund fraud: 1 unit at $10.00	($10)		14	140	11	$100	(10)
Totals	$820	$40	14	$140	11	$100	($40)

Figure 1.6. The history of a merchandise unit through several stocktaking periods

In reviewing this hypothetical stocktake, the results indicate that the five transactions have generated a stock loss of three units plus a dollar loss of $40.00. This example can attribute the causes of the loss as follows:

Human and administrative error

Failure to check incoming stock: 1 x unit loss valued at $10.00

Ticketing error: dollar loss of $5.00

Customer theft

Unknown loss: 1 x unit loss valued at $10.00

Employee malpractice

Deliberate(?) under-ringing: dollar loss of $5.00

Fraudulent refund: 1 x unit loss valued at $10.00

The total loss for this particular item is $40.00. In calculating a percentage figure, the $40.00 is expressed as a percentage of gross sales. In the example given, gross sales for the stocktake period was $820.00. Thus:

$$\$40.00 \times 100 \div \$820.00 = 4.87\%$$

The retail loss for this particular item is 4.87%. This is a figure which is far too high for any responsible store manager to accept. If this figure is indicative of the business generally, a massive problem exists which needs urgent attention.

For many retailers, the percentage figure is expressed as either 'Cost' or 'Retail'. Those having responsibility for loss-control management, should understand whether the figures being expressed reflect either the cost or retail method of accounting. Given that the retail selling price of merchandise can be anywhere between 10% to 200% higher than its cost value, it becomes clear that a 2% loss figure expressed in terms of cost is a far more catastrophic result than a 2% loss expressed in terms of retail.

Using the previous stocktaking scenario as an example, the difference between a 4.87% loss expressed at retail and one expressed at cost becomes painfully obvious.

It is not the intention of this book to detail the pros and cons of the cost and retail accounting systems, but to explain the basics of each.

The Cost Method of Accounting

The cost method of accounting is simply a system whereby all stock is valued at its original cost price. For some retailers, this system is utilised where there is high value of goods, in terms of dollar value, but low numbers of stock, such as white goods and furniture. Take for example the purchase of a fridge, most customers are eager to seek a better price. For these types of product, salespersons may have costs at their fingertips and can often negotiate a better selling price for customers in accordance with the known cost figures. Whereas in a modified system of the cost method, such as that which is applied to large volume sales of a major discount chain with a large product range and quick product turnover, it is more difficult to apply a set cost for each and every item. The modified version involves 'averaging out' the cost of merchandise across a particular range of similar stock. Overall, the stocktake figures will tend to balance the 'averaging effect', but on occasions, the effect of a large-scale mark-down on a particular line may 'skew' the averaging process and could result in an unfortunate administrative financial loss for one store but an administrative financial gain for another. This is good news for one store manager, but bad news for the other, particularly if incentives are partly based on retail-loss performance. Figure 1.7 highlights this problem.

In Figure 1.7, the 180 shirts represent a total value of $1,665.00. Although the cost price of each is slightly different, the averaging method of cost has produced a garment cost average of $9.25. The total value of the 180 garments remains the same at $1,665.00. Overall, the company balance sheets have not been affected, but the individual figures for both store A and B are skewed. Store A shows a 'loss' of $38.75, while store B shows an 'overage' of the same amount.

STORE	ITEM	COST ($)	NO.	VALUE AV. ($)	COST ($)	VALUE ($)	GAIN (LOSS) ($)
A	Shirt 1	$12.00	20	$240.00	$9.25	$185.00	(55.00)
A	Shirt 2	$9.00	65	$585.00	$9.25	$601.25	$16.25
B	Shirt 3	$10.00	40	$400.00	$9.25	$370.00	(30.00)
B	Shirt 4	$8.00	55	$440.00	$9.25	$508.75	68.75
TOTAL			180	$1665.00	$1665.00		

Figure 1.7. Effects of 'averaging' on the cost method of accounting

The Retail Method of Accounting

The retail method of accounting simply involves the recording of all merchandise at its retail selling price rather than its cost price. The retail selling price is what customers see on the actual price tags.

There are some schools of thought that believe that the retail method of accounting in terms of expressing retail loss is flawed due to the premise that the retail price includes gross profit potential not yet realised. This therefore presents an argument that it is not possible to show a loss on what as yet has not been realised. For example, if 100 bottles of Scotch whisky retailing at $27.50 were stolen by customers over a period, their retail value would be approximately $2,750.00. Given that the mark-up on spirits could be as high as 30% (or more), the actual cost of purchasing would be approximately $19.25 per bottle or $1,925.00. Should the loss be recorded at retail value of $2,750.00 or its cost price of $1,925.00? If the loss is recorded at retail price, that could be an untrue claim because the claim would also include the $850.00 of gross profit which is a theoretical figure not yet realised. The question is simply: How do you claim a loss of something that as yet has not occurred, that is, a gross profit of $850.00?

One view point is that the gross profit not yet realised includes a fair proportion of expenses needed to sell the merchandise in the first place. It is part of the 'cost of sales' formula. For example, although the selling price (gross profit) on a particular item may be 100% on top of its original cost (the amount spent on purchasing the item), the final retail selling price would reflect the 'cost of the sale', namely, wages, advertising, leasing of premises, utility expenses, administration costs and, of course, a net profit calculated on the top. The argument here would be that expressing losses at retail selling price is a far more realistic figure as it tends to reflect not only the actual cost of the original item, but also the costs that still need to be met regardless of the item being lost or not.

THE EFFECTS OF RETAIL LOSS

It should now be apparent to readers that retail loss is just not confined to the effects of known and unknown retail stock loss. Retail loss is a Pandora's box of financial and economic problems that requires a multitude of skills to overcome. In terms of merchandise that have otherwise been stolen or fraudulently refunded by customers or employees, the effects on the retail business can be quite dramatic and include:

- Loss of profit. If the stock is missing, retailers cannot sell it and have, therefore, lost the opportunity to maximise profits.

- Loss of trade. If the store does not have the stock in, customers become alienated and go elsewhere.

- Stock replacement. The stock needs to be replaced, causing resources to be unnecessarily extended.

- Negative wastage. Not only has the retailer lost the money originally paid for the stock, the retailer still has to incur add-on costs involved in the cost of sales formula, such as wages, transportation, displays, advertising.

At this point, most readers might ask the question: Is it happening to me? The preceding paragraphs have provided sufficient evidence to suggest that it is. Naturally, the degree of loss depends entirely on the prevention strategies employed. But as a basic guide, there are seven questions retailers could ask themselves to determine just how much is being lost:

- Is it occurring?
- Why is it occurring?
- What are its levels?
- Where is it occurring?
- When is it occurring?
- Who is doing it?
- How are they doing it?

SHIFTS IN CRIMINAL TRENDS

The face of today's modern retailing world has changed dramatically from what it was 10 years ago. The face of crime has also changed: criminals on both sides of the counter are working harder and smarter. Computer-based systems have certainly provided for better accounting, audit and discrepancy reporting results, but the face of crime has changed along with the technological improvements. Hardcore criminal action through armed robbery directed at targets such as banks, building societies and other financial institutions have undergone the process of what is generally referred to as 'target hardening'. Target hardening means that the prevalence of this type of crime has made it necessary to implement security measures that make the target harder to attack. Certainly the effect of target hardening has reduced the number of incidents of armed robbery on financial institutions, but a phenomenon known as 'displacement' has resulted. Displacement is the movement of targets from one area of industry to another. Where the financial industry was once a popular target, the effects of target hardening have displaced the criminality to the retail industry, resulting in an increase of criminal activity both internally and externally. Not only do retailers face being targeted for burglary and armed robbery offences, but other instances of 'soft crime', such as shop stealing, price swapping, cheque fraud, credit card fraud and refund fraud, are now more popular with criminals.

Retailers need to discover their weaknesses and determine strategies to minimise the impact of these weaknesses on retail operations. Retailers need to be able to answer questions on where their losses occur and what causes those losses.

Despite the shift in criminal trends, retailers cannot place all the blame for retail loss on external sources. Retailer complacency must take some of the blame. Retail loss prevention and security is largely a commonsense commitment, and without a doubt, some retail loss can be blamed on an organisation's operational deficiency.

Every commercial enterprise should operate on the basis of a sound business plan and, likewise, a retail business should have a sound loss prevention and security plan. Often, retail loss is simply due to management apathy, poor accounting systems, uncontrolled point-of-sale transactions, insufficient in-store administration, incomplete housekeeping and defective stocktaking processes.

RESPONSIBILITIES FOR THE MANAGEMENT OF RETAIL LOSS

The responsibility and accountability for retail loss comes from two separate directions: first, from management for the planning, organising, leading and controlling of loss-prevention strategies; and second, from every person within the organisation for the control and minimisation of in-store losses. It should be clear to every employee that the day-to-day control and minimisation of in-store loss is not just another task to be undertaken, but rather a part of every retail task already being performed.

Management Accountability

The management role in developing sound loss-prevention strategies is to make a commitment to prevent loss. This must be a specific statement, it must form part of the organisational operating philosophy and there must be a commitment from the very top. Management must lead by example and if loss prevention strategies are in place, these should be adhered to by every person within the organisation. The commitment to preventing known and unknown loss should be as absolute as is the commitment to maximising sales.

The main thrust of retail will always be sales: retailing operating philosophy will always dictate that sales come before security. Some retailers may find that statement odd, given that this book is being written from a loss prevention perspective, but if the primary objective of any retailer is to maximise profit, then obviously the minimisation and control of loss is going to have less emphasis than maximising opportunities for sales. Certainly, the minimisation and control of retail financial and economic loss is going be a contributing factor to the maximisation of profit and should therefore be given the appropriate priority.

Historically, there appear many examples where in good times and healthy sales periods, a retail loss of 2% or more may be considered affordable and acceptable and, therefore, more easily absorbed into the net profit of an organisation. The emphasis on loss prevention reduces and general standards quickly fall. However, in the lean years where there are depressed sales, frequent mark-downs, low profit margins, and where every dollar earned is hard earned, the prospect of a 2% retail loss could have disastrous effects on the weak financial position of a retailer. Suddenly, loss prevention measures take on a greater urgency to help post a healthier bottom line.

A commitment to loss prevention should not be just situational, rather it should form part of an organisational philosophy, no matter what the economic situation the country is at the time.

The following list highlights the basics of a management loss prevention strategy:

- Provide management commitment to prevent loss.
- Identify and analyse the issues that contribute to loss.
- Design and develop loss prevention, and security policy and procedures.
- Provide appropriate loss prevention and security skills and training.
- Constantly validate and review loss prevention strategies.

Employee Responsibility

As previously stated, loss prevention is the responsibility of every person in the organisation. Team work plays a vital role in any loss prevention program and it becomes obvious that for any loss-control strategy to be effective it must be treated seriously by every employee. By making loss prevention a responsibility of every employee and actively publicising that fact as organisational policy, all employees are provided with sufficient purpose to acknowledge the importance that management places on the loss problem. Every person's role in maintaining sound loss prevention strategies includes:

- Developing a commitment to prevent loss.
- Following closely laid down loss prevention and security policy and procedures.
- Passing on appropriate skills and knowledge training to others.
- Instilling accuracy attitudes.
- Regularly spot checking mark-ups and mark-downs.
- Paying attention to each task done.

REVIEW QUESTIONS

1. Explain the key statement: 'The primary objective of any retailer must be to maximise profits.'

2. Retailing involves benefits at three main levels. What are these levels? Show how each of the various levels might present opportunities for the retailer.

3. Why is an understanding of the three major retail operating principles important?

4. Compare the retail loss figures from overseas countries such as the United States, Canada and the United Kingdom. Conduct some basic research to explain possible reasons for the differences between countries.

5. Define retail loss.

6. Examine your own organisation's definition of retail loss. Does it include losses caused through mark-downs, wastage, spillage etc? How is the value calculated?

7. Comment on the essential differences between known and unknown losses.

8. Why is retail loss research necessary? Discuss sources of information on retail loss data. Is this data reliable? How will it assist you in determining loss prevention strategies?

9. Should the distribution of loss figures be applied to all retailers? If not, discuss why.

10. Discuss the concept of 'shrinkage' — what does it mean? Is the term 'shrinkage' relevant. Is there an alternative term that retailers could use? Why is the use of the term 'shrinkage' questionable?

11. Discuss the difference between the effects of a financial loss on a retailer as opposed to an economic loss. In terms of prevention strategies, why is it important to be able to separate financial loss from economic loss?

12. Is it important to know the means by which your organisation calculates its losses? If so, why?

13. Does your organisation know what its financial losses were during the last financial year? If it does, is the figure a stock loss figure, or a total financial figure? Does it incorporate a figure for economic loss?

14. How are losses calculated? Is the figure a true representation of the losses caused through careless, negligent or criminal behaviour?

2 Errors, Miscalculations and Inaccuracies

CHAPTER OBJECTIVES

1. To expose the potential risks of human and administrative error on retail operations.
2. To provide an overview of the potential areas for error.
3. To examine the cause and effect of some common problems.
4. To develop a framework for preventative strategies.

THE ERRORS PEOPLE MAKE

In his book, *Retail Security — Controlling Loss for Profit*, Curtis details a study undertaken by one retailer where it was found that one in ten in-store transactions were in error (Curtis, 1983, pp. 471–476). The study further revealed that over a single year, more than one million clerical errors were made which caused a net loss of $US440,000. This study revealed that there was little relationship between actual stocktake shortages and the figures revealed by the clerical error picture. These are some of the errors that were studied:

- wrong addition;
- wrong multiplication;
- wrong sales or excise tax charged;
- wrong employee discounts;
- under or overcharging;
- failure to register a sale;
- wrong designation of transactions;
- mixing up charge and cash transactions;
- allocating wrong department codes;
- registering wrong department codes on transactions; and
- transacting lay-by sales etc as fully paid-up items.

In Chapter 1, survey data from the Australian Bureau of Statistics, coupled with industry research, suggested that retailers lose some $2 billion per year to known and unknown retail losses. Further research suggests that anywhere from 20% to 25% of retail loss may be due to human and administrative error. If this 20–25% of loss is attributable to human error, then retail employees could be making huge financial mistakes which may be costing the industry up to $500 million per year, or over $1.3 million per day!

People make mistakes: human or administrative error made in the everyday functions of retailing are inevitable. Chapter 2 explores the potential for mistakes and what loss prevention practitioners can do to minimise and control instances of human and administrative error.

As human beings, we acknowledge these weaknesses and constantly prepare ourselves to minimise the impact of error and mistakes in our everyday lives by the accrual of knowledge, by learning necessary skills and by gaining experience to apply those skills. In retailing, we become proficient in what we are doing by applying the knowledge, the skills and the expertise in a variety of tasks, and this of course minimises the potential for errors and mistakes.

The administration process of retail is not a difficult concept to understand: stock comes in, it is sold; more stock is purchased and, once again, that stock is sold. This, of course, is a simplistic view. What generates the potential for error and mistake is the complexity of the task that accompanies the process of selling. Obviously, the more complex the task, the greater the potential for error, and the greater the potential for subsequent financial loss.

THE CONCEPT OF 'EQUALLING ENTRIES'

In effect, all retail transactions operate on a balancing equation. This forms the basis on which retail accounting works. In other words, for every transaction that occurs in retailing, there should be an opposite and balancing transaction. For example, during a sale, the action of processing the transaction includes either a manual or computerised act. If the transaction is correct, that act results in our levels of stock being reduced by one and dollar sales being increased by the value of that stock item, which, in effect, balances the equation. There is a 'minus' recorded against stock levels, but a 'plus' recorded against the value of goods sold. This is a simplified version of the double-entry system of accounting.

The effect of equalling entries:

Effect No. 1 (+):   There is an increase in cash equal to the selling or retail price of the stock.

Effect No. 2 (–):   There is a decrease in the level of stock.

An Example of Human Error

To demonstrate this concept further. A customer brings two identical items to the counter. Each has a retail selling price of $15.00. It is very busy. In her haste, the checkout operator rings-up only one item and charges the customer only $15.00 instead of $30.00. The customer wanders off without realising her good fortune.

Effect No. 1 (+):   Cash levels increase by the value of one stock item.
Effect No. 2 (–):   Theoretical stock levels are reduced by one.

The effect of the error:

Actual stock levels reduced by two.
Theoretical stock levels reduced by one.

Unknown retail loss:

One stock item valued at $15.00 retail price.

In the above example, the actual and theoretical stock levels do not balance and, therefore, the transaction has the effect of creating an unknown loss equal to the cost or retail price of the stock item depending on the accounting method used.

EXERCISE QUESTION — EFFECT OF SIMPLE ERROR

SCENARIO:

Thirteen quality books in a book store were mistakenly marked down from their correct selling price of $155.50 to $15.55. No-one has done a mark-down spot check. All the books were sold at the incorrect marked-down price of $15.55. Assume that the cost of the original books was $100.00 per unit. Calculate the value of the retail loss at:

1. cost price; and
2. retail selling price.

1.   ANSWER: COST PRICE

Cost price:

13 books x $100.00 (cost of each book)   = $1,300.00

Actual sales:

13 books x $15.50 (sold at incorrect price)   = $201.50

Actual loss:

Value of cost price – actual sales   = $1,300.00 – $201.50
          = $1,098.50

(continued...)

EXERCISE QUESTION — EFFECT OF SIMPLE ERROR (cont.)

2. ANSWER: RETAIL SELLING PRICE

13 books x $100.00 (cost of each book)   = $1,300.00

13 books x $155.50 (retail selling price)   = $2,021.50

Gross profit on each book = $55.50

Gross profit on total = $721.50

Actual sales:

13 books sold at incorrect price of $15.50   = $201.50

Actual loss:

Value of selling price – actual sales   = $2,021.50 – $201.50

Total loss: $1,820.00

To make up for the $1,820.00 loss, the book store would need to sell at least 33 additional books at the correct selling price:

33 books x $155.50   = $5,131.50

Cost price:

33 books x $100.00   = $3,300.00

Balance: $1,831.50

These are additional sales required over and above the normal daily budget requirements. But this is really a false hope, because no matter how many extra sales you might make, the loss has already occurred and will never be recovered.

THE FIVE AREAS OF POTENTIAL RETAIL LOSS

The concept of equalling entries generally applies to all facets of retail operations and is not just confined to the sales arena. When reviewed overall, retail operations can be divided into five main areas which have the potential to cause massive financial loss through genuine error, mistake, miscalculation or inaccuracies. These five areas are:

* receipt of incoming stock;
* POS transactions;
* credit, exchange or refund transactions;
* mark-up and mark-downs; and
* returns to distribution centres or to suppliers.

Receipt of Incoming Stock

Incoming stock includes:

* normal replenishment stock;
* interstore transfers; and
* vendor deliveries.

The most common error in any of the incoming stock events is not necessarily caused by short deliveries, but rather by the failure to independently check each and every shipment, carton, box, item or delivery that arrives into a store. The retail experience generally reveals that the correct processes of delivery are often largely neglected. In a multidepartment or multistore environment, the failure to correctly account for all deliveries may result in major losses for one member of the chain but major gains for another.

One example involves a transport cost-saving exercise experienced by many multistore retailers. A managers' meeting is called at a State office location and store managers are asked to bring in all their interstore transfers to swap with other store managers. This stock is gathered up, leaves the store unrecorded, is placed in private vehicles (voiding insurance conditions on transit stock loss) and is carted off to the designated meeting place. At the end of the meeting, a frenzy of activity results in merchandise being handed over and exchanged.

This sets up perfect opportunities for error, miscalculation and inaccuracy. How often does the follow-up transfer documentation record the transaction? Many examples abound of managers preparing transfer documentation but forgetting to deliver the stock causing a gain for themselves, but a loss to the receiving store. Conversely, the manager might send stock but forget to transfer it administratively, giving the receiver a gain, but the sender a loss. Overall, the company books may well balance, but in the meantime, it becomes a nightmare for a loss-prevention manager, a stocktake controller or financial accountant to sort out the resulting mess.

Case Study No. 1

One major discount store in Melbourne received two semi-trailer loads of stock per week, but as a result of staffing restrictions, accepted on good faith the entire shipments without verification. Retail losses in this discount store reached over 10% for some stocktakes. As part of a loss control program, a proportion of the loads were randomly checked. Major discrepancies were ultimately identified for every single load.

An investigation revealed that the results of periodic stocktakes at the Distribution Centre always showed substantial gains. In other words, there was always more stock than theoretical levels showed. No formal investigations were ever undertaken, and excess stock was usually just added to the opening stock level for the next accounting period.

Acting on final recommendations, the retailer immediately implemented stock-control measures. Allocation of stock systems, verification processes and quality control checks in product and carton counts were upgraded and tested which dramatically reduced the error rate in semi-trailer deliveries.

The key controls for the receipt of incoming stock, whether through a general stock-delivery replenishment system, vendor deliveries or interstore transfers, are all basically the same. The physical property needs to be thoroughly checked against accompanying paperwork.

Key control objectives include:

- accurately recording incoming stock quantities;
- recording and appropriately claiming for all shortages, overages and damaged stock;
- verifying vendor deliveries for appropriate payment; and
- recording all stock deliveries at the correct retail selling price.

Basic Principles of Receipt

General Store Deliveries

On the receipt of all incoming stock from any delivery source, whether the retailer's own carrier, a delivery contractor or through a special courier service, the delivery cannot be regarded as being complete until:

- Every individual unit of stock shown on an accompanying shipping note, delivery docket or invoice has been checked and verified.
- All shortages and damaged units have been accurately recorded on all relevant documentation.
- The delivery documentation has been actioned by the appropriate authority for recording purposes, adjustment of stock levels, and recovery of claims (if necessary) against the delivery source.

Vendor Deliveries

Vendors attending a store location should be escorted to the appropriate name-brand display product and a store employee should remain while the vendor replenishes the stock. Wherever possible, the following procedures should be adopted:

- All vendor delivery notes must be checked against the actual levels of stock replenished.
- Receipt documentation should be forwarded to the appropriate authority for recording purposes, adjustment of stock levels, and recovery of claims (if necessary) against the vendor.
- Invoices must be checked against the delivery documentation for proper addition and retail cost data before final approvals are made for payment.
- The verification process should also include a capability for detecting duplicated vendor invoices by matching previously paid invoice numbers.

Interstore Transfer Deliveries

The fundamentals for interstore deliveries are quite simple. The major key control element is that:

- All products being transferred from one location to another must be accompanied by appropriate transfer documentation detailing total number of items, product description, stock-keeping codes (SKU) and current retail price.

Product + Documentation = Interstore Transfer

Unless this equation is complete, there is no interstore transfer, and a shortage for one store is virtually guaranteed.

Most interstore transfers follow either a manual or computerised system or procedure for accounting purposes. Whatever the procedure adopted, it is vital to ensure that:

- both the product and accompanying documentation properly reach their ultimate destination;
- the delivery is verified; and
- both actual and theoretical stock levels are accurately adjusted at head office, for both the sending store and the receiving store.

Segregation or Separation of Control

Segregation or separation of control is a standard control measure designed to minimise opportunities for accidental error, deliberate malpractice or straightforward fraudulent criminal action. Both the sending store and the receiving store have a financial interest in the product being transferred and, unless an independent third party is involved, the opportunities for deliberate or accidental error could be seized upon and taken advantage of. For this reason, both the sending transaction and the receiving transaction need to be independently monitored to ensure that stock levels are adjusted accurately. This segregation of control also allows for independent arbitration in the event of disputes or discrepancies arising and for correct stock adjustments made to the store responsible. Thus, the process of control links three vital elements:

- the sending;
- the receiving; and
- the validation through a stock controller.

Figure 2.1 illustrates this link.

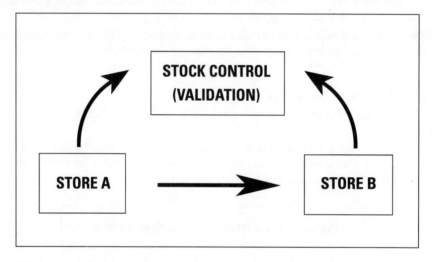

Figure 2.1. Flow chart of control functions of stock controller

Transfer Form Requirements

To ensure that the interstore transfer process flows smoothly and efficiently, a four-part transfer document is required. This document should be sequentially numbered and designed to show:

- sending store;
- receiving store;
- time and date sent;
- the method of transportation;
- quantity of product being forwarded;
- full details of the product being forwarded; and
- the names of the persons both sending and authorising the transfer.

Time Frame Controls

Additionally, time frames need to be built in to the system to enable investigations to be carried out quickly in the event of any discrepancy or delivery dispute. A suggested time frame may require the sending store to notify the stock controller immediately a transfer is forwarded. Similarly, the receiving store must 'action' the incoming transfer within 24 hours. Given a standard delivery time of, say, two to three days, the stock controller has a four-day transaction period in which to examine discrepancies. If either the sending or receiving store fails to meet the time frames in despatching necessary transfer details, then they automatically incur any losses. This obviously provides some incentive and motivation for store managers to meet their interstore transfer obligations.

Flow of Events

The flow of events through the interstore process is as follows:

STORE A (SENDING STORE)	1.	Prepares both the product and the 4-part documentation (Copy A, B, C & D) ready for transportation.
	2.	Retains Copy D for in-store verification.
	3.	Despatches product together with documentation (Copy A & B) to Store B at receiving destination.
	4.	Forwards documentation (Copy C) to Stock Controller at Head Office for independent verification.
STOCK CONTROLLER	1.	Receives dispatch advice from Store A, and lists dispatch as outstanding transit stock pending verification of delivery.
STORE B (RECEIVING STORE)	1.	Stock arrives in store.
	2.	Stock is checked, and any discrepancies listed on both Copy A & B of documentation.
	3.	Copy A is forwarded to Stock Controller for acquittal.
	4.	Copy B is retained with Store B for verification purposes.
STOCK CONTROLLER	1.	Receives Copy A from Store B and compares receipt of stock with details forwarded by Store A (Copy C).
	2.	If all details are correct, theoretical stock levels are adjusted accordingly.
	3.	Non-delivery of transfer is indicated through process of deficiency analysis reporting, ie, the non-receipt of verification documentation after 4 days.
	4	Any deficiencies are investigated within the agreed time frame and stock shortages adjusted where necessary.

POS Transactions

Point of sale (POS) transactions account for all incoming and outgoing cash, electronic funds transfer at point of sale (EFTPOS), and other negotiable securities used to purchase, exchange or refund product. These include:

- cash purchases;
- cheques;
- credit-card transactions, either manual or EFTPOS;
- gift vouchers;
- welfare orders;
- incentive bonds;
- promotional sales; and
- lay-by transactions.

Entering the incorrect cost of items or allocating an incorrect transaction code can cause either financial loss or unnecessary embarrassment for the salesperson. Errors occur in handing back change, failing to check credit-card warning lists, failing to question suspect or counterfeit currency, and accepting doubtful cheques, to name but a few.

Controls to Minimise Errors at POS

The major controls to minimise the potential for human and administrative error in any point of sale transaction include the implementation of sound policy and procedures that cover:

- all sales transactions;
- preferred register practices;
- lay-by transactions;
- end-of-day procedures; and
- internal random audit function.

Controls for all sales transactions:

1. Ensure that all sales transactions are transacted through a cash register.
2. Ensure that all sales are rung on the cash register at the time of the transaction (not some time later).
3. Ensure that all sales are supported by either manual sales dockets or computer-generated receipts which need to be both sequentially and numerically encoded. The receipt or sales dockets should also identify the store, describe the product, include the identity code and retail price paid.
4. Ensure that sales are verified by verification imprint from the cash register which includes time, date and salesperson transaction data.
5. Implement policy that customers must be given a receipt for any transaction. Any receipts left behind are to be retained in a secure place and destroyed under supervision at the end-of-day's trade. (Destroyed does not include mean merely throwing receipts into a rubbish bin!)

6. Allow for a system to be implemented for transactions not properly coded or marked or if pricing appears to be incorrect. This would require a temporary and non-allocated code being used to record the transaction. This effectively records the sale of the item, but the recording of a temporary code will not adjust theoretical stock levels, and, unless a policy exists to acquit all temporary or non-allocated codes with a 24-hour period, the recording of an non-allocated code against a stock item will result in a theoretical stock loss.

7. Prohibit sales staff from working from an open cash-register drawer. This will deny opportunities for salespersons to accidentally or intentionally fail to ring-up, under-ring, or void a legitimate sale.

8. Ensure that all computerised cash registers are programmed to be inoperative if the drawer has been left open from the previous transaction.

9. Ensure that all 'No Sale' and 'Void' receipts are accounted for and attached to a daily reconciliation report.

Preferred register practices:

1. Implement policy that deters sales staff from leaving keys in registers.
2. Ensure that someone other than the sales staff have the keys to control the locks and the function-mode switches of each register.
3. Wherever possible, have only one register operator per register.
4. Have staff sign registers in and out.
5. Regularly spot check floats balances.
6. For additional register operator security, consider the use of private codes or PIN numbers.
7. Clear registers several times per day.
8. Set a limit of maximum cash holdings per register.
9. Prohibit employees from ringing up purchases for family members.
10. Require all employee discount purchases to be authorised by store managers.

Control measures for lay-by transactions:

1. Lay-by transactions should be treated as a full sale and theoretical levels should be adjusted accordingly.
2. All lay-by purchases should be housed in a special lay-by area using both a numerical and alphabetical recording system for cross-referencing, internal auditing and ease of customer collection.
3. All lay-by sales that are voided, forfeited or cancelled need to be verified by the store manager.
4. Non-return of lay-by stock: A common problem for voided, forfeited or cancelled lay-bys is that although the transaction documentation may be complete, the physical return of the lay-by item may not be carried out. This creates a retail loss simply because theoretical levels of stock have been increased by the action of

the return transaction, but the actual level of physical stock has remained unchanged as the unit may still be in a lay-by reserve.

End-of-day procedures:

1. Examine the day's sales transactions and obtain all manual sales dockets, voids, and no-sale slips and compare these with the reported number provided by most registers.
2. Ensure that the reason for each 'No Sale' and 'Void' is written on the back of each receipt and is verified at the time of the transaction by management.
3. At end of day, a Daily Cash Register Reconciliation Report should be completed by two independent staff members. One to balance the register transactions, make up the next trading period's floats and reconcile credit-card vouchers, cheques, EFTPOS transactions and other negotiable documentation against the recorded figures; while the other person counts all the cash. Results should be recorded on the manual Daily Cash Register Reconciliation Report and a cash count sheet. These two items should then be reconciled against any computerised figure. If it is incorrect, the report and the cash count should be doubled checked for accuracy by another person, not the person initially finding the mistake. Any corrections should then be made and recorded. If discrepancies still exist, the matter should be reported to the next higher authority.
4. Maintain a daily 'Under and Overs' log for each register or register operator.
5. Ensure that 'unders and overs' are thoroughly investigated and monitored to determine whether they are either an error or theft.
6. Determine if patterns or trends exist in the occurrence of any 'unders and overs'.

In-store audits:

An in-store audit function should also be developed that monitors the following areas:

*   a review of the previous period's register's 'unders and overs';
*   daily bank deposits reconciled with end-of-day takings;
*   excessive voids transactions;
*   excessive no-sales transactions;
*   excessive refunds transactions;
*   excessive errors in price discrepancies;
*   missing and lost documentation;
*   missing and lost lay-by purchases or documentation;
*   balancing register totals with bank deposits;
*   credit voucher books;
*   gift voucher books;
*   customer holds and orders;
*   petty-cash staff discount purchases;
*   sales journals, where applicable; and
*   interstore transfer sheets.

A sample In-store Audit Report is contained in Chapter 5, Internal Controls.

Credit, Exchange or Refund Transactions

Most major retailers allow for a commonsense approach for the exchange, credit or refund of faulty merchandise. Without detailing the obvious opportunities for dishonesty on refunds in this chapter, opportunities for staff to inadvertently create error are numerous.

Case Study No. 2

A customer returns a garment without a receipt which, in the meantime, has been marked down from $49.00 to $39.00. The staff member returns the garment on the on-line terminal and advises the customer that in the absence of a receipt, she can only refund the marked-down price. The customer accepts and leaves, but a day later finds the original receipt and returns to the shop requesting her additional $10.00.

The salesperson pleasantly completes another return transaction on her on-line terminal and refunds the customer her $10.00. Result: this apparently innocent transaction has created a retail loss of one garment by increasing the theoretical level of stock by one.

Transacting Refunds as Sales

Another common refund error occurs when a salesperson transacts a $25.00 refund, but inadvertently records the transaction as a sale, thereby causing a $50.00 shortage of cash at the end of the day. The mistake incorrectly advises a computer-operated terminal that $25.00 has been placed in the till, when in fact $25.00 has been taken out, creating the double dilemma. Let's look at how this happens.

Effect of correct refund transaction:

Item 345876 valued at $25.00 is refunded. Refund is transacted through computer or manual stock-card system.

Balances before transaction		Balances after transaction	
Cash in register:	$345.00	Cash in register:	$320.00
Theoretical stock levels:	12	Theoretical stock levels:	13
Stock in hand:	12	Stock in hand:	13

Effect of incorrect transaction:

Item 345876 valued at $25.00 is refunded, but inadvertently rung-up as a sale.

Balances before transaction		Balances after transaction	
Cash in register:	$345.00	Cash in register:	$370.00
Theoretical stock levels:	12	Theoretical stock levels:	11
Stock in hand:	12	Stock in hand:	13

Cash of $25.00 is taken out of the register, reducing level to $320.00, but the error has raised the theoretical level of cash to $370.00, creating a $50.00 shortage and a unit discrepancy of two.

Corrective refund action:

To correct this error, the transactions need to be reversed. Two actions are required. First, the actual error needs to be corrected by reversing, or in other words, transacting another refund. This results in the following.

Theoretical levels before 1st adjustment		Actual levels after 1st adjustment	
Cash in register:	$370.00	Cash in register:	$345.00
Theoretical stock levels:	11	Theoretical stock levels:	12

This corrective action has resulted in re-establishing the situation just prior to the error been made. What is now required is the second step to enable the correct transaction to take place, that is the original refund to adjust all the theoretical and actual levels as follows.

Theoretical levels before 2nd adjustment		Actual levels after 2nd adjustment	
Cash in register:	$345.00	Cash in register:	$320.00
Theoretical stock levels:	12	Theoretical stock levels:	13

Mark-ups and Mark-downs

Failure to record mark-ups and mark-downs is one of the greatest sources of unknown loss. In Chapter 1, the cost and retail methods of accounting were described. An example of 'averaging' the cost method has already shown the potential for individual store loss in a large retail chain; likewise, the problems associated with mark-ups and mark-downs can drastically affect the retail method of accounting. Particularly when marking down the wrong product or marking down the product with the wrong price.

For example, if the selling price of 20 items of merchandise was recorded at $35.00 each, their total book or theoretical value would be $700.00. If, however, sales were slow and the selling price was marked down to $25.00, their book value would reduce to $500.00. But if the mark-down was not recorded and the theoretical book value not adjusted, the stock would record a loss of $200.00. Conversely, the effects of unrecorded mark-ups can cause similar havoc as unknown swellages or overages also create major problems.

Returns to Distribution Centres or Suppliers

Quite often, faulty or unsuitable merchandise being returned to suppliers for one reason or another does not instil the same degree of attention as would say the receipt of stock. Returns are regarded as a negative aspect of retailing and as this function is not revenue generating, the accounting and recording processes are often treated haphazardly. Take for example, 25 faulty toys stacked in a corner awaiting processing and return to a supplier. No credit returns are completed, no further action undertaken. Come stocktake time, a stocktake checker sees the toys, but as they are earmarked for return, does not count them. If the paperwork has not taken them off the stocktake-accountable list, then the 25 faulty toys would still be regarded as 'theoretical' stock and would appear on the stocktake report as an unknown loss.

REASONS FOR ERRORS

There are a thousand reasons why human and administrative errors occur. No doubt readers could supply a substantial list of their own, but it would appear that the main reason why human and administrative error occurs is simply that the majority of those working in the retail industry are unaware of the effect that their actions have on the retail accounting equation and this comes back to the question of training.

It is a basic right of employees to be trained to satisfactorily do their tasks correctly. Often is the case where an employee is given a set of notes, told to read them and is then expected to be an expert on the subject. This is clearly wrong.

For employees to perform their tasks correctly, it is imperative that they understand the how, the when, the where and the why tasks are done they way they are.

Human and administrative error results from a lack of knowledge. Certainly error is compounded by apathy, carelessness and negligence, but a fair proportion of administrative error must be attributed to the lack of practical and relevant training provided to employees.

Skills Training Requirement

In his book, *The Training Handbook*, Gordon Rabey (1990, p. 6) states that 'All staff have a right to expect adequate training before being held responsible for their work'. He adds that training is linked through two main purposes: the production of work and the development of staff. To achieve high levels in the former, due attention must be provided to the latter. This makes good sense. We have already seen some examples of how human and administrative losses occur and the probability of their frequency (1 in 10 transactions or an error rate of 10%). It now becomes obvious that without the appropriate skills, knowledge and expertise, sales will suffer, costs will increase, losses will escalate and the business will fail. Rabey (p. 37) suggests that a good sequence for training is to:

- create interest;
- explain the job;
- demonstrate the method;
- assess the performance; and
- review progress.

PREVENTION STRATEGIES: HUMAN & ADMINISTRATIVE ERROR

Although the aim of this chapter is not to set down precise guidelines for the analysis, design, development, conduct or validation of a set training program, prevention strategies must include a review of current performance levels to ascertain the levels and degree of impact that human and administrative errors have on the organisation's financial loss. Once these have been verified and the major contributing factors identified, training programs should be designed, developed, conducted and regularly validated to test effectiveness.

Development of an Error Control Plan

There are many models of plan development and any reasonable management reference book will provide advice on a considerable number of different strategies. In very basic terms, the development of an error control plan follows three basic steps:

1. The first step involves the development of an appropriate policy that must state a senior management commitment to minimise and control the effects of human and administrative error.

2. The policy should include directions to all managers, supervisors and other employees that everyone is responsible and accountable for establishing and maintaining accuracy in the accounting process.

3. Finally, if managers, supervisors and other employees are to be made responsible and accountable, then it is necessary to provide them with the necessary skills, knowledge and expertise to effectively allow them to perform those tasks. Policy must reflect three elements to achieve those necessary outcomes:

- effective training;
- continual supervision; and
- the development of staff disciplines.

Bob Curtis (1983, pp. 474–475) suggests that any error-control program should be a practical and realistic approach to the prevention of error. He recommends gathering error data from its source as follows:

- sales audits;
- incorrect delivery documentation;
- lay-by audits;
- cash-office operations; and
- accounts receivable and accounts payable.

Information on repetitive error could be collated by an Error Control Centre or a supervisor having responsibility for error control. Action plans can then be implemented for elimination and control of common error causes.

An action plan might include:

- Policies and procedures implemented and thoroughly promulgated to all employees that state precisely the standards required and the action taken in the event of continued poor performance.
- Individual interviews with employees who have more than the average error rate.
- Retraining for employees with poor performance.
- Counselling for continual poor performance.
- Job relocation to an area where accuracy standards have a lower priority for those with continual poor performance.
- Employment termination or dismissal as a final option rather than a solution for those with continual poor performance.
- The redesign of complex administrative procedures for those that create opportunities for unnecessary error.
- The development of appropriate audit and spot checking plans.
- Instilling accuracy attitudes and behaviour by encouraging employees to:
  - ask what effect this transaction will have on known or unknown losses;
  - conduct only one transaction at a time;
  - listen to all instructions;
  - ask questions if unsure of a procedure;
  - avoid 'cutting corners'; and
  - take the time to do every job properly.

The effects of a sound error-control plan are quite clear: errors can be reduced at their source, operating costs become lower and through increased controls and supervision, the potential for maximising profit is increased.

REVIEW QUESTIONS

1. There is a delivery stock shortage, where the shortage has been identified, a claim has been raised and has been accepted by a supplier. What effect (if any) has the shortage on your stocktake figure?

2. An employee has deliberately damaged a new guitar and marked down its selling price accordingly. The mark-down is recorded as damaged stock and the guitar is sold to the employee's friend at the recorded marked-down price. Does the sale transaction itself affect any retail loss figure? If not, why not? Is there a loss? If so, where?

3. A customer has recently purchased product at a sale price. A month later, the customer returns to your store and requests a refund at the normal pre-sale price. The refund is given. What effect (if any) has this transaction on either theoretical and actual stock levels or the dollar value of theoretical and stock levels?

4. A staff member records the mark-down of 20 checked shirts from $15.00 to $10.00, but forgets to change the price on the swing tags or price tickets. All the stock is sold at the original selling price of $15.00. How would this transaction affect any retail loss figure?

5. During a stocktake count, one staff member listed 24 table cloths, SKU 234765, as 234675. Would this apparent error affect the final stocktake figure? If so, how?

6. It is a very busy day, and staff are serving two customers at a time. The manager sees a traffic jam at the register and orders that all transactions are to be done manually from the open till until it quietens down. Over the next hour, 28 units of merchandise are sold for a total value of $1,568.00. Discuss the implications (if any) that have resulted from that one hour of frenzied trading.

7. A new sales person is given a book, listing 67 names and addresses. The sales person is told that the 67 names are current lay-bys that are in the lay-by reserve. He is told to audit them. On completion of the audit, he advised the manager that he has in fact found 72 lay-bys, but only 63 of those relate to the names and addresses that he was given. Another check confirms that this is correct. Is there any retail loss? Discuss and list the possibilities that may have created this situation.

8. A carton of stock arrives in your store or department. It is correctly addressed. The carton contains no paperwork whatsoever, but it is obvious that the contents relate to you. You are not very busy, so you take the stock and do a great job merchandising it ready for sale. What are the consequences (if any) of your actions?

9. Your manager tells you that she has been asked to help design a form for the company that will ensure delivery and receipt of all interstore transfers. She asks you to complete a list of key elements, and asks you to explain why you would list them.

10. A customer comes in with a toaster valued at $43.00 and tells you that it is faulty and she wants to exchange it. The management team are all out to lunch. You find another toaster, but not the same brand, selling for $42.00. As a gesture of goodwill, you offer her the alternative toaster, which she accepts, and you give her $1.00 from the till. You do nothing further except replace the faulty toaster on the shelf. The customer is so happy with your service she writes your store manager a letter. When you are called in to her office, instead of the expected accolades, you receive admonishment. Why?

3 Employee Malpractice

CHAPTER OBJECTIVES

1. To understand the extent of employee malpractice in retailing.
2. To identify operational areas that might provide shortfalls and loopholes.
3. To investigate the levels of employee fraud.
4. To understand the three ingredients of the fraud triangle.
5. To establish avenues of inquiry.
6. To develop Codes of Conduct for retail employees.

DEFINITION OF EMPLOYEE MALPRACTICE

Employee malpractice is any direct or indirect careless, negligent or criminal conduct by any employee that causes or has the potential to cause financial or economic loss, or denigrates the goodwill or reputation of his or her employer whilst serving in any position of trust.

Employee malpractice includes:

- theft of cash or property;
- damage to property or abuse to property belonging to the company, its employees or its customers;
- misuse of discount privileges;
- abuse of company time (getting paid for more hours than were actually worked);
- under-ringing of sales for friends and family;
- fraudulent business expense claims;
- excessively long breaks or lunches taken without approval;
- constant late starting or early finishing of work without approval;
- the use of sick leave entitlements when not actually sick;
- breach of company policies, procedures and confidentiality;
- poor appearance;
- poor attitude to customers;
- careless, irresponsible, negligent, offensive or illegal behaviour; and
- abuse of alcohol or illegal substances which affect work performance or the safety and wellbeing of other employees or customers.

THE EXTENT OF FRAUD

Employee activities attributable to malpractice can severely limit any retailer's ability to meet its operational objectives. Unless controlled, the effects of employee corruption, fraud, malpractice, misconduct, dishonesty or criminalism will ultimately affect the following four major elements in a retailer's performance:

- organisational image;
- quality of service;
- employee productivity; and
- employee morale.

This revelation is certainly not new and, although not strictly referring to the retail industry, these four major elements are included in the opening lines of the Criminal Justice Commission's (Queensland) excellent publication *Corruption Prevention Manual* (1993). This resource guide was mainly written for government departments, yet its relevance to the retail industry becomes quite apparent as the processes which motivate government employees to commit fraud are virtually the same as those which motivate employees in the private sector. Fraud and corruption data in Australia remain unclear and although actual figures are simply not known, there are some 'guesstimates' available as to the extent of the problem.

In 1986, the Federal Special Minister of State Mick Young was reported to say: 'Figures ranging from $5 billion to as high as $30 billion have been cited, the simple fact is we don't know…Press advertisements placed Australia-wide in 1993 claimed that the figure was closer to $10 billion' (Criminal Justice Commission, 1993, p. 1). Even more recently in September 1994, Commander Allen Bowles of the Victoria Police Major Fraud Group told a Melbourne Channel 10 news conference of the need to educate employers and employees on a code of conduct to report fraud. The report also revealed that fraud and corruption cost Australian employers some $4–5 billion annually (McMinn, 1994).

As a general comparison, the FBI and other US federal agencies estimate total fraud losses in the United States to be between $60 billion and $200 billion annually (Davis, 1995, p. 47).

These figures relate to public and private industry sectors as a whole rather than the retail industry specifically.

The Extent of Employee Malpractice in Retailing

The information in the preceding paragraph reveals that fraud figures are generally unknown and this is also the case for the retail industry. But with the high level of research capabilities available today, a range of statistical analytical processes can be applied to known crime data on internal frauds, numbers of employees charged, value of cash and property misappropriated, and other general information provided by law enforcement agencies to produce fairly accurate statements.

In Chapter 1, some survey data were examined and, when averaged, revealed that losses attributable to internal retail amounted to 67% of the total loss figure. This included some 23% attributable to human and administrative error, with the remaining

44% being attributed to employee malpractice. Like the national fraud figure, the actual loss to retailers from employee malpractice will never be known, but if the 44% is any guide, it does provide some indication as to the potential for dollar loss (see Figure 3.1).

AUSTRALIA

Gross Annual Sales: $108.3 billion

Losses: 2% of Gross Sales = $2.17 billion

Employee malpractice: 44% of Losses = $955 million

Figure 3.1. Employee malpractice: estimates of loss

(Source: ABS retail trade figures, Jan-Dec1994.)

This 44% figure is probably incorrect as it only reflects loss attributable to what we have previously described as known or unknown financial loss. The real loss will never be actually known because it is simply impossible to calculate each and every item that has ever been misappropriated, or to calculate the economic damage of other intangible losses suffered as a result of a careless or negligent action by an employee. The extent of employee malpractice will also never be known but there are claims that employee malpractice is responsible for up to 30% of business failures in the United States (Walsh & Healy, 1982, pp. 1–4). That's not good news for Australian or New Zealand retailers.

General Levels of Employee Malpractice

On page 13 of Chapter 1, sample formulae for estimating both shop stealing and employee malpractice were provided for use as a training tool for staff awareness programs. These formulae provide some very general indicators but it must be stressed that they are subject to assumptions made, that is, the number of employees who will steal on any given day. All the same, there is some evidence revealed by general research and individual organisations to quantify the levels of employee malpractice.

In his book, *Retail Security and Loss Prevention*, Hayes states that although 'shopstealing occurs more frequently then employee theft, the financial loss from dishonest employees is 15 times greater' (Hayes, 1991 p. 3). The earlier reference on the distribution of losses as shown in Figure 1.2 in Chapter 1 tends to support that statement. Customer dishonesty accounts for only 33% of the total loss figure, whereas employee malpractice suggests a much higher 44%. This is further supported by Barry Harris, the Security Manager of a major supermarket chain. In an address to a retail conference held in Sydney, Harris revealed major differences between the value of goods stolen by employees and those stolen by shop stealers. For one financial period, his comparisons revealed a greater theft value resulting from employee dishonesty than from shop stealing (see Figure 3.2).

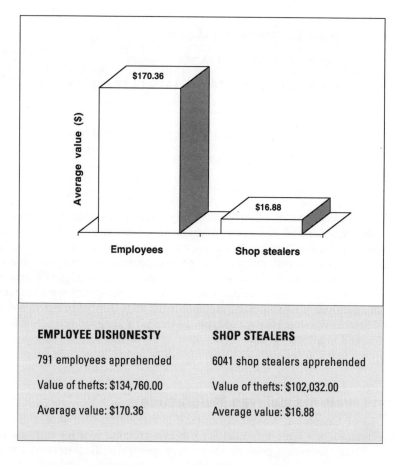

Figure 3.2. Comparison of employee and shop stealer retail theft

Given this kind of data, it would appear beneficial for retailers to maintain accurate information on the number of employees apprehended and the value of cash and stock stolen and recovered to provide some basis for future analysis.

Studies on Employee Malpractice Levels

There is research available that generally supports the theory that although instances of shop stealing are more prevalent, the value of employee dishonesty is far greater. Of course many authors differ on the extent of employee malpractice, but here are just a few estimates provided by a number of loss prevention practitioners and researchers who have conducted research on the levels of malpractice. In an early work entitled *Managing Employee Honesty*, Charles Carson suggests that 25% of employees are likely to steal and cites financial needs as the main cause (Carson, 1977, p. 14). In the same year, Denis Byrne and Peter Jones differed from this figure and suggested that 60% of employees steal from the workplace (Byrne & Jones, 1997, p. 2).

In 1983, Clark and Hollinger (p. 5) wrote their popular book *Theft by Employees* and suggested that there were no reliable statistical data to quantify actual figures, however they suggest that anywhere from 9% to 75% of employees engage in some form of theft from the workplace. They cited five major reasons for this:

- external economic pressures;
- youth and work (peer group pressure);
- opportunity;
- job dissatisfaction; and
- the knowledge that little or no punishment will be given in the event of discovery.

In 1984, Krupka suggested that 25% to 80% of employees of a particular business will become involved in employee theft if no active measures are in force (Krupka, 1984, pp. 146–148). More recently in 1993, Peter Berlin advised that employee theft can be responsible for as much as 80% of a store's shrinkage or as little as 10%, but it falls most often in the 20% to 25% range (Berlin, April 1993a). These references are certainly wide ranging, from a low of 9% to a high of 80%, with the average being around 46%. But what is important is the general theme that accompanies these results. Whatever the individual result of an organisation might be, it would appear that the level of employee malpractice is governed by the degree of control that the organisation has over its operating procedures.

A GREATER OPPORTUNITY FOR THEFT

The preceding paragraphs have shown that employee malpractice has the potential to cost retailers far more in terms of financial and economic loss than losses attributable to dishonest customers. The logic for this statement is quite simple. A dishonest customer needs an appropriate environment of opportunity to steal from a retailer. Timing must be right, the environment must be right and the opportunity must be right. The dishonest customer must run a gauntlet of anti-shop stealing initiatives to avoid detection. Locked display cases, store surveillance officers, closed-circuit television cameras, alert staff, electronic article surveillance systems and a host of other loss prevention precautions taken by a retailer to prevent and detect customer dishonesty. On the other hand, retailers allow staff far greater freedoms. Staff control the keys to locked display cabinets. They know when store surveillance officers are on duty, they know if their closed-circuit television systems are dummy or real. They know the limitations of their electronic article surveillance systems and, more importantly, they know and understand the organisation's policies, procedures and systems and all its inherent weaknesses and strengths.

The path to dishonest behaviour for customers has far more obstacles to deny theft than the path for a dishonest employee. Employees are in a far better position to commit fraud than customers, simply because they have the opportunity to exploit the system to a far greater degree than any would-be shop stealer. Opportunities for internal theft can only be limited by the level of internal controls imposed. Certainly, a retailer could design, develop and implement systems, policies and procedures that portray a total siege mentality and put into place rigid and uncompromising checks and balances that will, no doubt, prevent instances of loss. But the resulting effect on employee morale and the perception of mistrust will almost certainly affect the productivity of staff. On the other hand, the lack of internal checks and balances would provide many more opportunities for dishonesty to occur. Somewhere in the middle lies the correct answer: policy and procedures which not only provide for sound and functional checks and balances, but which are also designed to acknowledge trust and faith in the organisation's staff.

MORALITY, MOTIVATION AND EDUCATION

Morality and Motivation

The attitudes, ethics, morality and integrity of any population depends largely on its sociological history. What may be totally abhorrent for one person may be completely acceptable for another. A person, who has recently arrived from an overseas location where high level administrative corruption leads to crime as an accepted way of life and where survival depends entirely on the cunning and ingenuity of its population, may exploit the many apparent weaknesses in his or her new society as a means to an end. The attitudes and ethics of an integrated multicultural society will always differ and these differences may well be reflected in a workplace environment.

This concept tends to be supported by Stephen Ross in his book *Moral Decision* (1972). He suggests that social relations are influenced by politics, laws and customs, and that customs exert powerful influences on members of a society. He presents a case that people are born without basic moral attitudes. As they grow, they naturally acquire skills, habits, affections, loyalties and feelings as a result of conditioning. People learn through imitation and indirect influence.

Parental education is often quoted as being the major influence on children's lives and that it is the responsibility of parents to teach children the difference between right and wrong. But what is right or wrong? Can parents themselves differentiate between the two?

Case Study No. 3

Police were called to an incident involving some 10-year old children throwing rocks onto a main highway. One vehicle was hit, causing a huge dent in the bonnet. If it had gone through the windscreen, the driver or passenger may have been killed. Whilst police were en route, the driver had pulled off the road saw the young offenders and gave chase. He grabbed one by the arm. The boy was only 10 years of age and admitted to throwing the rocks. He gave his name and address and provided the name and address of his accomplice. The driver then let him go.

When police arrived at the scene, the driver gave the officers the information and whilst doing so, he saw the boy walking back accompanied by an angry looking adult male. Without any display of guilt, remorse or shame for what had occurred, the man's first words were, 'You grabbed my son and I'm going to sue you'. When police tried to explain that the driver and his passenger were nearly killed by the incident, the father replied, 'That's not the point, he grabbed my son and I'm suing'.

Despite a brief lecture on the menace of rocks flying onto roadways, the irate father continued to threaten that he was not only going to sue the driver for assaulting his son, he was going to sue the police for false arrest and just about everyone else. When told that if he wouldn't pay the damage caused to the truck, he would have to go to court, he said that he would sue the court as well. The police officer concerned stated that it was one of the worst displays of parental misguidance she had ever seen: 'If parents don't teach right from wrong, who's going to do it?' (Condensed and reprinted with permission from *The Chicago Tribune*, 1994.)

Moral and Ethical Education

On the question of moral and ethical education, Ross seeks assistance from the ancient Greek philosophers Plato, Socrates and Aristotle. He suggests that their teachings indicate three general methods for teaching morality (Ross, 1972, p. 210):

1. **Habit.** That which is acquired by practice and imitation.
2. **Social interaction.** Through the discovery of principles, justice, equality and fair play.
3. **Evaluation.** '…Man learns what is good or bad by studying the most effective means for gaining his desires, fulfilling his loyalties and realising his affections.'

The implications for retailers are very simple. Ross suggests that if people grow up in a society with well-defined social customs and norms, ethics and morality will tend to conform with those customs and norms (Ross, 1972, p. 207). If the Greek philosophers suggest that morality can be taught through habit, social interaction and evaluation, it then follows that retailing operating philosophies should aim for educational and training outcomes that promote these desired ideals.

Theories of Motivation

Some of the most discussed theories on motivation are Douglas McGregor's Theory X and Theory Y and, more recently, William Ouchi's Japanese management style of Theory Z (Figure 3.3).

THE X, Y, Z THEORIES OF MOTIVATION

Theory X

In theory X, an employee works:

- as little as possible;
- is resistant to change;
- has little ambition;
- is self-centred;
- passive; and
- indifferent, and wants to avoid responsibility.

This employee, with a lack of ambition is not motivated by doing the job, but rather by financial incentives. This employee does not object to being led or directed.

(Continued…)

Figure 3.3. The X, Y, Z Theories of Motivation

THE X, Y, Z THEORIES OF MOTIVATION (cont.)

Theory Y

A more enlightened approach, which gets better results is Theory Y. This humanistic approach to job motivation recognises that employees:

- do not dislike work;
- find work natural; and
- will expend physical and mental efforts at their jobs.

These employees:

- are capable of assuming responsibility;
- are capable of creating ideas;
- are ambitious;
- have potential for development; and
- want to do a good job.

Here, management provides an environment where the employee can exercise control and achievement.

Theory Z

Theory Z suggests that Japanese companies have a special way of managing employees so that a Z company culture exists. The company has a commitment to its workers that includes:

- humanised working conditions;
- long-term employment;
- long-range staff development;
- consensus decision making; and
- attention to human relations.

It also deals in trust, intimacy, and close personal relationships, and assumes that the worker's life is whole (rather than just 'nine to five'). It also touts 'Management By Walking About', a self-explanatory term.

Figure 3.3. The X, Y, Z Theories of Motivation

(Reprinted in part from Barefoot & Maxwell, 1987, *Corporate Security Administration and Management,* with permission and courtesy of Butterworths.)

The preceding paragraphs have provided some insight into basic issues of morality and motivation and it becomes quite obvious that the variables of human nature are extremely complex. The psychology of a person is as diverse as the universe and to attempt to understand every aspect of human nature is well beyond the scope of this book. The primary element to remember here is that retail employees are just as much affected by the activity of sociological processing as any other member of society. For these reasons alone, readers may well presume that the majority of retail employees will strive to be honest, but it is important to accept the fact that not all retail employees will have an honest approach. In their book *Fraud Auditing and Forensic Accounting*, Jack Bologna and Robert Lindquist provide some food for thought:

- some people are honest all of the time;
- some people (fewer than the above) are dishonest all of the time;
- most people are honest some of the time; and
- some people are honest most of the time.

There is one theory in the retail loss prevention industry commonly known as the '10/10/80 Theory' (Figure 3.4). Despite canvassing colleagues regarding the source of the following quote, its origin remains a mystery for now. Over the past 10 years or so, most industry loss prevention personnel have heard it repeated in one form or another. Whether there is any basis of fact for the theory is another question, but linked with the revelations of Bologna and Lindquist, it begins to take on a certain truism.

> 10% of any population will steal no matter what.
>
> Another 10% never would.
>
> The remaining 80% of the population would steal, but only if the threat of apprehension had been removed.

Figure 3.4. The 10/10/80 Theory

This provides for a new dimension on the question of morality and motivation. If the 10/10/80 theory has any substance, it tends to support all the assumptions made in the preceding paragraphs, but now adds a demotivating element: the possibility of apprehension or detection. Society would appear to be one of conformity: one of doing the right thing, to follow accepted habits and behavioural traits that society allows. It would seem that members of a society will follow these patterns, but once opportunities arise that allow individual members of the society to break away without fear of being caught, then individuals may well take that option. Justification for that deviation from the norm is then introduced and the reasons for lying, cheating and stealing become numerous. Some of the more common reasons include:

- people may believe that they can get away with it;
- people may consider that stealing is a challenge;
- people may feel frustrated or dissatisfied with their job;
- people may believe that everyone else does it, so why not them;
- people may feel abused by their employers and want to get even; and
- employees may think that a company is so big that stealing from it does not really matter.

IDENTIFYING THE FRAMEWORK OF FRAUD

Indicators of Malpractice

An analysis of the reasons given by many dishonest and corrupt employees who have been apprehended for a wide range of property offences indicates the existence of certain characteristics. These characteristics also existed before these employees were apprehended. These characteristics can act as red flags to provide a warning that something may be wrong and are not those usually displayed by the average employee. Dishonest employees may:

- have excessive gambling habits;
- be very close to clients or suppliers;
- have unusually high levels of personal debts;
- believe that rules are for other employees;
- enjoy lifestyles that appear well beyond their means;
- associate with people who tend to display deviant behaviour;
- display higher than normal desires for material possessions;
- be influenced by family, friends or suffer other peer group pressure;
- believe that their wages or salary are inconsistent with their responsibilities; and
- are always early, go home late, rarely take time off and are reluctant to take rostered days off, annual leave or other due holiday leave.

These 10 characteristics by themselves do not necessarily mean that an employee is engaged in widespread malpractice. What the list does provide is a 10-point general guide for potential problems. If an employee displays three or more of the characteristics listed, those facts alone should raise an alarm for management. Discreet inquiries should follow that will establish the need (if any) for further investigation. Managers can use a 10-point checklist for employee malpractice to test the potential for employee dishonesty. See sample checklist provided in Chapter 6.

The Three Ingredients of Malpractice

Many theories abound on why employees steal, but that is a question best left to psychologists, sociologists and criminologists. One loss-prevention manager suggests that internal malpractice occurs because people are naturally, 'greedy, needy or just plain seedy'! A more practical and simplistic explanation is offered by experienced loss-prevention consultants throughout the industry and, although there are many variations to the general theme, it would appear that employee malpractice becomes evident when a combination of three factors arise. W. Steve Albrecht and Gerald W. Wernz suggest that these involve 'situational pressure (usually a financial need), a perceived opportunity to commit and conceal a crime and a way to rationalise the dishonest act' (Albrecht & Wernz, 1993, p. 95). The following combinations are the common denominators for employee malpractice:

- need and a desire;
- opportunity; and
- rationalisation.

Need

To apply need as an excuse to steal in a Western society does pose some problems. In countries where there are relatively few welfare agencies, high levels of unemployment and no social security benefit systems, there is a real case for the justification of theft for people to survive. But to apply an excuse of need for those living in so-called civilised Western societies such as Australia and New Zealand, the abundance of welfare organisations, and the availability of government financial assistance would usually preclude any excuse of need. Certainly there would be cases where justifiable reasons are tendered and excuses of financial needs accepted, but more often than not, need is generated by a particular situation such as the payment of an outstanding and urgent gambling debt, or a sudden and overwhelming economic circumstance such as the cost of a funeral or a child's wedding. The need could be related to simple peer group pressure from family or friends or for a plain and simple thrill or for long-term criminal gains to maintain high lifestyles.

Opportunity

The 10/10/80 theory suggests that the society of today is an opportunistic one. Is there general support for this theory? Do employees work in an opportunistic workforce?

Case Study No. 4

In 1992, residents in Los Angeles, California, went on the rampage after a not-guilty verdict was entered against four white police officers charged with the brutal assault of a black motorist. The rampage quickly turned into a racial riot and it took a number of days for civil order to be restored. During the course of the events, looters and opportunists took advantage of the lawlessness and looted everything within the district. Shops were burned to the ground, windows were smashed and entire supermarkets, speciality shops and department stores were emptied. Certainly there was anger and frustration at the jury's decision, but it wasn't the decision that emptied the stores of cash and stock, it was simply that an opportunity had arisen and the threat of apprehension had been removed.

Case Study No. 5

In 1923, over 600 members of the Victoria Police Force went out on strike over pay and superannuation conditions. The news quickly spread throughout Melbourne that no police were on duty and resulted in:

> ...a wave of violence and looting on a scale never before witnessed in Melbourne. Two men were killed and hundreds more injured as mobs of roughs fought and looted in an orgy of violence. A tram was stopped and set on fire, and dozens of shop fronts were shattered by brazen looters who tried garments on for size before clearing all shops of stock! [Haldane, 1986, p. 180]

Once again, this had occurred because an opportunity had arisen and the threat of apprehension had been removed.

Case Study No. 6

During the mid-1980s, a spate of political incidents culminated in the bombing of the Turkish Consulate in Melbourne on 23 November 1986. The blast blew out neighbouring shop fronts and, despite the flames and having to dodge bits and pieces of the unfortunate bomber who had been blown up with his own bomb, looters suddenly appeared and carried off sunglasses, magazines, jewellery, cigarettes and clothing ripped off store dummies. A bystander stated: 'I saw people taking advantage, being greedy, acting like let's go for it, it was really disgusting!' (Cave & Botton, 1986). Why? Because an opportunity had arisen and the threat of apprehension was not present.

Lessons for Retailers

These examples suggest that retailers should be conscious that possibly 90% of their workforce (80% that might steal, plus the 10% that will steal) have the potential to wreak a substantial amount of financial and economic havoc. Unless, of course, there is a reduction of opportunities by the implementation of sound internal controls. Criminology research indicates that the greatest deterrents for malpractice to occur is the fear by the employee of detection and punishment.

Rationalisation

Rationalisation is simply the method by which a dishonest employee will justify an act of dishonesty. The rationalisation of the action will explain his or her behaviour or attitude in a rational and logical manner. It is a simple excuse or reason for dishonest employees to maintain their standing within their work group, a self-gratifying justification that states: I did nothing wrong! Some examples of rationalisation are shown in Figure 3.6.

Triangles of Loss

This three-way recipe for disaster is not unlike the Fire Triangle. The processes of combustion require the presence of combustible material (fuel), the presence of oxygen (air) and the attainment and maintenance of a certain minimum temperature (heat). These three elements represent the three sides of the Fire Triangle. Remove one or more sides of the Fire Triangle and combustion cannot take place. The practice of fire fighting is based on this simple principle. Albrecht and Wernz (1993, p. 95) suggest that the fire-triangle rule should be applied to the three sides of the Fraud Triangle.

Albrecht and Wernz state that although fraud or malpractice will never be completely eliminated from workplaces, the removal of need or opportunity or rationalisation from the Fraud Triangle may either collapse it entirely or, at the very least, substantially diminish it.

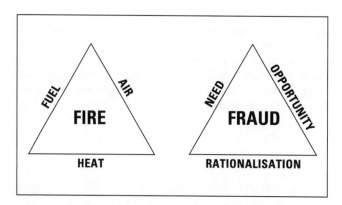

Figure 3.5. The Fire Triangle and the Fraud Triangle

Theft of stock, cash, property belonging to the company, its customers or other employees.	'I'm only borrowing it — I meant to pay it back!' 'I'm not hurting anybody!' 'The bosses would understand if they knew!' 'But everybody here does it!' 'The money Is being used for a good purpose!' 'But it's not that serious!' 'But if I don't give my friends a discount, they'll think I'm a wimp!'
Anger against managers, fellow employees or at the company generally.	'I can't stand my boss, I'll sneak off early once in a while just to keep out of the way.' 'It's only a job, besides they're ripping off customers with their high prices.'
Revenge for real or imagined grievances.	'Until they start liking me and accepting me, I'll just keep taking some of the tattslotto money from the staff funds. They never miss it anyway!' 'How dare they play with my emotions like that, I'll show them, I'll tear up this batch of cheques that have come in from debtors — I'm leaving anyway — so who cares!'
Restitution believed owed or earned, or a perception that the organisation does not pay enough.	'I'll just reward myself with the small change from the till every day!' 'The wages are so lousy, but I short change little old ladies by a 20-cent, 50-cent, a one or two-dollar coin, 10 or 15 times a day; they never check it; and why should the company care, they don't have a loss!'
Fear of demotion, redundancy or retrenchment.	'I'm going to get them, before they get me!'
Frustration at being overlooked for promotion.	'I didn't get the promotion, I deserved it, they didn't reward me, so I will just take enough to compensate what really is rightfully mine anyway.'

Figure 3.6. Examples of rationalisation

DISCOVERING THE LEVEL OF FRAUD

There are numerous measures available to determine the levels of employee malpractice. The following is a simple list of indicators and tests that provide clues that the organisation is suffering from the effects of careless, negligent or criminal actions:

- adverse company profit and loss statements;
- adverse stocktake results;
- staff questionnaire surveys;
- integrity testing; and
- mystery shopping operations.

Adverse Company Profit and Loss Statements

The end-of-year report will always indicate any major differences between operating loss or profit. There are retailers who do not stocktake throughout the year but monitor their progress through the calculation of operating profit. If the percentage profit differs vastly from previous years, and there is no ready explanation for the possible decline, then the possibility of malpractice is present.

Case Study No. 7

One retailer had a national chain of some 15 shops, and based his annual retail figures on a net profit margin of 18% rather than through an actual stocktaking process. The retailer purchased another chain increasing his outlets to 30. Although his operating philosophy was improved, his net profit dropped from 18% to 12%. A full investigation by retail loss prevention consultants revealed major discrepancies in the operating procedures of the newer stores and that store managers had taken advantage of the weaknesses to help themselves to a daily percentage of store takings.

Adverse Stocktake Results

Retailers conducting regular stocktakes are provided with data to compare theory and actual levels of stock. Progressive build-up of data over time provides for the identification of trends in retail loss results. The methods of stocktake are many and varied, and range from manual systems to highly sophisticated electronic data interchange systems. Stocktake results can be used to track suspect managers.

Case Study No. 8

A store manager in New South Wales who was suspected of gross malpractice was transferred to three different stores over a four-month period. Stocktakes were conducted on a monthly basis and the results indicated that whenever the store manager went into a new location, the sales figures would drop and the retail loss would increase. A question of dishonesty or just poor performance? The manager was counselled and was offered another position, but one which held fewer responsibilities. The offer was not taken up and the manager resigned. Losses immediately reduced and sales began to increase.

Other identifiers that suggest something may be wrong is a reordering or stock replacement system based on units being sold, not on a reorder system. This system is one where stock is replaced only when it is actually sold. The computer system is such that the sales transaction also activates the reordering process. If manual ordering systems are suddenly activated or spot checks reveal an out-of-stock situation, the question should be asked: why is there an apparent discrepancy? The disappearance of the stock suggests that it occurred in some other way than by a sale!

The sophistication of a modern stocktake process now provides for far greater accuracy in determining actual stock losses. But there is still some difficulty in determining the cause. As one store audit manager put it: 'As some 90% of our stock is bar-coded to size and colour, the "what" which has gone is not too hard to identify. However, the "how" we are still working on!' (Bullen, 1994, p. 10).

Staff Questionnaire Surveys

These surveys provide retailers with a snapshot view of their own employees' attitudes to and perceptions of the business. Quite often, senior managers and business owners perceive that their management and communication techniques provide a good workplace environment, that their employees are adequately paid, that training levels are high and that morale is well established. In some cases, management are so far removed from their employees and the in-store operations of the business that they not only fail to see declines in standards, but also become shop-blind to other problems such as a lack of morale, supervisor apathy and other concerns which affect shopfloor retailing.

The commissioning of staff questionnaire surveys often reveals massive problems of which senior managers are totally unaware. These types of surveys can be conducted either internally or externally, anonymously and voluntarily. The questions can provide answers to career structures, management involvement, employee commitment, communication, training and loss prevention attitudes. The attitudes and perceptions of staff sometimes provide startling results and, if used correctly, can provide management with a means by which to increase profits, reduce costs and control retail loss.

Integrity Testing

Also called honesty tests (not to be confused with honesty testing in pre-employment screening), these tests are designed primarily to confirm or negate the suspicious actions of employees. They should never be used at random. Employers should bear in mind that a commonsense approach must be adopted. Honesty and integrity testing is used when other evidence or information suggests that something is wrong. Integrity tests need to be conducted carefully and with professionalism. Entrapment of employees or the use of 'agent provocateurs' to seduce staff into committing fraud is both unethical and unlawful.

'Entrapment' simply means to lure into danger, difficulty or self-incrimination. An 'agent provocateur' is a person employed to associate with other employees or groups suspected of malpractice and other fraudulent or criminal activities and to incite them to commit illegal acts so as to incur a punishment.

Integrity tests need to be designed to allow employees a free choice either to commit an act or not to commit an act. Integrity testing should only be conducted by professional personnel and not by a misinformed supervisor. This is a very volatile area which could create considerable hostility from magistrates and industrial commissioners if not handled with fairness and frankness toward the suspect staff member.

Case Study No. 9

Complaints from elderly customers regarding a checkout operator frequently short changing them led to this Victorian retailer to conduct integrity tests. The issue needed to be dealt with sensibly and with sensitivity. In this case, the suspect cash register operator was tested on five separate occasions in one day by several elderly undercover operatives. Each visit was completely documented and every detail and transaction noted. The operation was captured on a hidden closed-circuit television camera and on four occasions, the operatives were short-changed $2.00

each. The cash register operator was confronted with the evidence in the presence of a witness of her choice. She initially denied the accusation, but when videotape was shown to her, admitted that she had in fact short-changed the elderly pensioners.

Case Study No. 10

In one NSW situation, a staff member was thought to be pocketing the proceeds of sales. A very simple operation followed with an undercover operative purchasing a single product, but suddenly remembering that his parking meter was about to expire, threw down the appropriate amount and bolted. The subsequent actions of the salesperson were then observed by another operative who watched as the money disappeared into a pocket. Policy in this store was simply that all cash transactions had to be placed in the till. This policy was taught at induction training and re-enforced throughout the year at awareness seminars. The magistrate hearing the case threw it out, because the operatives challenged the staff member immediately after he placed the money in his pocket. It was the magistrate's view that the operatives failed to allow the staff member sufficient time to put the money into the till. He gave the employee the benefit of the doubt as he stated that the operatives should have waited until after closing time to challenge the staff member. Beyond that time, the staff member had no legal right to retain possession of the cash and his intention therefore would have been beyond reasonable doubt.

Case Study No. 11

A Western Australian retailer was ordered to pay $7,000 in compensation to a shop assistant after she had admitted to stealing $200 per day. The Federal Industrial Relations Court was told by the retailer that the employee had admitted to a co-worker the theft of cash by using the no-sale key. An integrity test was carried out and found that the till was in fact short. When confronted, the employee admitted to not having rung up the sale. An investigation revealed that the no-sale key had been used eight times in one 90-minute period. The court found against the retailer for the following reasons:

- the employee was not advised during the investigation that her job was at risk or of the criminal implications;
- the retailer's investigation was seen as amateurish sleuthing and almost entrapment;
- the register roll should have been removed in the presence of the employee and an independent witness and signed by all parties;
- the employee had not been warned about the use of the no-sale button; and
- there was a clear difference between the retailer's policy and what happened in practice.

Honesty and integrity testing has its place, but a warning is given that some retail managers view these tests as a means by which to rid themselves of unproductive staff or other employees who no longer fit the image or culture of the organisation. They apply a 'three strikes and you're out' performance test on undesirable staff members whose only sin is that they no longer meet senior management's expectations. These tests become subjective rather than objective and do little more than provoke unnecessary industrial disputes. Although there is some evidence that this practice still occurs, they are the exceptions rather than the rule. Testing the efficiency and effectiveness of store operations is one thing, but unethical integrity tests are plainly unacceptable to any responsible retailer.

Design of Integrity Tests

Honesty and integrity testing is a contentious issue and can be the cause of serious concern between retailers, employees and respective union representatives. Prior to implementing any honesty or integrity test, retailers should seek both legal and industrial relations advice for their particular State and prepare honesty and integrity contingency plans based on mutually acceptable ground rules. There must be is a level playing field that takes into account both the rights of the employee and the employer. Readers are cautioned that in the event of any prosecution for dishonesty following the conduct of an honesty or integrity test, any unqualified action may be viewed by some magistrates as highly provocative. Many cases have been thrown out as a result of hasty operations being put together without proper planning.

Mystery Shopping Operations

These types of operations are quite popular for testing the efficiency and effectiveness of in-store operations and cover such areas as telephone techniques, customer service, POS techniques, selling skills, fitting room controls, loss-prevention awareness, etc. These operations may also be known as 'Training Needs Analysis Surveys' or 'Store Evaluation Surveys'.

If used correctly, they can provide high level data for management that highlight deficiencies in training which will allow the organisation to design and develop future training needs.

In short, the conduct of mystery shopping or training needs analysis surveys is a review or validation process. Some retailers have set programs in place and the surveys are conducted regularly. For store managers, the surveys are often a guide as to their own management success in maintaining store efficiency. Results are often promulgated in company newsletters and financial rewards are provided as incentives for managers and employees demonstrating high levels of service. For store managers that show repeated poor performance, the surveys may result in counselling, retraining, transfer, demotion or, at worst, dismissal.

One of the many side benefits these types of reviews have on loss prevention strategies is that they are extremely useful to determine staff attitudes toward loss prevention. For example, if a particular store shows unacceptable levels of retail loss, a survey might reveal that loss-prevention awareness levels are low because staff

failed to follow basic loss-prevention conventions such as:
- facing the front of the store most of the time;
- being conscious of all customers entering the store;
- failing to deny shop stealers opportunities to steal;
- leaving the shopfloor unattended; and
- failing to remove keys from registers.

These factors may identify either a lack of training or plain apathy by staff. If, however, loss-prevention training levels were high, then the failure to maintain loss-prevention awareness may also reflect poor attitudes for internal procedures which may lead to further evidence of dishonesty or malpractice.

INVESTIGATION RESOURCES

Sometimes it is very obvious where crime, fraud and malpractice lie. It may be at point of sale, in a particular department or a particular store, office, a warehouse or in a distribution centre. It could be in all of these areas. How do retailers find out where it is? Through the use of all the resources at their disposal. Retailing technology is becoming more and more advanced and computer deficiency analysis is capable of determining areas of discrepancies quickly and efficiently. Major retailers now employ highly technical and sophisticated computer software programs that analyse statistical data on customer flow and cash flow. Retail statisticians can produce histograms, frequency polygons and measure averages, modes and medians to determine variations and deviations on bell curves that will cause the average loss-prevention practitioner's head to spin.

Deficiency analysis technology is certainly making the investigation process more efficient and is fast becoming one of the main aids in loss-prevention strategies. But despite these technological advances, more often than not malpractice is discovered by pure accident.

Case Study No. 12

A female customer attempted to cash refund a particular line of product in a shop in Victoria. An area manager in the store at the time had extreme suspicions about the product. Thinking quickly and without fuss, she authorised the refund, obtained formal ID and obtained a vehicle registration number. The reason for her suspicion was that the product was a special line developed for future sale in New Zealand. It was not going to be sold in Australia. The area manager knew that the product was still in the Distribution Centre. So how could it suddenly turn up for refund in a Melbourne store? An investigation followed and resulted in a connection being made between the refunder and a female supervisor working at the Distribution Centre. Inquiries revealed that the supervisor was often allowed to work alone and unsupervised in the Distribution Centre after everyone else had left. After she had been arrested, product worth thousands of dollars was recovered at her home address.

The indicators which may have provided clues that malpractice is occurring in the workplace include:

- reports by employees;
- random audits;
- spot checks on tills;
- regular deficiency analysis;
- pure accident;
- low morale;
- regular absenteeism;
- constant register imbalances; and
- irregular stocktake results.

It must also be stated that any one of the above indicators is more often than not innocent and can be explained, but when two or more of these factors appear frequently throughout the investigation process, it may well be a good indication that malpractice is evident.

AN AROUND THE CLOCK APPROACH

An assumption must be made here that malpractice occurs whenever opportunities permit. These include periods when supervision is not present and controls are relaxed. The 'when' of fraud equals 'any time'! Malpractice will always occur unless the opportunities for malpractice are denied by the development of sound and practical internal loss-prevention controls. For example, when the authorisation, custody and accounting functions for stock are separated, malpractice is less likely to occur. But simply having controls is not enough: they must be enforced.

In one study, the most common element contributing to fraud was not so much the lack of internal controls, but the failure to enforce the existing ones (Albrecht & Wernz, 1993, p. 95). The actual timings of malpractice can also be important. For example, a crucial time for dishonest employees involves two elements:

- the actual theft of the item; and
- the removal of the item from the scene.

Experience suggests that the critical hours for a thief are:

- the hour before a store opens; and
- the hour immediately following its closure for the night.

It is during these periods when the thief is most likely to commit his or her crimes.

Case Study No. 13

A convenience store manager was well liked by all his staff. He would frequently let his staff go home early, and would always offer to clean up himself after the store closed. 'Don't worry about the rubbish', he would tell them, 'I'll fix it'. Staff thought he was being kind and considerate, until he was checked by security staff placing a rubbish bin full of unpaid groceries into the boot of his car after everyone else had left for the night.

THE ETHICS OF ACCEPTABLE BEHAVIOUR

Pilfering or Fringe Benefits?

The influences of need, greed and the other motivators that induce employees to steal emerge only when operating systems allow them to. Every employee within any given organisation comes under the influences of dishonest behaviour if the climate is right.

Of course, there are more opportunities for some to commit fraud than there are for others. The opportunities for fraud increase with seniority, as the greater the seniority and the greater the knowledge of the operation, the greater the degree of access an employee has to company assets.

Questions that are often asked at this point concern the degree by which fraud is viewed by some organisations. There is often a complete misuse of the terms 'pilfering' and 'fringe benefits'. Senior management can fall into the trap of allowing senior or key personnel a far greater degree of tolerance and indulgence for the misappropriation of assets than they do for much lower ranked employees.

An organisation should have the same policy for all employees, but the variables of life are such that there may be a real or perceived corporate moral dilemma. Certainly the question of individual employee worth would enter any argument. A senior manager who directs unauthorised company funds to maintaining his private residence may be forgiven for his 'indiscretion' as his economic worth to the company may far exceed the value of the funds misappropriated. However, the logic of this argument is of no consequence to the back dock supervisor formally dismissed for misappropriating out-of-date magazines. There are solid arguments for and against the complex issues involved in corporate ethics, but the bottom line is simply that the same rules must be applied to all employees.

Codes of Conduct

The majority of major retailers have now introduced codes of conduct for all employees which start with the chairman of the board. Codes of conduct set standards and dictate policy of what is acceptable in the company and what is not. Some companies dictate policy that prohibits the receiving of any gifts by any employee from clients, suppliers or anyone else. These prohibitions may extend to invitations to lunch, gala exhibitions, sporting events in corporate boxes, free flights interstate or other fringe benefits that some position of responsibility might invite. Some companies actively promote their codes of conduct in reception areas that publicly advise clients and suppliers that the acceptance of gifts by employees is prohibited and all gifts will be returned with a curt note advising the policy. Codes of conduct are included in employment agreements and all employees are then subjected to the same set of rules, guidelines and codes.

Case Study No. 14

A fraud investigation resulted after allegations that company A had 'poached' customers from company B when employees left company B to join company A. The investigation resulted in no criminal offences being disclosed relating to the original allegations. However during the investigation process, it was revealed that a senior production manager had been issuing false invoices to his new employer which had gained him some $30,000. Management was in a dilemma. Here was a senior person on whom the company relied. Profits were up under his guidance, and although his actions were dishonest and unacceptable, they were done out of apparent need rather than greed, but his actions were still not considered justifiable. Management made a decision: the senior manager was terminated for gross misconduct, was arrested, charged and convicted. He was sentenced to imprisonment. On his release, the company rehired him in a junior position allowing him to repay the loss incurred.

NON-COMPANY PERSONNEL AND THEFT

Often, retailers believe that only their own employees may be involved in malpractice, experience shows, however, that this is not the case. Malpractice is not only associated with employees working directly for the company, it also involves indirect personnel working within the company's environment. Direct and indirect theft is committed by:

- shopping centre security personnel;
- maintenance staff;
- delivery drivers;
- head office staff;
- warehouse personnel;

- managers; and
- supervisors.

In other words, any person within a given retail environment.

Case Study No. 15

A security guard who always helped to do the daily till balancing and helped staff put the night wallets into the bank night safe was also always removing a $20 or $50 note from the wallets. This continued for about 12 months. The store was never told about any banking irregularities by head office. Head office had no reconciliation system and the thefts mounted to $2,500 before the bank became suspicious. Who was at fault?

The store manager: for allowing an unauthorised person to do the balancing and banking.

Management: for failing to have a daily banking reconciliation system to check store deposits against register sales receipts.

Case Study No. 16

A very happy maintenance worker was always willing to clean out the back room and take out the rubbish for staff after attending to minor repairs such as replacing neon tubes, fixing door latches etc. It was not until a staff member, on returning from lunch, noticed the helpful friend putting the rubbish in his vehicle instead of the dump master bins that suspicions were aroused. The incidents were reported to security. On his next job he was followed, and as he placed the rubbish into his vehicle, security requested a check of the contents. The 'rubbish' turned out to be $800 worth of stock. This man had been regularly stealing for years and selling all the stolen stock at country markets.

Case Study No. 17

Two delivery drivers, who had regular runs to service stations, discovered that it was company policy that discrepancies valued below $10 per delivery would not be investigated. Each had about 25 deliveries to do, so each stole about $150 of stock each day, which they sold to customers in a pub every other Friday evening. That was until product was offered to the company security man who just happened to be in the pub to send off a friend.

REVIEW QUESTIONS

1. One theory on the extent of retail loss intimates that employee malpractice may have a greater and more disastrous effect on retailers than the effects of shop stealing. Explain.

2. Read the following case history, and discuss and answer the following questions:

   • Why did it occur?

   • What would you do to prevent it happening again?

   • How would you sell your plan to senior management?

Case Study No. 18

Twice a year the buyers for this particular company went overseas to select appropriate style and fashion garments for future seasons. They brought back many and varied samples which would be analysed and scrutinised for suitability. These were all being kept in various samples rooms spread around the buyers' offices. At one management meeting, an anxious buyer asked if anyone had seen a particular jacket which had apparently gone missing from her office. This prompted other buyers to report missing samples. An investigation followed that revealed a wide range of samples was apparently missing from every department. There were no real sample garment control measures in place, so stocktakes could not be conducted to confirm the loss, but estimates by the buyers indicated a major loss. This was obviously an inside job, but who was doing it? The buying staff themselves? Or was it the cleaners? Other employees from other departments?

An action plan was devised. The security manager decided to tempt the thief into thinking that opportunities to continue stealing the sample stock were being limited, but the action plan allowed for only one further and final week for the thief to steal. It was a gamble, would the thief take the bait?

A notice was promulgated to all staff stating that all sample product was about to be secured into one specially designed samples room. That staff had one week to place all samples into that room, and that after a certain date, the room would be locked and only authorised personnel would be allowed access via a magnetic card swipe reader. In the meantime, a closed-circuit television camera and time-lapse video recorder were secretly installed into the samples room which provided a 24-hour monitoring function on all those that entered the room.

Over the ensuing week, the video tapes revealed people coming and going, taking in and taking out sample product, all of which was authorised. The overnight tapes revealed nothing, except on one occasion when the door opened at 3.10 am one morning causing some excitement. However, it was a conscientious cleaner, who noticed the light on and entered the room to turn it off. On the final day, however, the day before the swipe readers were to be activated, the thief struck. It was late on a Sunday afternoon, the tapes showed a male enter the room, turn on the light and begin to make selections. He placed his selections on a box. The tape showed him clearly selecting samples, rejecting this one, keeping that one. As he did so, the tape showed him smoking a cigarette. He even held up some garments to the light to judge colour and styles providing excellent profiles to the hidden camera. In all, the thief selected some 43 shirts and jackets. He then left with his booty.

On the Monday morning, the video tape was shown to his superior. The company had a no smoking on the premises policy, and as he watched the thief helping himself, he commented: 'Well, if we can't get him for theft, we'll get him for smoking on the job!' The thief was a trusted computer programmer with access to all areas of the company premises at all times. His job was to monitor on-line computer processes from around the company's operating sites. Police were called and shown the tape. A magistrate subsequently authorised a search warrant on the employee's home and when the warrant was executed, police discovered more than $10,000 worth of stolen stock in his garage.

3. Conduct the following exercises at your next employee malpractice awareness training session.

Exercise No. 1

Suppose you are alone in a quiet coffee shop. Nobody is in view and you see a wallet on the table beside you, nobody is present. The wallet contains no identification, but there is $75 in notes in it. There is no possible way to identify its owner, despite the fact that it may have belonged to a pensioner who needed the money for weekly groceries and medicine.

Ask your participants to be honest, and ask who would keep the $75.00? At the very least, your audience will look nervously around to see if anyone else has put their hand up. Chances are, your entire group may take the opportunity to take the money. Why, because there is no threat of discovery — the threat of being found out has been removed: nobody saw you find it. Opportunity has given you $75.

Exercise No. 2

Same situation, but on this occasion, you have two friends with you. What would happen in this case? Most likely, all three would be instilled with a good dose of morality and hand the wallet into police. Why, because if the threat of appre- hension for a thief is present, the thief will not steal. Similarly, the wallet will be handed in, because the threat of being found out is present through the presence of the two other people.

4 Employee Malpractice: Prosecution Policy

CHAPTER OBJECTIVES

1. To understand the arguments for and against prosecution.
2. To identify the difference between a criminal justice system and a corporate justice system.
3. To consider the basics of 'right and wrong'.
4. To provide a justification for the setting of a standard.

REPORTING WORKPLACE OFFENCES

During the 1993/1994 financial period, the Statistical Section of the Queensland Police Service released figures for the number of charges laid against employees for the commission of internal offences (see Figure 4.1).

The Queensland figures indicate that on every working day during 1993/94, nearly 10 employee workplace offences were reported to police for investigation. Though not a large number, it is one which, when added to every other task police are required to do, places more and more strain on police resources. These figures are generally reflected across other Australian States and to New Zealand. The figures provide additional support that employee crime is alive and well. But a number of major questions arise out of these statistical figures. If those 2,793 Queensland workplace crimes are those that are known, how many crimes were actually committed in the workplace that were not reported? On the balance of probabilities, the real figure would have to be significantly higher.

Every reader of this book could no doubt relate a story that involves someone within the retail industry whose position was terminated for a dishonesty offence that would have resulted in charges being laid by police had the incident been reported. The reasons why they were not charged are perplexing. Retailers find numerous reasons which, in one way or another, are quite valid. The question whether to prosecute those found stealing requires consideration of attitudes toward human understanding, compassion, consideration for the employee's immediate family, loss

OFFENCE GROUP	NO. OFFENCES REPORTED
Steal as a servant	2237
Fraudulent false accounting	354
Fraudulent disposition of trust property	11
Misappropriation by officers of companies	191

Figure 4.1. Charges laid against the Commission of Internal Offences, 1993/94, Qld

(Source: Information provided by the Statistical Section, Information Resource Centre, Management Information Division, Queensland Police Service, May 1995.)

of respect for the employee from fellow employees and many other aspects. Conversely, the failure to report workplace crime could also be seen as detrimental to the operating philosophy of the company because other employees may see it as a weakness or the application of double standards if only some employees are reported.

CORPORATE OR CRIMINAL JUSTICE

Prosecution: The Criminal Justice System

A criminal justice system is simply a State or federal system of law enforcement agencies, legal processes and prison systems through which an individual prosecuted for an offence punishable by law may pass. A retail employee may become involved in the criminal justice system, if for one reason or another, he or she has been charged with an offence by police or other authorised officer empowered by an Act of Parliament. This may have been as a direct result of a complaint made to authorities by a retailer or, in less likely cases, where the police have actually detected the offences themselves.

The criminal justice system involves dealing with the police processes that include:

- the taking of statements;
- subsequent interrogation;
- fingerprinting and photographing suspects; and
- the formal laying of charges.

It includes all subsequent court appearances, bail applications, legal appeals and any time spent within a prison system. In summary, the criminal justice system is the normal legal process and procedure involved from the time a person may be arrested, processed, charged, tried, imprisoned and paroled, to the moment he or she is unconditionally returned to society as a free person.

Internal Management: The Corporate Justice System

The corporate justice system deals with retail employee dishonesty at an internal management level rather than the retailer reporting the act of alleged dishonesty to legal authorities. Corporate justice has become a recognised method of dealing with the fraudulent behaviour of employees, as existing criminal justice systems have been seen by some to be largely 'expensive, counter productive and ineffective' (Stenning 1984, p. 85). That conclusion may suggest an alternative course of action open to retailers. But is corporate justice a real attempt to overcome some of the perceived deficiencies of the criminal justice system as suggested by Stenning?

FOR PROSECUTION	AGAINST PROSECUTION
• The implementation of positive prosecution policies is a natural deterrent for all employees.	• Prosecution is both too expensive and too time consuming.
• Not seeking to prosecute a staff member for criminal offences only saves money in the short term.	• Prosecution of employees might lead to strained relationships with unions.
• A clear prosecution policy provides a level playing field for all employees.	• Police do not have the time or the resources to do the prosecution properly.
• Prosecution policies communicate the company message that it will not tolerate criminal acts.	• Prosecution invites unfavourable press for a retailer.
• Positive prosecution policies reinforce the Codes of Conduct.	• A vigorous prosecution policy might be seen as damaging to a retailer's image.
• Retailers have a civil duty to prosecute.	• A retailer may have a lack of confidence in the criminal justice system.
• Prosecution protects employers from allegations by future employers of failing to display a 'duty of care' toward the retail industry.	• A retailer might not believe in whistle blowing and would rather just get rid of the problem. • A retailer might consider that, on occasions, corporate justice is better served than criminal justice.

Figure 4.2. Arguments for and against a prosecution policy

RETAILERS' INTERPRETATION OF CRIME

In 1978, a well-known criminologist, Edwin Sutherland, in his book *Criminology*, accused mining, manufacturing, mercantile and financial corporations as being the greatest of all criminals. He suggested that criminal offences committed by the larger organisations included:

- misrepresentation in advertising;
- infringements of patents;
- financial frauds; and
- other miscellaneous activities (Sutherland, 1978, p. 46).

Sutherland believed that these types of organisations may be the most dangerous to society as they impinge on human rights and democratic institutions. He concluded that those organisations that practise fraud feel no pangs of conscience, therefore their apparent illegal practices are not regarded by them as being criminal (Sutherland, 1978, p. 47).

This presents an interesting scenario for retailers. If Sutherland's assessments are correct, it may well follow that retail employee malpractice might not necessarily be regarded by some retailers as being criminal in the accepted sense of the word. There may even be reluctance to pass on alleged offenders to law enforcement bodies if the retailers themselves could not justify their own interpretation of what was criminal and what was not.

Retailers have one primary objective and that is simply to maximise profit. In any case of fraud, or other criminal act where money was stolen by staff, one of the first considerations for the retailer would be an attempt to regain the funds misappropriated. Retailers may have little interest in long, drawn-out court battles which may or may not arrive at a result favourable to them. There is little satisfaction in the knowledge that the employee who is handed over to authorities and sentenced to two years' imprisonment will, as a result, be unable to repay the thousands stolen. A retailer, for that reason alone, may be more inclined to negotiate the matter internally to the satisfaction of all parties concerned. But what are the moral and legal justifications of corporate justice?

MORAL VIEWPOINTS ON PROSECUTION

Duty to Report Crime

In earlier times, it was a common belief that any criminal act deserved punishment and the ancient code of 'an eye for an eye' prevailed (Duffee 1976, p. 72). These views were widely accepted by moralists who believed that dishonesty was against God's laws. Moralists took the commandment 'thou shalt not steal' in a very literal sense and sought to regulate the morals of others. Historically, the failure to report offences was not only considered morally wrong, but specific laws existed to prosecute those failing to report crimes.

Prior to 1974, it was a misdemeanour in Common Law to abstain from prosecuting an offender who had committed a crime (Paul 1969, p. 94). Similarly, earlier British law indicated that the offence of 'compounding' was committed if promises were made to thieves not to prosecute if stolen goods were returned or restitution made. Common thoughts of the day indicated that 'mercy should be shown — not sold!' (Turner, 1952, p. 323). It would seem then that a duty existed, at that time, for criminals to be reported in order to have them properly dealt with according to both the law of the land and, more importantly, God's law. This viewpoint is further expounded through the classical school of criminology which held that mortal beings possessed an innate sense of what was right and what was wrong. This was regarded as absolute because people have an inborn moral sense. Therefore, it was impossible to justify a wrong act and such an act deserved punishment (Duffee, 1976, p. 72). Duffee further stated that some individuals equated crime with sin and tended to make crime a moral issue: 'The laws of man become the laws of God and therefore man must suffer for breaking both the moral order of society and the commandments of God' (Duffee, 1976, p. 73).

Utilitarianism

The question of morality can provoke a great deal of philosophical argument. Moralists may well argue that to steal is wrong and is against 'God's basic laws'. But what is right and what is wrong? J.S. Mill, an exponent of utilitarianism, wrote:

> the creed which accepts as the foundation of morals, Utility or the Greatest Happiness Principle, holds that actions are right in proportion as they tend to promote happiness, wrong as they tend to produce the reverse of happiness. By happiness is intended pleasure and the absence of pain: by unhappiness, pain, and the privation of pleasure. [Quoted in Flew, 1979, p. 335]

These moral principles beg some questions. If a staff member were to steal cash from his employer, the actual theft and the appropriation of the cash may well give the employee intense pleasure: does that make the theft right? If the employee were caught and handed over to the police, the actions of handing over the employee may give someone else great pleasure. For that person, the action was right, but the same action would cause the employee great pain: does this make the action wrong?

Here, there is a great dilemma, this one action of theft has created a paradox. In theory, the single action is either right or wrong, it cannot be both. This utilitarian viewpoint on moral principles may be described as being rather one sided in that morality is being analysed entirely through 'actions and their consequences, never through motives or intentions' (Flew, 1979, p. 335).

A Different Approach

In his book *Moral Decision,* Ross (1972, p. 29) states that, 'loyalty to a moral principle without qualification or exception is plain[ly] wrong'. Ross (1972, p. 30) continues: 'justice is best, not in terms of virtue in general, but concretely in the lives of men and the order of society.' Perhaps this view has been taken up by present-day rational thinkers and has encouraged law makers to remove the offence of 'compounding', thereby no longer making it an offence for retailers failing to report acts of fraudulent behaviour to legal authorities.

There are, however, some exceptions to this rule. For example, specific statutes exist that require pharmacists to report the theft of controlled substances (certain categories of classified drugs) by employees or any other person to both their State controlling bodies and the police. This requirement also applies to New Zealand pharmacists.

The preceding paragraphs establish that corporate justice is seen perhaps as a suitable alternative to criminal justice and that the question of morality may not even be relevant. If senior management in a retail environment believe, after taking into account the possible variables, that the interests of all parties concerned are best dealt with at a corporate level, then that decision may not be described as being unethical or inappropriate. On the other hand, the retailer may well decide that the interests of the business are better served if the matters are dealt with by the authorities — this decision would be equally correct.

SETTING STANDARDS FOR EMPLOYEES

Situational corporate justice might provide solutions in determining each and every individual case of malpractice on its own merits, but one major problem that conflicts with this philosophy may be a perception by other staff that double standards are being applied. This is a difficult situation for employers. If employees believe that a level playing field does not exist within their own organisation, then respect and trust for their senior management could diminish, morale could suffer and productivity levels could reduce.

For retailers, malpractice means one of two outcomes. First, it can be an event which may be contrary to the retailer's code or conduct or in breach of a company policy or procedure, but is not necessarily criminal in nature. The incident may be resolved through retraining, counselling or applying other internal disciplines. Second, it can be an event which is also regarded as employee malpractice but which may be far sinister in nature and one that may well breach the law of the land.

It is in these cases that retailers need to apply a standard formula. If a retailer believes that sufficient evidence exists to support a case for prosecution and that prosecution is in the retailer's best interests, then all the facts of the matter need to be collated and presented to police for their further investigation. At the very least, retailers need to make a firm statement on their internal standards of behaviour. This should be included in all workplace employment agreements, be reinforced through signage (see Figure 4.3) and be an integral part of induction and general company training.

NOTICE TO ALL EMPLOYEES

Any employee who breaches company Codes of Conduct or any policy or procedure without reasonable excuse will face a hearing which may result in disciplinary action being taken, dismissal, criminal prosecution or other legal recourse.

Figure 4.3. Example of Employee Code of Conduct Notice

Moral decision making is an individual concept. It is completely situational — it can change as situations change. What may be a definite moral principle for one retailer may not be to another. Yet the same retailers could have similar moral standards on other issues. Whatever event occurs that requires an examination of the moral and ethical standards of retailers, it needs to be examined on its own merits using rational thought processes.

In today's society, the norm is the standard expected by the majority of reasonable free thinkers. If a particular situation is considered acceptable by a cross-section of the community, which reflected the overall views of society, then this would be regarded as an acceptable standard of behaviour. The processes of corporate justice will be allowed to continue as long as it is not considered as being either morally or ethically corruptive.

REVIEW QUESTIONS

Case Study No. 19

A senior employee was caught out after she had conducted a fraudulent and fictitious refund to the value of $40.00, despite her annual salary being substantial. The incident was reported to the head of the company who said the final decision should be left to you.

The Investigation

Interviews with all parties had revealed that the employee had been with the company for many years, and in recognition of her service had been transferred on promotion to a remote location. Her husband gave up a good job to go with her. After some time at her new site, she was again transferred to another remote location on promotion and once again her husband gave up his new job to accompany her. At the latest transfer, no work was available for the husband, suitable accommodation was hard to find and expensive. The cost of transferring was high and the couple's reserve funds were depleted. The action took place between paydays when the 'cupboard was bare' and the weekend loomed. There was no cash around, so she illegally took the $40.

The Case for the Employee

Need. Overwhelming economic need due to loss of spouse's income.

Opportunity. A senior employee with open and unlimited access to company regional sites and cash registers.

Employee rationalisation. 'They owe it to me for all the moves I've made, besides I'm only "borrowing" the money, and I'll repay it when we're back on our feet.'

The Case for Management — Company Preventative Strategy

- **Need.** Management had a responsibility and an accountability not only to the proprietors of the organisation, but also to their employees to ensure they had sufficient policy and knowledge on their employee's current financial needs. This also extended to the provision of making available temporary emergency cash loans.

- **Opportunity.** Cash handling controls and refund procedures were being monitored through independent deficiency analysis by central computer monitoring. Sound paperwork trails that needed to be verified through review resulted in this act of malpractice being reported to management.

- **Rationalisation.** Company codes of conduct, and clear statements relating to employee malpractice were promulgated throughout the organisation and reinforced by competency-based fraud awareness training. Generally, employees of this organisation were explicitly told that malpractice would not be tolerated under any circumstances. The employee's records, however, did not indicate attendance at any malpractice-related training course.

Syndicate Discussions
Discuss the situation and the following:

1. Did management fail to take into account the high costs involved with transfer, or to ensure that the staff member had sufficient capital in the short term to meet the interim costs of the transfer? Explain your answer.

2. Did management fail to convey to the staff member that emergency staff loans were available to any staff member who needed temporary cash funding? Explain your answer. What are the implications here?

3. Should your Managing Director, Chairman of the Board, or whoever will determine this case and take on the role of a judge and jury, have all the facts at hand? Is he or she really qualified to handle the complex issues that are involved?

4. What effect will a corporate justice decision have on other staff?

5. What effect will a criminal justice decision have on other staff?

6. In your opinion, whose interests are best served here and why?
   a) the employee
   b) the employer
   c) the community

7. *Result A*

   A decision has been made to terminate the employee's position and to prosecute. Two months later, you receive a phone call from another retailer who wants to hire her. The inquirer is unaware that the former employee lost her job and was charged. You have been told to address the issue. What are you going to tell the retailer?

8. *Result B*

   A decision was made to keep her on. She was given a loan to help her over her immediate financial needs, but also told that no further promotions would be given. After eight months, she left the company of her own accord.

   Another inquiry is received asking you about this former employee.

   What is your response?

9. Do you have a duty of care or legal obligation to tell the prospective employer what you know?

5 Employee Malpractice: Internal Controls

CHAPTER OBJECTIVES

1. To understand the concept of risk management.
2. To design an internal control plan.
3. To identify the difference between proactive and reactive controls.
4. To examine examples of control measures.

RISK ANALYSIS

Internal controls are implemented to safeguard against error, mistake and fraudulent activity. Determining the levels of risk within any organisation is dependent upon a thorough risk analysis of the entire operation. The value of complete risk analysis provides for future loss prevention and security strategies that may limit the effects of expected and unexpected financial loss. Risk analysis may take the form of security reviews, surveys or audits that reveal weaknesses in the operating system. The *Best Practice Guide*, a fraud-control document provided by the Fraud Policy and Prevention Branch of the Federal Justice Office of the Attorney-General's Department, suggests that the process of risk analysis can be either simple or complex (Figure 5.1).

Probability, Frequency and Cost of Potential Loss

As with government departments and agencies, the complexity of risk analysis is entirely dependent on a retailer's exposure to the risks involved. Risk analysis involves surveying the vulnerabilities that the retailer may be exposed to. Once all possible vulnerabilities have been identified, the probability of the event occurring, the frequency at which the incident may occur and the financial impact it would have on the organisation are then calculated.

For example, a retailer might conduct a risk analysis on the probability, frequency and cost factors of a fire occurring at one of their retail outlets.

COMPLEX RISK ANALYSIS

'There are a number of valid methodologies that have been applied to Commonwealth departments and agencies. Some use multifaceted questionnaires or a spreadsheet with complex weightings to produce a mathematical assessment of the risk factors based upon the qualitative assessments of the managers responsible for the function.'

SIMPLE RISK ANALYSIS

'Others are little more than a number of key factors that the person undertaking the risk assessment applies.'

'The nature of the functions that the department or agency performs will determine which is the most appropriate methodology.'

Figure 5.1. Simple or complex risk analysis methods

(Source: Fraud Policy and Prevention Branch, Federal Justice Office, Attorney-General's Department.)

Probability

The probability of a fire occurring may be high, medium or low, and depends upon on the level of fire-prevention equipment available and the level of fire-prevention training given to staff. The degree to which fire-prevention standards have been maintained is also included here.

Frequency

The frequency of fires largely depends on particular situations, but calculations can be made through historical and statistical data that might suggest that the frequency of a fire event at a given location may be once every 25 years.

The Cost Factor

The cost of a fire might be calculated at half a million dollars, and therefore the retailer may decide that he will offset the risk by taking out insurance to cover the possibility of fire. In a similar way, the effects of other financial disasters such as earthquakes, floods and even burglary and robbery may also be covered by insurance.

The probability, frequency and costs of employee malpractice can also be assessed, but a retailer may offset this risk by the implementation of internal controls rather than by expensive insurance policies. Some insurance companies may provide cover against employee fraud through professional indemnity policies, or extended fidelity guarantees. Some employment bodies, such as those which govern the legal profession, are required by law to provide financial restitution to victims who have suffered the effects of 'defalcations' (fraudulent misappropriation of funds) committed on them by their solicitors.

But for retailers, the reality of offsetting employee malpractice by insurance may be too expensive an option. A better option for retailers is to examine their own exposures to risk and implement internal controls that deny or minimise opportunities for internal error, mistake or fraud in the first place.

INTERNAL CONTROL PLANS

There can never be one single security or loss prevention measure that will defeat each and every loss contingency. Just as military strategists plan for the defence of strategic positions, so too must retailers plan for the defence of their assets.

Defence in Depth

The concept of defence in depth is not a new one. Military generals have applied these principles for hundreds of years. The concept of defence in depth is the application of a multiple layer of barriers that denies an enemy strategic ground, or in the case of retailers, denies opportunists seizing company assets.

For example, in 1941, during the Second World War, the Australian 9th Division, commanded by Major General Morshead, successfully defended Tobruk harbour in Italian North Africa against repeated attacks from superior German forces led by Lieutenant General Rommel. The success was due to many factors, but one vital factor included the use of a strategic defence in-depth plan which consisted of mine fields, anti-tank ditches, wire obstacles, concrete weapon pits, booby traps, antipersonnel mines, and road blocks (Hall, 1984 p. 52).

Figure 5.2. Defence of a strategic battle field

The success of the defence in-depth strategic plans at Tobruk can be similarly applied by retailers. As stated earlier, it is not one single factor that will act as a catalyst to prevent malpractice. It is the use of a multiple layer of barriers that will ultimately deny the opportunists.

Figure 5.3. Defence of a strategic asset protection plan

Proactive and Reactive Approaches

As already shown, there are many different approaches in countering malpractice in the workplace, but two basic elements feature regularly as common factors in any internal control plan. These involve both 'before the event' measures and 'after the event' measures. These elements are more commonly referred to as being either proactive or reactive. Proactive means creating or controlling a situation by taking the initiative, or doing something before an anticipated event occurs. Reactive is the opposite: doing something after the event. The adoption of both a proactive and a reactive approach is crucial for any internal control plan to be effective. Both are closely linked and neither will succeed without the other.

A proactive or reactive approach can utilise a number of different corruption prevention models. The Criminal Justice Commission (Queensland) offers several approaches which are shown in Figure 5.4.

PROACTIVE APPROACH

1. Management-based model

Where supervisors are required to be aware of those elements that are at risk and take proactive steps to discourage staff from becoming involved in corrupt activity.

This model is viewed as an integral part of:

• prevention strategy;

• behavioural modification; and

• enlightened staff management.

REACTIVE APPROACH

1. Accountancy-based model

Where the skills of auditors and accountants are employed to examine financial systems to make it more difficult for people to embezzle or defraud.

[Note: This can be either proactive or reactive. Proactive in designing the initial system. Reactive in examining the results.]

2. Policing model

Where allegations of malpractice are investigated and action or prosecution is instigated against those found offending.

Figure 5.4. Proactive and reactive approaches to corruption prevention

(Source: Corruption prevention models are reprinted courtesy and permission of the Criminal Justice Commission (Queensland) and derived (and edited in part) from their *Corruption Prevention Manual* 1993.)

PROACTIVE INTERNAL CONTROLS

Five-Phase Systems Approach

In considering proactive controls, it is the *before* element that is crucial. For this reason, it is a retailer's responsibility to ensure that measures are designed that aim to minimise, control and, where possible, eliminate opportunities for error, mistake or fraud. For retailers, the emphasis is on a five-phase systems approach, involving:

• analysis;
• design;
• development;
• conduct; and
• validation of proactive internal control programs.

The systems approach is one where each of the five elements interlocks with all of the others (Figure 5.5). The emphasis is on results, and the system has an in-built flexibility for the process of change. This system is in a constant rotational state. Its processes are one where validation is followed by further analysis, redesign, and redevelopment for continual improvement.

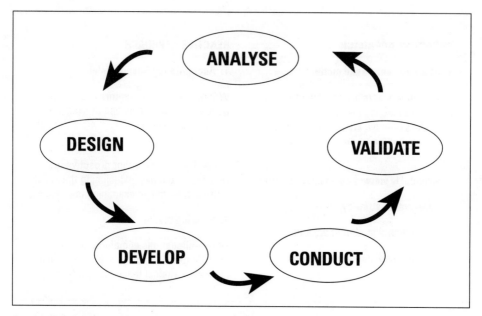

Figure 5.5. A five-phase systems approach

A retailer aims to provide its customers with an effective and efficient service that maximises sales and profit. A retailer's chances of success in a highly competitive industry can only be based on its ability to be prepared to adapt within a constantly changing environment. This is only achieved by monitoring the market, knowing your competitors and understanding client needs. This also involves many other initiatives that will enable the retailer to maintain market share. Naturally, this is reliant on the retailer's internal operating systems, the level of expertise of its staff, its training systems and the levels of its internal controls. A retailer's ultimate aim should ensure that each of its employees is capable of performing his or her job with high levels of expertise. Those employees who are well trained in their job have high morale, have positive and active management and communication links and are far more likely to perform more productively than those who lack good leadership, are untrained and suffer poor morale.

Although every person within a retail organisation has a responsibility for the elimination of opportunities for malpractice, senior management retains the responsibility for the planning, organising, leading and controlling of employee malpractice prevention strategies which may include:

- a senior management commitment;
- pre-employment screening;
- induction programs;
- company policy and procedures;
- awareness training; and
- stock and cash controls.

Senior Management Commitment

Not only must retail management make a commitment to develop strategic loss prevention plans, but they must also be seen to be actively supporting proactive control strategies. If there is little or no commitment from the top, how can store managers or other supervisors expect support from subordinates? Management needs to consider the issues shown in Figure 5.6.

DELEGATION OF LOSS CONTROL MANAGEMENT	This may be in the formation of a loss prevention department or the delegation of internal controls to external consultants and auditors, or the implementation of spot checks and audits by supervising staff.
COMPANY CODES OF CONDUCT	The development of standards that clearly provide all company personnel with a statement of what is and is not acceptable behaviour.
ROTATION OF DUTIES POLICY	A policy which may direct the rotation of staff involved in the ordering, receipt and payment of merchandise.
EMPLOYMENT CONTRACTS	Employment contracts that provide clear guidelines for staff, store managers and other personnel which may include: • duties and responsibilities; • performance standards; • codes of dress and standards of behaviour; • rates of pay/salary and staff discount entitlements; and • retirement and termination of employment conditions.

Figure 5.6. Senior management commitment

Pre-employment screening

Pre-employment screening is now considered a major tool in ensuring the right retail staff for the right job. Often, emphasis is only placed on the person's apparent ability to perform the task. Sadly, honesty and integrity attributes of prospective applicants are often neglected. In the retailing industry, employees are virtually given free access to thousands of dollars' worth of cash and merchandise.

Case Study No. 20

The manager of a shoe store in Queensland's Pacific Fair shopping centre was suitably impressed by an applicant's excellent reference. It described him as being punctual, a snappy dresser, great with customers, and having higher average sales than others. He generally appeared to be the best candidate for the job. The manager even rang the referee, who was quite happy to verify all of these wonderful characteristics. The applicant was hired. Some time later, the shop started to show higher than usual refunds and an investigation revealed fraud. At about that time, rumours were circulating that the new employee had lost his position from his previous employer for fraudulent refunds and had been arrested and charged by police. The manager once again rang the writer of the reference, who replied, 'Well you asked about his ability to do the job, not about his honesty or integrity!'.

One fact that is often overlooked by retailers is that retail employees whose previous positions have been terminated for offences of gross misconduct involving theft of cash or stock, usually attempt to find work in similar retail employment. The next applicant that might seek employment with your organisation may have extremely high levels of knowledge, skills and expertise to perform the duties required, but the applicant's ethical and moral attitudes may also need some scrutiny.

Application Screening

Applications for employment involve two major elements: first, the job or position description; and second, the person specification or person selection criteria (see Figure 5.7).

POSITION DESCRIPTION	PERSON SPECIFICATION
A job or position description outlines what the actual job requires. It states:	A person specification or the selection criteria for the position relate to the applicant's ability to be able to do the job. It states:
• the duties required;	• the experience required;
• the qualifications needed ;	• leadership ability;
• the hours to be worked; and	• demonstrated sales records; and
• any other information that specifically relates to the job itself.	• knowledge of retailing systems.

Figure 5.7. The two elements of employment applications

The Application Form

The vital aspect to remember here is that any application for employment must be submitted in writing. Employment application forms need to be designed and administered that allow for the following information about the applicant to be processed:

- the applicant's name;
- home address;
- home phone number;
- an emergency contact number;
- tax file number;
- previous work history (past three to five years);
- educational qualifications; and
- a selection of referees.

EEO Guidelines

State and Federal equal opportunity legislation prohibits questions that require an applicant's age, marital status, religion, race or other information which is not relevant to the position being applied for. This also includes questions that relate to criminal convictions. The question 'Have you ever been convicted of a criminal offence? — if so, provide details' is now considered unfavourable by civil liberty groups and against the general thrust of equal opportunity legislation. However, some retailing positions require a great deal of trust and it may be more appropriate to seek written approval from an applicant allowing a retailer to apply to the local State Commissioner of Police for the release of any information, such as criminal or driving convictions, that may be relevant to the position being sought.

Other considerations on the application form may be the inclusion of the requirement that during the course of employment, all employees may be required to open their personal bags, lockers and vehicles for random inspection by authorised company personnel. A code of conduct with regard to breaches of company policy could also be included.

Finally, the application form should conclude with words that suggest that the applicant has completed the application form accurately and is aware that any false or deliberate omissions may result in the application's rejection, or if the applicant is employed on the basis of information supplied which is consequently found to be false, his or her position may be terminated.

Case Study No. 21

A senior retail manager was employed on the basis of his previous experience and that he held retail tertiary qualifications. His references were checked and his experience was proven to be correct. He was duly appointed to a senior position. After a few months, the manager's performance did not reflect the level of qualifications that the manager stated he held. A subsequent investigation revealed that he had provided false documentation of his qualifications to secure the position. The retailer took legal action and the offender was charged by police with the Victorian offence of obtaining a financial advantage by deception. The retailer also sought restitution of part of the salary paid to the manager. The offender was subsequently convicted, fined and ordered to repay a portion of the salary earned.

Employment Verification

The application form needs to be carefully scrutinised and any gaps in time frames need to be explored. If, for example, a prospective employee stated that he or she was overseas for three months, that information needs to be checked thoroughly. It may have been the case that the applicant had spent that time other than where stated. This is simply done through the last point of reference. Contact all establishments listed, verify the dates, the positions held and the reason for leaving. Ask the most vital question for pre-employment screening: 'Would you employ this person again? If not, why not?'

Reference Checking

As the majority of references written do not accurately reflect the characteristics of the person described, it is necessary to contact the referee for a personal discussion. Many people write references for family, friends or former employees largely as an obligation or a favour. The writer therefore may feel it necessary to write something more favourable for the applicant than is actually the case. The only way to ascertain the sincerity and truthfulness of the reference is to seek verification from the writer. Most reference writers tend to open up more with a verbal report. Ask them such questions as 'Why do you say that?' or 'Can you give me an example of what you mean when you say…?'.

Integrity Interviews

Some retailers utilise integrity interviews that aim to test the honesty and integrity attitudes of prospective employees. These are usually in the form of psychological profiles that require prospective employees to answer a set of questions that can gauge the applicant's inclination toward dishonest behaviour. The results are then determined through computer analysis or by trained counsellors.

Any indication that the prospective employee may have dishonest tendencies automatically rejects the application. The types and format of integrity testing interviews need to be fully scrutinised before any retailer attempts them. There is some controversy over their degree of success, and retailers are advised to seek professional guidance from human resource agencies, employer organisations such as the various employers' chambers of commerce and industry found in each State or local retail trading associations.

Employee Induction Programs

Induction programs are those that new employees attend on joining the company or attend shortly afterwards. Induction programs provide in-house training for all new staff on all aspects of the business and includes loss and crime prevention issues. It is during these induction sessions that the company's standards are explained.

Employee induction programs:

- ensure that all participants understand company policies and procedures relating to employee malpractice;
- can be used to validate and verify whether participants have read and signed codes of conduct and their employment contracts;
- teach staff the why, where, when and how of loss prevention strategies;
- describe to staff the company policy on prosecution;
- educate staff about the reporting of malpractice as a commitment and responsibility, and that the failure to report shows a lack of interest in the wellbeing of the company and for other honest staff; and
- advise staff of the procedures for reporting malpractice through either hotlines or reward lines or other means of communication.

Company Policy and Procedures

Policies should prevent malpractice by denying, deterring or delaying the three elements of employee malpractice. Policies should be developed for:

- staff discount purchases;
- staff purchases generally;
- staff hold and staff lay-bys;
- access and key controls;
- banking procedures;
- after-hours attendances;
- combination safe access;
- cheques and credit cards; and
- cash refunds and exchanges.

Additionally, specific policies on the prosecution of employee offenders and legal courses of action for the restitution, compensation or recovery of financial loss need to be considered.

Employee Malpractice Awareness Training

Unlike induction courses, awareness courses need to be conducted with line managers and store managers in the prevention and detection of employee malpractice. Training should be linked with other loss prevention and security-related programs. These courses should aim at providing line managers with the ability to recognise and react to instances of malpractice. All training should be linked to other internal programs dealing with cash and stock controls. Well-trained line managers have far greater opportunities to detect employee malpractice than any other employee, and that includes loss-prevention staff, simply because they tend to be closer to the source.

Stock, Cash and Physical Controls

Internal stock, cash and physical controls need to be implemented. Some examples are shown in Figure 5.8.

CASH CONTROLS
- Register roll reviews.
- Change should always be called out aloud.
- Customers should always be given their receipt.
- Excess cash should be cleared to a drop safe.
- Staff should focus on one transaction at a time.
- Cheques and credit cards controls.
- Cash refunds, exchanges and credits controls.
- Void and no-sale transaction controls.
- Cash register shortage controls.
- Price variation reports.
- Bank deposit controls.

STOCK CONTROLS
- Accounting controls for all incoming stock.
- Interstore transfer controls.
- Stock urgently out of store, ie, fashion parades, displays, police exhibits, alterations, dry cleaners.
- Stocktake procedures.

PHYSICAL CONTROLS
- Staff purchases controls.
- Staff lay-by controls.
- Staff holds controls.
- Staff bag checks.
- Unauthorised use of or wearing of store stock controls.
- After-hours alarm attendances.
- Combination safe access controls.
- Access and key controls.
- Rubbish removal controls.

Figure 5.8. Examples of stock, cash and physical controls

COMMUNICATING THE MESSAGE

Communication throughout the organisation is fundamental in raising loss prevention and crime prevention awareness levels. Raising these levels through proactive controls can be achieved by:

- loss prevention seminars;
- 30-minute in-house instant sessions on various loss prevention topics;
- monthly bulletins or weekly one-page flyers to maintain awareness;
- 'message of the week' flyers included in pay slips;
- loss prevention and security posters displayed in stores, warehouses, distribution centres and office areas;
- computer-based loss prevention games;
- poster programs;
- warehouse awareness meetings;
- active encouragement;
- the formation of loss-prevention committees; and
- loss-prevention bonus incentives or competitions.

REACTIVE CONTROL MEASURES

This usually involves the two corruption prevention models of accounting and policing measures that are designed to provide for a reporting function and an auditing and deficiency analysis service. These 'after the event' measures include both internal measures and external responses which may involve the use of a law enforcement agency to further investigate or process employees where evidence suggests that prosecution is necessary. However, prior to this event, the reactive measures for retailers could include:

- introduction of a company hotline or reward line;
- the use of an external agency for the reporting of employee malpractice;
- mystery shopping operations;
- honesty testing;
- deficiency analysis reporting;
- spot checks;
- stocktakes;
- investigation policy (which includes courses of action open on discovery of malpractice);
- prosecution policy; and
- point-of-sale exception monitoring (POS/EM).

Figure 5.9. POS/EM (point of sale exception monitoring) automatically monitors all POS terminals for suspected shortages, register theft, and collusion

(Photograph courtesy and permission of Sensormatic Australia Pty Ltd)

The Use of Law Enforcement Agencies

The assistance of law enforcement agencies can also be utilised through contact with local Crime Prevention Bureaux which can provide useful advice on crime prevention measures. In some cases, they might even attend retailer's premises for the conduct of seminars or general crime presentations involving personal safety and security issues.

Police are also utilised in a reactive measure in providing crime-related data for statistical review and analysis and, where necessary, the processing of employees apprehended for fraudulent activity.

SAMPLE IN-STORE AUDIT CHECKLIST

Store: _____   Date: _____

Manager: _____   Auditor: _____

Period under review: _____

	(Auditor to tick box either yes or no)	YES	NO

1. CONDUCT REGISTER BALANCE. Did you balance?
    If No, please explain: ☐ ☐

2. VOIDS, REFUNDS, CREDITS. Were they authorised?
    If No, please explain: ☐ ☐

3. OBTAIN LIST OF CURRENT LAYBYS. Balance against reserve?
    If No, please explain: ☐ ☐

4. CREDIT VOUCHER BOOK. All apparently correct?
    If No, please explain: ☐ ☐

5. GIFT VOUCHER BOOK. Did you balance?
    If No, please explain: ☐ ☐

6. CUSTOMER HOLDS AND ORDERS. Are overdues acceptable?
    If No, please explain: ☐ ☐

7. STOCK TRANSFER SHEETS. Are all current transfers actioned?
    If No, please explain: ☐ ☐

8. PETTY CASH. Check vouchers and receipts. Do they match entries?
    If No, please explain: ☐ ☐

9. Does theoretical petty cash balance correspond with actual cash total?
    If No, please explain: ☐ ☐

10. Have all STAFF DISCOUNT PURCHASES been approved?
    If No, please explain: ☐ ☐

11. END-OF-DAY RECONCILIATION SHEETS. Do they balance?
    If No, please explain: ☐ ☐

12. CHECK ALL BANKING DEPOSITS. Do they correspond with:
    (a): End-of-day Reconciliation Sheets (b): Bank Statements?
    If No, please explain: ☐ ☐

13. Is the back room neat and tidy? ☐ ☐

14. Is all excess stock cleared and put out for sale or placed in reserve? ☐ ☐

15. Is the store free of food and drink? ☐ ☐

16. Are all staff dressed appropriately? ☐ ☐

17. Is the store selling-floor neat and tidy? ☐ ☐

EVALUATION REPORT

TOTAL NO. OF SCORES: ☐

Retailing demands high standards, any store achieving anything less that 17 'yes' responses is considered to be unacceptable. This store is:

ACCEPTABLE: ☐   **UNACCEPTABLE:** ☐

If store is scored as unacceptable, list unacceptable matters:

_____

_____

_____

_____

Conduct meeting with manager or person in charge of the store to develop positive action plans to achieve an acceptable result.

ACTION PLAN AGREED UPON:

_____

_____

_____

_____

I acknowledge the above action plan to achieve an acceptable result on my next store audit. I am aware that such an audit may occur any time within the next 30 days. I have received a copy of this audit report.

_____   _____   _____
(Manager's signature)   (Auditor's signature)   (Date signed)

REVIEW QUESTIONS

1. What impact will a risk analysis have on store operations?

2. You are a new manager opening a small store in the suburbs, can you use the police in determining any loss-control plan you may be considering? If so, what information could the police provide and how is this useful to your operations.

3. Explain the concept of defence in-depth. How does this help retailers?

4. What is the main factor in a proactive prevention model? Explain your answer.

5. A five-phase systems approach for internal control is one which is in a constant state of change. What are some of the benefits for such an internal control system?

6. How would you obtain a senior management commitment to an internal loss prevention plan?

7. Conduct a survey of four major retailers in your area and obtain their Codes of Conduct for their employees. Compare your results and discuss. How do these Codes of Conduct assist in controlling loss?

8. Examine the manner in which your company conducts its register operations. Are there any apparent weaknesses that show a potential for loss. If so, draft up a proposal for control. Be prepared to justify your recommendations.

9. You have been authorised by your company to increase awareness on the benefits of internal controls. Develop the following:

   a) A 10-minute motivational talk on the benefits of internal controls, with particular emphasis on how internal controls protect employees.

   b) Design a poster with an internal control 'message of the week' that reflects your 10-minute talk.

6 The Processes of Investigation

CHAPTER OBJECTIVES

1. To examine the types of retail investigation.
2. To establish a preliminary framework for the conduct of an investigation.
3. To consider the options and avenues open for inquiry.
4. To understand the importance of information and evidence and its relevance to court proceedings.
5. To provide guidelines for the conduct of an investigation into allegations of employee malpractice.
6. To provide guidelines for the preparation of investigative reports.

INTRODUCTION

An investigation is a logical process of reasoning through which the person conducting the investigation may consider all the circumstances. An investigation involves a search for the truth to ascertain the proof or disproof of the circumstances being investigated. An investigation examines questions of what, when, where, how, who and why.

Investigations take on many different forms. An investigation might be a simple inquiry relating to a carton of stock that has gone missing. It may involve allegations of unusual discrepancies in a particular line of stock or accusations of sexual harassment. Investigations may include:

- theft of cash or stock by employees or customers;
- employee malpractice;
- stocktake discrepancies;
- exit interviews
- pre-employment screening;
- sexual harassment;
- employee discrimination;

- background investigations;
- workers compensation claims
- workplace accidents;
- customer compensation claims; and
- competitor profile investigations.

ESTABLISH THE NEED FOR AN INVESTIGATION

Before the conduct of any investigation, a number of preliminaries need to be established to determines whether or not an actual need for an investigation exists. Three questions need to be asked:

1. Did an incident actually occur?
2. Who was responsible for committing the incident?
3. Can the incident be connected to those identified as being responsible?

Case Study No. 22

An allegation was made by the new proprietors of a timber import business that employees were responsible for missing timber valued at more than $250,000. The new proprietors stated that stocktakes revealed apparent timber discrepancies equalling two semi-trailer loads. A preliminary investigation conducted to establish if a theft had actually occurred, revealed that there was no theft and no discrepancy. This timber business received bulk shipments of logs from overseas which needed to be sawn into appropriately sized planks. The new proprietors based their assumptions on the pre-sawn value of the timber, not the post-sawn value. The discrepancy was soon explained by the two-storey high pile of sawdust in the rear of the yard.

THE INVESTIGATION

Internal or External Agencies

Large retail organisations usually have their own internal loss-prevention and security departments. Security practitioners and investigators employed by these organisations usually conduct a variety of investigations and perform other duties for their individual employers.

For the smaller retailer, however, the role of investigator is often passed on to a line supervisor or other employee who may not have the necessary skills to conduct investigations to a satisfactory conclusion. Some retailers seek assistance from outside organisations and use private agents or licensed inquiry agencies to conduct these investigations on their behalf.

Before contracting external agencies to conduct any investigation, a number of issues need to be addressed. In Australia and New Zealand, any person who carries out an investigation on behalf of a third party for a fee and is not directly employed by the third party, may be required at law to hold a specific licence to conduct investigations. Investigation agencies such as these are generally referred to as inquiry agencies and their investigators are generally referred to as inquiry agents. The term private detective is not generally used in Australia or New Zealand. Both the investigation company and the person conducting the investigation may need to be licensed. Before out-sourcing any external investigations, retailers should consider the following:

- set a budget for the investigation;
- obtain a number of quotes from prospective inquiry agencies;
- ensure that both the inquiry agency and the private inquiry agent hold a government licence to conduct investigations;
- ascertain from the inquiry agency and the private inquiry agent if either belong to an industry association;
- establish if the association has a Code of Ethics;
- verify the bona fides of the agency or agents with the association;
- obtain references from the agency;
- reference check all inquiry agencies and agents before final approval;
- once an inquiry agency has been selected, agree on a price;
- insist that all results be documented and a full report forwarded by an agreed date; and
- ensure that all proprietary rights are maintained for all information gathered in the course of the investigation.

Attributes of an Investigator

The processes of an investigation must follow a logical sequence where an investigator needs patience and diligence.

Any process of investigation requires an analytical mind and a genuine interest in pursuing an answer. Not just any answer, but rather the correct answer. An experienced investigator relies on facts and the ability to gather and evaluate these facts. There are no magical crystal balls, wishing wells or mysterious sixth senses to assist investigators. Only experience can develop the ability in investigators to detect fraudulent behaviour, deceit, and inconsistencies in evidence and information to provide the links that direct an inquiry to a successful conclusion. A good investigator needs to:

- be experienced in investigation techniques;
- be independent and detached;
- be totally objective;

- be able to distinguish fact from fiction;
- be able to analyse the consequences of the investigation; and
- be able to recommend a suitable outcome.

An Objective Investigational Approach

Police detectives are taught to conduct investigations using an objective approach which might take the following forms:

- collate all the available facts;
- consider the facts and let these facts present their own theories;
- avoid attempts to distort the facts to fit a preconceived notion or theory;
- as other facts emerge, use them to test the validity of the theory;
- avoid jumping to conclusions;
- proceed methodically, avoiding procrastination;
- maintain an open mind; and
- be aware that deciding to do nothing is making a decision which may be the right decision in the circumstances.

Undercover Agents

Undercover operations utilise the services of licensed inquiry agents as undercover operatives. These may be employed to infiltrate retail workplaces, shops, warehouses and distribution centres to identify sources of theft or other matters requiring investigation.

These operations are expensive to conduct for a number of reasons. A good undercover operator is extremely hard to find. Personnel employed in these operations are often required to lead double lives and may be required to establish several identities to ensure the integrity of operations. Undercover work is often hazardous and a totally professional approach is required to be able to handle the many contingencies that may be encountered while acting as an undercover agent.

Usually, the need for an undercover operation is immediate and good operatives are difficult to obtain on short notice, often resulting in poor choices being made. In trying to assist a client, an inquiry agency may call upon an unemployed friend of a friend who may not have any real experience. The inexperienced person might then be given a two-minute briefing and dumped at the site. Undercover operations are inherently emotive, and if discovered may result in industrial action or the operative being physically injured. For these reasons, only professional investigators should be used. If an inquiry agency cannot provide a suitably qualified and experienced undercover agent, then the proposed operation should not proceed.

There are occasions when it is more sensible to defer an investigation rather than proceed and create a difficult situation.

EVIDENCE

All investigations involve the gathering and analysis of information in one form or another. The information gathered may consist of facts, testimony, documents and/or physical exhibits. The source of this information usually originates from:

- the site of the incident or 'the scene of the crime';
- the examination of exhibits such as register rolls, delivery notes, refund vouchers;
- interviews of all personnel involved or those who witnessed the event;
- general information received from:
  - customers,
  - workplace colleagues, or
  - members of the general public;
- the examination of records such as audit reports, discrepancy reports and exception reports;
- the surveillance of suspects through direct observation or through the use of closed-circuit television; and
- final interviews when allegations are put to suspects.

Admissible and Inadmissible Evidence

Evidence is the means by which facts are proven. It is the information that is presented at court to prove the commission of a criminal offence, the person committing the offence and the connection between the offender and the offence. In a court of law, some forms of evidence are accepted and others are not. That which is not is regarded as inadmissible evidence and therefore cannot be presented. There are many rules that dictate what is admissible and what is not, and investigators often have problems with this concept. Far too often investigators will reject or refuse to examine information or other evidence simply because they believe that, for whatever reason, the evidence may be inadmissible in a court of law. This belief is wrong. The only test an investigator needs to apply to a question concerning admissibility is simply: Is this information or evidence relevant to the facts under inquiry? If the answer is yes, then the investigator must include it.

The question of admissibility must be left to the legal processes which determine what is admissible. Investigators must not assume the role of court prosecutor, magistrate or judge. An investigator's role is to gather all the facts of the matter and present them in a logical sequence.

Before the court hearing, a case prosecutor will preview all the facts and advise the investigator of any contents that may or may not be presented. In any case, a court will be the ultimate authority in determining the status of any questionable evidence.

THE INVESTIGATION PROCESS

Any incident where malpractice is alleged must be investigated. An investigation is a search for the truth, and must be done professionally, compassionately and fairly. The facts of the matter must be clearly understood before any action is taken. The following guidelines, although not exhaustive, are provided to assist retailers with a basic investigation process.

STEP 1   Receipt of information suggesting employee malpractice

Once information is received or malpractice is suspected, a number of options are open. The retailer can task a competent member of management who has an open mind and possesses the appropriate investigative attitudes, experience and authority to make management decisions. Alternatively, the retailer could out-source the investigation to a professional inquiry agency to report back to a senior manager with an investigative report.

STEP 2   Information and evidence gathering

The investigator gathers and analyses all available facts, documents, testimonies and exhibits. This includes analysing the signs that suggest something is wrong, for example:

- changes in an employee's work behaviour from punctual to tardy;
- constant financial difficulties;
- reduced employee performance problems; or
- an employee's emotional problems, such as trauma caused through a family death or divorce.

All the evidence must then be reviewed and any irrelevant information discarded.

The elimination process

In any investigative process where there are numerous suspects, rather than attempting to identify the offender outright, it is often better to eliminate other possibilities.

Take the example shown in Figure 6.1 where nine register shortages totalling $250.00 have occurred. Seven employees worked in the store over the 14-day period of the shortages. By checking staff attendances against shortages reports (Figure 6.1), several eliminations can be made.

First, Robert was on rostered days off on two occasions that the shortages occurred. John was on rostered days off and on leave for four occasions. When the theft occurred, Tony was present each day. Both Elizabeth and Denise were also on rostered days off on three occasions the thefts occurred. Maxine worked every day. The elimination process has indicated two main suspects: Tony and Maxine.

Action plans may now be developed that might test these theories further to establish if one or the other, or both are responsible.

This example is a demonstration of the process of elimination in a very simple form. It is based on the assumption that no-one else was involved. If, however, other staff were also randomly removing cash from the till, the elimination process may become more complex.

Once all relevant evidence is evaluated and conclusions are reached, it may substantiate an allegation of malpractice, or result in no action being taken. There may be some information, but insufficient to draw significant conclusions. If this is the case, the incident should be closed and details filed. At the completion of the investigation process, four courses of action are usually open.

1. No further action and the matter closed.

2. Counselling or disciplinary action taken against the employee concerned and the behaviour corrected through retraining and the implementation of positive action plans.

3. Dismissal on grounds of breach of company policy, ie, Gross Misconduct.

4. Dismissal and subsequent reporting of offences to law enforcement agencies.

If the information suggests that no further action is warranted and management closes the investigation, that is the end of the matter. If however, the investigation suggests that further action is warranted, then the employee should be allowed to have the allegations placed before them.

STEP 3   Interviewing the suspect employee

Once the facts of the inquiry have been established, the allegation should be put before the employee. This should be done in private. However, consider the presence of a witness who is the same sex as the employee to avoid any accusations of impropriety. The employee is also entitled to have a witness present.

During the interview:

*   take notes;
*   have all physical exhibits available;
*   keep in mind every known fact;
*   let the facts decide the issues and invite explanations;
*   avoid accusations;
*   check every explanation for validity;
*   check all details; and
*   avoid tangents, but stay with the facts.

Figure 6.1. Fortnightly Cash Register Shortage Report

JAN 1996	Mon 1	Tue 2	Wed 3	Thu 4	Fri 5	Sat 6	Sun 7	Mon 8	Tue 9	Wed 10	Thu 11	Fri 12	Sat 13	Sun 14
SHORTAGES	—	$15	$20	$45	$30	—	—	$35	$35	—	$20	—	$20	$30
ROBERT	—	RDO	—	—	—	—	RDO	—	—	—	—	—	—	RDO
JOHN	—	—	—	—	—	RDO	RDO	ON LEAVE			—	—	—	—
TONY	RDO	—	—	—	—	RDO	RDO	—	—	—	—	RDO	—	—
ELIZABETH	—	—	—	—	—	RDO	—	—	RDO	Sick	—	—	RDO	RDO
ALEX	—	RDO	RDO	—	—	—	—	RDO	RDO	RDO	—	—	—	—
MAXINE	Sick	—	—	—	—	—	—	—	—	RDO	—	RDO	—	—
DENISE	—	RDO	RDO	—	—	—	—	RDO	RDO	RDO	—	—	—	—

RDO = ROSTERED DAY OFF

STEP 4   Is the employee's explanation consistent with the facts?

Is the employee telling the truth? Body language experts suggest that people who may not be telling the truth will:

- act nervously;
- fidget;
- touch their noses;
- tug at their collars;
- avoid looking people in the eye; and
- perspire.

Although this behaviour may be normal for some people, usually body language may provide indicators.

STEP 5   If dismissal eventuates

Ensure a policy exists for an exit questionnaire which may reveal operational weaknesses in the system. If the recovery of stolen cash or other property is involved, ensure that a recovery plan has been agreed upon.

Case Study No. 23

The loss prevention manager for one company had his position terminated for failing to comply with company directives. As part of the separation process, the employee was graciously allowed to retain use of the company car for one month. On the day the car was to be returned, the vehicle mysteriously rolled backward down a hill, hit a fire hydrant and suffered major damage. Accident or design? The vehicle should have been returned on the day of separation.

Complete an end of engagement check list to ensure that all company property is returned such as:

- company vehicles;
- identification cards;
- company credit cards;
- keys and access control cards; and
- staff discount cards.

Also arrange for such things as outstanding staff credit purchases to be acquitted.

STEP 6   Prosecuting and involving the police

Management can easily fall into the trap of rationalising criminal behaviour, but the decision to prosecute must still be left for senior management. However, if senior management has decided that charges are warranted, then avoid any compromises that the employee may offer. If a criminal offence has been detected and senior management express a desire to prosecute, then police must be called. Advise the employee to that effect, but if an employee chooses at that point to leave, there is no power to detain them unless a citizen's arrest has been made. This can only be done if the person making the arrest was the person who actually found the employee committing the offence. If an employee indicates an intention to leave the premises, allow them to do so. Any deliberate attempt to hold an employee could result in counter charges of:

- false arrest;

- false imprisonment;

- assault; or

- a combination of all of the above.

If an employee does leave prior to police arriving, then provide the investigating officers with all the information and evidence and follow their further instructions.

INVESTIGATION REPORTS

In his book *The Process of Investigation*, Sennewald states that an investigative report should be a:

> clear, comprehensive, written documentation of facts, presented chronologically, which is an objective, first person recording of the investigator's experiences, conversations and observations regarding a specific assignment and from which the events of the investigation can be reconstructed even after a lapse of time. [Sennewald, 1981, p. 157-158]

In brief, the investigator reports need to be clear, concise and correct. The investigative report should follow the basic principles outlined in Figure 6.2.

Take notes and write them at the time of the event.	A good investigator always carries a small ruled note book that readily fits into any pocket for details of conversations, events, incidents & observations. Although small electronic notepads are becoming popular, keeping notes in their simplest form is often more practical.
Keep language simple.	Avoid the use of technical or professional terms, if required, explain them. Instead of writing: 'He decamped from the scene', write: 'He left the scene'.
Record only what was said or what was observed	1. 'He told me that he saw Andrea put the money into her left pocket.' 2. 'I saw the person cross Smith Street from north to south in front of Crouch's chemist shop.'
Keep to the facts of the matter — avoid assumptions.	A fact: 'I saw him pause, look at the object and then walk away'. An assumption: 'I think he had it in his mind to steal it'.
Make the report understandable.	What actually happened? 1. 'The figures, although in discrepancy, told me that all was not as it should have been because the tapes were missing.' OR 2. 'Although the register roll was missing, backup data on daily takings confirmed the discrepancy.'
Prepare the report in a sequential format.	Allow the report to flow naturally without losing the continuity of the events.
Ensure that the report does not leave unanswered questions.	'...and in conclusion, I plan to take some positive steps to ensure that this doesn't happen again!' Question: What positive steps?

Figure 6.2. Basic investigative report-writing principles

CONCLUSION

The processes of investigation are not rigid. Certainly there are guidelines to follow, but investigations tend to direct themselves. One vital clue or piece of information may lead the investigation to another. An investigator's role is to be able to develop expertise and skills in steering the investigation in the right direction to a successful conclusion. Keeping the right focus and avoiding tangents are features that good investigators apply.

An investigation is not unlike a large jigsaw puzzle. An investigator takes each piece at a time, examining it for relevance and suitability before linking it with another piece. Slowly, the puzzle takes shape as more of the pieces are joined together. The greatest satisfaction for the investigator is to make all the pieces fit to complete the puzzle.

10-POINT CHECKLIST FOR EMPLOYEE MALPRACTICE

(Tick the appropriate box) YES NO

1. Does this employee display an unusually close or over friendly attitude to any of our clients or suppliers?

2. Is there any evidence that suggests that this employee has excessive gambling habits?

3. Is there any evidence to suggest that this employee has unusually high levels of personal debts?

4. Does this employee display an attitude that suggests that company rules are only for other employees?

5. Is there any evidence that this employee enjoys a lifestyle that appears beyond his/her usual means?

6. Is there evidence that this employee associates with people who tend to display deviant behaviour?

7. Does this employee display higher than normal desires for material possessions?

8. Is there evidence of undue influence by family, friends or other peer group pressure in relation to dishonesty?

9. Does this employee display an attitude that his/her salary is inconsistent with his/her responsibilities?

10. Is this employee always early, goes home late, rarely takes rostered days off, leave or other holidays due?

If three or more YES boxes have been ticked, further investigation is warranted. A discreet action plan to monitor the performance of this employee also should be considered. Discuss with senior management.

Figure 6.3. A 10-point checklist for employee malpractice

REVIEW QUESTIONS

You are a regional supervisor for a multinational retailer specialising in small appliances. The managing director of the company has tasked you to investigate the following case.

Case Study No. 24

Information provided indicates that a male person has been attending at the company's outlets at coastal towns from Townsville to Coffs Harbour. His method of operation is always the same. He enters the store with what appears to be a valid company Credit Note for goods purchased between $45 and $75. He explains that he needs to cash the Credit Note as he is in desperate financial need. The company has a cash-back policy on Credit Notes. Information suggests that the first Credit Note was refunded six weeks ago; the last, just yesterday. You have been given the following information:

- you have 16 Credit Note Vouchers from outlets that have already been refunded;

- the Credit Notes are a genuine company print;

- your preliminary assessment reveals that the Credit Note serial numbers suggest there are three Credit Note books being used. Each book has 50 Credit Notes;

- you are getting married next week;

- the total value of the refunds now stands at $1,040;

- the times, dates and places of the transactions suggest to you that the offender is heading south; and

- you recall that about four months ago, a manager of one of your Brisbane outlets was dismissed for hostile and antagonistic behaviour toward his staff.

Your managing director advises you that your objectives are:

- to stop further instances of fraud;

- to identify who is conducting the frauds; and

- to prepare a case to instigate criminal proceedings against the offender.

Your managing director also states that she wants a full briefing within 48 hours on what you have accomplished thus far.

Prepare an investigative plan of action on what you would do to meet your managing director's objectives.

7 Customer Dishonesty

CHAPTER OBJECTIVES

- To examine the extent of customer dishonesty.
- To identify categories of shop stealers.
- To examine the methodology of theft.
- To develop strategies to prevent shop stealing.

INTRODUCTION

Historical Attitudes to Stealing

In the early days of Australia's first settlement, food and clothing were relatively scarce. Although supplies were on the way, the new colony was suffering and came close to starvation. Stealing became more prevalent and harsher penalties were being imposed.

Case Study No. 25

Take the case of Calvin Simpson. He was sentenced to 50 strokes of the lash for theft. A witness reported:

Blood flowed at the 4th, the convict cried out at the 18th, and continued crying for a few succeeding lashes; his skin was considerably torn and blood flowed during the whole of the punishment (Little, p. 24, 1972).

His crime: stealing a pair of shoes.

Case Study No. 26

Not so lucky was young Thomas Barrett who, at 17 years of age, had the dubious honour of being the first person to be executed in New South Wales. 'I have led a very wicked life,' he lamented shortly before he was hanged from a branch of a eucalyptus tree. Two days before, the Criminal Court found him guilty of having stolen bread, butter, peas and salt pork (Gordon, 1987, p. 91).

113

Case Study No. 27

The harsh punishments of the day were not just limited to males. In 1789, members of the first Australian police force (a night-watch formed from selected convicts) caught a female convict stealing clothes. On being given the death sentence, she claimed to be pregnant, but a panel of 12 of the 'discreetest' women soon found that she was not. The forewoman, a grave personage between 60 and 70 years of age, pronounced her state by this short address to the court: 'Gentlemen! She is as much with child as I am.' Sentence was accordingly passed and the thief was executed (Taylor, 1982, p. 84).

Case Study No. 28

These severe penalties were not just limited to convicts. In March 1789, six privates in the Marines were convicted of stealing from a public store in Port Jackson and were hanged (Crowley, 1980, p. 12).

Present-Day Attitudes to Shop Stealing

Certainly the restrictions of a bygone era appeared excessively harsh and often cruel. Yet in extreme cases where supply could barely fulfil the demand of a new settlement, severe punishment was often seen as the only way to maintain law and order. Two hundred years later, circumstances have changed considerably. No longer does society live in an environment where demand cannot be met by supply. The focus of society has changed, retailing and marketing strategies have changed, and attitudes towards dishonest behaviour have changed. Shop stealing is 'viewed with passing tolerance as part of a consumer-orientated society' (Lawrence and Hore, undated, p. 2).

Although some members of the community condemn shop stealers, others see it as a game, and some even regard shop stealing as the least serious crime of all (Lawrence and Toh, 1989, p. 3). Criminologists are now more concerned with why shop stealing occurs and strategies are being designed that tend to de-motivate shop stealers to steal, rather than demands being made on the criminal justice system to impose heavier penalties (see 'Shopstealers Walk an Emotional Tightrope in your Store', p. 123).

CUSTOMER DISHONESTY

The Extent of Customer Dishonesty

In Chapter 3, the question of an opportunistic society was raised. Retailing is big business and all retailers desire market share. While fierce competition is beneficial for consumers, business margins become tighter and tighter. Staffing levels are constantly being reduced, and a by-product of the concept of self-service is exactly that. Self-service operations have attracted not only increased sales and reduced margins, but have also created huge opportunities for customer dishonesty.

In Chapter 3, it was stated that the average cost of a supermarket shop stealing incident was estimated to be $16.88 (Harris, 1994, p. 3). Albert Baumgartner, Executive Officer of the Retail Traders' Association of NSW suggests that each shop stealing incident costs retailers currently $45.00 and further suggests that there are between 10 to 13 million incidents of shop stealing each year (Baumgartner, 1994, p. 3).

The national shop stealing figure for Australia may never be completely and accurately assessed, but if the formula for calculating shop stealing figures is applied (2% of gross annual sales, of which 33% is attributable to shop stealing), the 1994 national shop stealing figure could be as high as $716 million per annum. Estimated shop stealing losses from January to December 1994 for each of the States are shown in Figure 7.1.

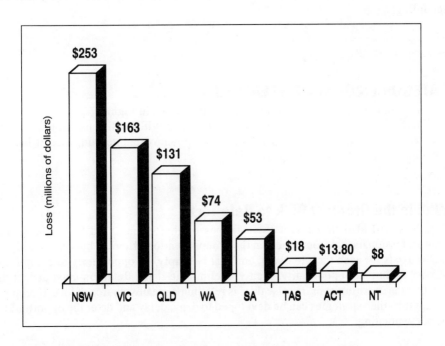

Figure 7.1. 1994 State loss estimates from customer dishonesty

Definition of Shop Stealing

Shop stealing is simply theft. Whether the item is a washing machine, a coat, petrol, oil or a low-priced confectionary item. For retailers, theft may come in a variety of forms including false pretences, obtaining property by deception, obtaining a financial advantage, robbery and burglary. Theft may also be known in some State areas as *larceny*. Although the wording and essence of these offences vary from country to country or from state to state, the definition of theft remains largely the same:

> Any person who dishonestly appropriates property belonging to another with the intention of permanently depriving the owner of such property is guilty of the act of theft or larceny. [Neill 1981, p. 3]

Who Do Shop Stealers Target?

All retailers are being targeted, but the varying exposures to risk, probability, frequency and cost factors place retailers into different categories. These risks can be high, medium or low. As a general rule, the more popular the item, the more portable the item, and the more profitable it is, the higher the exposure to risk. The fact which determines an item's theft worthiness depends not only on its popularity, its portability or its profitability, but also on the level of control a retailer places over it. In Chapter 3, the common denominators for employee malpractice were highlighted. The same motivating factors that encourage employees to steal, also encourage shop stealing. If loss prevention controls are weak, then the levels of risk increase accordingly.

CATEGORIES OF SHOP STEALERS

The five general categories of shop stealers are shown in Figure 7.2.

There is no golden rule as to what a shop stealer will steal. A useful guide is the 'nail and paint' test. If the item is not nailed down or painted on, then it has the potential to be stolen by a shop stealer!

Who is the Greatest Risk to Retailers?

Retailers will also be subject to instances of theft committed by professional, semiprofessionals and from others in the groups mentioned above, but one underlying factor exists for each theft to occur, and that is simply the opportunity to commit the offence. Eliminate opportunity, then you eliminate theft. Retailers must accept the fact that the opportunist or impulse thief is retailing's greatest source of loss. If retailers accept this, then strategies can be developed to deny, delay and deter the opportunities from eventuating.

PROFESSIONALS

A select group of professional shopstealers who usually steal high priced or high volume merchandise that is quick and easy to sell. Professional shopstealers usually do not bother with distractions or other diversion tactics. They simply hit in a single, mass attack. These high value or high volume thefts are usually identified shortly after the event.

SEMIPROFESSIONALS

Shop stealers who are usually working as family units, husband–wife etc. Merchandise is usually stolen for cash refunds to support drug habits or to improve lifestyle. Major retailers usually are aware of the identity of these shopstealers. These semiprofessionals constantly test retailers for refund policy and shop stealing awareness.

ADOLESCENTS AND TEENAGERS

Young people usually still at school and very much influenced by peer group pressure. Thefts are carried out as a dare, or as a sign of bravado. Some gangs require certain items of apparel to be stolen, eg the wearing of certain brand name jeans must be accompanied by the stain of a dye-tag anti-theft device to prove that the jeans had been stolen.

OPPORTUNISTS OR IMPULSE THIEVES

This group is by far the largest statistical group of shop stealers and causes the greatest losses. Opportunists and impulse thieves are normal everyday shoppers who usually go shopping with an honest intention. However, when direct or indirect opportunities are created, these customers turn into shop stealers. For the impulse thief, an object that is portable, popular and profitable suddenly becomes an item worthy of theft and if an opportunity avails itself, theft will result. It is generally recognised that the most effective measure of dealing with the opportunity and impulse thief is the use of plain and simple customer service techniques.

OTHER

Those who are either very young or very old. May also include those suffering from personality or psychological disorders or who may suffer from alcoholism or from the effects of drugs.

Figure 7.2 Categories of shop stealers

HOW TO RECOGNISE THE SHOP STEALER

There are three categories of customers:

- the genuine buyer;
- the browser; and
- the shop stealer.

Buyers and browsers tend to look at products. They feel, they touch, they poke and generally appear to be preoccupied with it. Eyes are down or up, but looking at the product. Any sales person looking at a genuine buyer or browser would see them focus on the product. When customers are in this mode, they will be using what loss-prevention practitioners call their 'comfort zones'. This simply means that when a genuine buyer or looker is shopping, they shop 15–30 cm away from aisles, pyramids, four-way units, shelves, display counters and any other area where merchandise may be displayed. This allows buyers a natural area of space in which to use their hands in the process of feeling, touching, poking and prodding merchandise. Labels will be checked, prices would be compared, discussions would be held, all of which is a display of normal shopping behaviour that suggests to staff that the customers are genuinely shopping. If assistance is needed, the buyers and browsers will attempt to make eye contact with a sales person to conclude the transaction.

Buyers and browsers

On the other hand, when shop stealers are about to steal, they want to hide their actions. To do so, they need to disguise what their hands are doing. The shop stealer will tend to lean onto the product to conceal their actions. Their hands are busy attempting to hide the article and while doing this action, they must lean into pyramids, racks and other fixtures. There is no 'comfort zone'. Eyes purposely look at ceilings, when a staff member attempts to make eye contact, a shop stealer's eyes quickly dart away.

A shop stealer

The Giveaway Signs of the Shop Stealer

Impulse shop stealers will generally display their actions or telegraph their intentions by:

- acting nervously or hesitant — or just the opposite by appearing 'cocky' or overconfident;
- displaying jerky eye movements used to 'scope' or 'scan' the store;
- looking at ceilings;
- perspiring;
- returning continually to a particular spot;
- avoiding the gaze of a salesperson;
- leaving premises with undue haste;
- hanging around foyers, forecourts and toilet areas inside premises — especially in toilets adjacent to stock;
- loitering around counters that display easily picked-up items;
- congregating in large groups — especially groups or gangs of youths;
- using bags, boxes, coats, newspapers or other articles in their possession that could provide means of concealment;
- working together in groups of two or more — one trying to distract a salesperson while the other steals;
- wearing baggy clothing, especially out of season;
- reaching into display areas or walking behind counters;

- appearing not to know what they want and roaming around the premises;
- appearing to be uninterested in articles they have inquired about; and
- wearing items such as sunglasses, scarves etc, at times when there is no need. They may be trying to conceal their identity or to avoid descriptions being taken.

Methods of Theft and Concealment

Shop stealers are often ingenious in their methods of theft and concealment. Common methods include:

- straight theft of stock;
- straight theft of cash from a till;
- straight theft of the till;
- using a useless cheque or stolen credit card to purchase goods;
- using a useless cheque or stolen credit card to purchase goods then obtaining refunds moments later;
- straight theft of stock then returning the item for a refund;
- gathering discarded receipts, finding the corresponding item listed on the receipt, then stealing the item and obtaining a refund;
- swapping price tags for a lower priced item;
- purchasing merchandise on sale from one store, then obtaining a refund at another store at a higher price;
- palming small articles into rolled up newspapers, coats, gloves and other things carried in the hands;
- carrying umbrellas, prams, bags, large purses, paper bags, magazines, briefcases, coats or similar devices to conceal stolen property under their clothes;
- carrying 'booster boxes' which are large cartons or specially converted bags or briefcases with one end cut open to make a hinged flap through which articles can be pushed and concealed by shop stealers;
- using slit pockets in outer garments;
- using hooks sewn inside coats, jackets and loose or baggy trousers;
- putting items on whilst in the shop and simply leaving without paying, creating an impression that the shop stealer was in possession of the items when they came in; and
- placing a small expensive item inside a larger less expensive one and paying for the latter.

STRATEGIES TO PREVENT SHOP STEALING

All strategies to prevent shop stealing need to be directed toward:

- denying the opportunity for theft;
- delaying the opportunity for theft; and
- deterring the opportunity for theft.

The most effective proactive measures are a combination of:

- good customer service skills (described below);
- the skilful use of anti-theft systems (described in Chapter 9); and
- implementation of sound policies and procedures (described in Chapter 8).

Maximising Customer Service Skills

So why is customer service basic in preventing theft? Because shop stealers need opportunities to steal. If they are offered hospitality and service, opportunities are removed. The more opportunities removed, the less thefts occur. The less the thefts, the healthier the retailer's bottom line

Case Study No. 29

A new manager in a Burnie specialty shop, who was recently promoted, made it a point to greet every one of her customers who walked into her shop. When a young mum pushing a pram came into her shop, the manager called out, 'Hi! Great day isn't it? Gee I like your top'. The young mum looked surprised and said, 'Nobody here ever greeted me like that'. A friendly conversation ensued and a happy mum walked out with a $60 purchase saying, 'I really only came in here to browse'.

Maximising customer service has a major effect on honest customers because it:

- acknowledges the existence of customers;
- establishes a motivation for customers to buy;
- increases sales;
- increases staff morale; and
- increases staff awareness.

On the other hand, good customer service denies shop stealers. It is detrimental to shop stealers because it:

- removes the opportunities to steal;
- de-motivates the desire to steal;
- removes staff indifference; and, therefore,
- removes the environment conducive for theft.

Attentive Staff

The thing most hated by shop stealers is an attentive sales person. The one sure-fire measure that stops them every time is good customer service skills. If salespersons see a shop stealer stealing or about to steal, a direct approach should be used. Go straight to the suspect and offer assistance. Be direct, never bluff, but be assertive, use 'aggressive hospitality'. This could be in the form of a simple statement:

'Hi there, beautiful day isn't it?'
'That's a great top, where did you buy it?'

Open questions such as this always invite an answer. Closed questions such as 'Can I help you?' always invite a yes or no answer which closes the conversation instantly. Keep the conversation open. If this customer is a buyer, he or she will appreciate your friendly greeting and it may lead to a sale. Follow up the lead and use taught sales skills. However, if this customer has just stolen something or is about to steal, two things might happen. First, if a theft has taken place, the thief may think:

'My God, they've seen me pinch it. I've got to get rid of it!'

The thief will dump the merchandise somewhere, usually in a fitting room or in an area where that type of merchandise is not usually found, for example, a toaster in the linen area. Second, if the customer is about to steal, a shop stealer may think:

'Oh! They think I'm going to pinch something, I'll head off and try it somewhere else.'

Positive Body Language

In both cases, aggressive hospitality has probably prevented a major loss or generated a major sale. That is the principle behind good customer service. When salespersons talk to customers, they use body language all the time, people use body language to motivate or de-motivate, approve or disapprove. When dealing with potential shop stealers, salespersons tend to display their feelings through body language. Naturally feelings of hostility such as clenched fists, venom or anger will generally trigger the same in the person to whom all this hostility is directed. Affirmative body language needs to portray control and assertiveness. A smiling open-handed approach with comments such as these, tend to make the salesperson in control.

Hi, that's a great skirt you've got under your armpit, let me show you some shirts that go with it!   OR
G'day — that's our best selling book you've just stuffed into your bag. How would you like to pay for it — cash, credit card, cheque?

The key here is simple. If a sales person has seen dishonest behaviour and is absolutely certain where the merchandise is, a salesperson has nothing to lose but everything to gain by taking the initiative. Sales staff should realise that in situations where theft occurs, it is not they who are in the wrong. Salespersons are only in the wrong if they fail to take the initiative to do something. Thieves cost retailers dearly. Offer all thieves total quality service, treat them with smiles and salutations, and provide them with complete customer service. Why? Because they cannot steal. Every time a salesperson approaches a potential thief to greet them or to just talk to them, a theft may be prevented.

Using the Shop Stealer's Emotional States

In an 18-month study reported in the Peter Berlin Report, Shopstealers Anonymous (a US-based organisation) conducted a survey on apprehended shop stealers. The results enabled researchers and consulting psychologists to determine that, from the moment shop stealers enter a store and see an opportunity to steal, they become supersensitive to their surroundings. Otherwise normal and everyday events trigger a series of psychological reactions which range from sheer panic to elation. The researchers charted reactions to the otherwise normal and everyday events to depict the emotional state of a typical impulse or opportunist shop stealer during each phase of a theft incident. The report is reproduced here with permission.

SHOPLIFTERS WALK AN EMOTIONAL TIGHTROPE IN YOUR STORE

Store managers and salespersons stop shop stealers from stealing every day, but most of the time they're not aware that they did it. The little things salespersons do make a difference to the shop stealer because the shop stealer walks an emotional tightrope while in a store and just like any other guilty person, is constantly preoccupied by the fear of getting caught. It is precisely this fear that gives managers and salespersons the power to stop them, often just by acknowledging their presence. We see examples all the time when we see a sweater on the floor under a rack of blouses, or find a bottle of vitamins tucked behind a box on a shelf. Sure, it could have been a lazy shopper who changed her mind, but more often it's a sign that a would-be shop stealer became uneasy and decided to 'ditch' the merchandise rather than try to head for the door. What caused the shop stealer to abort the attempt could have been any number of different things.

From an 18-month study of apprehended shop stealers conducted by Shoplifters Anonymous, a US-based non-profit organisation specialising in shop stealer research and rehabilitation, researchers were able to determine that from the moment a shop stealer enters a store, or tries to steal an item, the shop stealer becomes supersensitive to his or her surroundings and otherwise normal events trigger a series of psychological and physiological reactions ranging from sheer panic to extreme elation. It is the extreme elation or 'emotional high' which nonprofessional shop stealers say is the primary factor causing their behaviour to become habit-forming or addictive, where they can no longer resist stealing merchandise from a store.

Shoplifters Anonymous charted the progression of these reactions to graphically depict the emotional state of a typical nonprofessional shop stealer during each phase of a theft incident, from entry into the store through completion or abortion of the attempt. It is especially valuable for store managers and employees to be aware of what shop stealers are thinking and how they are likely to react because this knowledge can also help store personnel to understand what they can do to prevent theft and why their actions will be effective.

(continued...)

Figure 7.3. Shop stealers walk an emotional tightrope

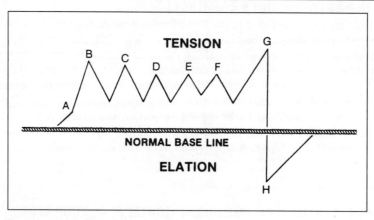

Figure 7.3 (a). How shop stealers react

(Figure reprinted courtesy & permission of the Peter Berlin Report, Berlin, 1990b.)

Figure 7.3(a) charts a typical venture through a drug store. When the prospective shop stealer enters the store, not yet aware that she will steal, she is at some 'normal' baseline tension level as are other customers who enter the store. When she selects a target, her tension level rises and she suddenly becomes acutely sensitive to her surroundings (A). Her tension level continues to rise as she prepares to take and conceal the merchandise.

Is anyone watching?

However, before she makes another move, she must ask herself one important question, the same question that all shop stealers ask themselves: 'Is anybody watching?'. You can actually see the shop stealer asking this question of herself when you see her eyes sweep the floor and see her turn her head quickly to the left and then right. If the coast is clear, she makes her move to conceal the item, usually within a split second. Her tension level rises to its highest point yet (B). It's important to know, however, that the shop stealer's decision to take the item is not a commitment to keep it. If things don't go exactly right and she perceives a risk in leaving the store with the stolen merchandise, she will either 'ditch it' or buy it.

(continued...)

Oh, my God, he's seen me! It's all over!

Having concealed the item, the shop stealer now turns to walk slowly down the aisle and the tension level drops a little, but never down to the baseline. Suddenly, she sees a salesperson or manager turn the corner, quickly walking towards her. Her tension rises as she says to herself, 'Oh my God, he's seen me…it's all over!' (C). But then the manager smiles and says, 'Hello, how are you today?' and simply passes by. The tension drops. Suddenly the shop stealer hears a siren outside from an ambulance or police car and immediately thinks to herself, 'They're coming' to get me!', and the tension rises (D). The sound goes away and the tension drops.

They must have called the cops!

As she looks toward the door, the shop stealer sees a policeman enter the store. The tension rises again as she says to herself, 'They must have called the cops after all!' (E). But the policeman approaches another young lady, gives her a kiss on the cheek and they both leave the store together. The tension drops when she realises that the policeman simply came into the store to pick up his wife.

(continued…)

Why is he staring at me?
— He must be waiting to
see what I'm going to do.

The shop stealer then turns to the left and notices a man staring at her. 'Why is he staring at me?' she asks herself as the tension begins to rise (F). 'He must be waiting to see what I'm going to do.' A few moments later the man is greeted by a friend and they both leave the store. The tension drops. By this time the shop stealer is a nervous wreck.'

Any of these experiences or many others like it, such as a salesperson acknowledging the customer's presence, a salesperson making eye contact, a PA announcement which says 'Security to section four', an alert cashier or guard at the door, could all be responsible for causing the shop stealer to 'ditch' the merchandise or buy it. According to Shopstealers Anonymous, the shop stealer, with rare exception, will elect to abort the theft rather than risk detection. But, what if none of these things happens and it becomes readily apparent to the shop stealer that no-one is aware of her presence or cares what she is doing? Then the shop stealer will head for the door. As she approaches the exit, past the point of purchase, saying to herself 'Steady, don't panic', she pushes open the exit door and the tension rises to an almost unbearable level (G) as she imagines a hand coming down on her shoulder and a voice saying 'I'm store security, you'll have to come with me!' But after about 25 feet past the store front, she cautiously turns to look back, sees no-one is following her and for the first time realises that she actually got away with it. She is so proud of herself that her tension turns to elation and excitement (H), which many claim is the true reward for the nonprofessional shop stealer. This feeling of elation described by shop stealers is hard for a layperson to understand, but it is easy for a store detective to understand, because the store detective experiences the exact same feeling of elation when he or she catches the shop stealer.

The findings of Shoplifters Anonymous help to clarify how prevention works and why salespeople do not have to be 'super-sleuths' to outwit a shop stealer. A little attention of acknowledgment is all that is needed to make a would-be shop stealer decide to 'shoplift elsewhere'.

So the next time you find merchandise out of place, think about what it means. You might want to suggest to your employees that it could be the evidence that they are doing a great job toward deterring shop stealers in their store.

Figure 7.3. Shop stealers walk an emotional tightrope

(This article is reprinted with permission from *The Peter Berlin Report on Shrinkage Control — Executive Edition*, Feb. 1990b.)

Behavioural Skills to Prevent Thefts

The results of this survey allow us to develop strategies to utilise these behavioural tendencies. Any experiences that generate positive loss-prevention reactions (such as good aggressive hospitality, acknowledging a customer's presence, making eye contact, smiling at a customer) could all be responsible for causing the shop stealer to ditch the merchandise or, more importantly, to pay for it. According to Shoplifters Anonymous, the impulse or opportunist shop stealer, with rare exception, will elect to abort the theft, rather than take the risk of detection or apprehension.

As part of their training, salespersons may have already enhanced their own individual style of selling. Customer service skills may already be well developed and salespersons, if trained in selling skills, should be totally at ease when approaching, greeting and talking to customers. Selling-skills training will also have given salespersons an insight into the many variables of human behaviour. Not only will they have developed selling skills and customer service skills, but will also have developed people skills. That is, the ability to read people through the way they look, the way they act and the way they behave. Through behavioural characteristics, a salesperson can determine whether a person is in a buying mood, just looking, or displaying the previously mentioned signs that indicate a potential for theft.

As part of an ongoing loss-prevention awareness training program, retailers can extend the principles of customer service skills by understanding the processes that occur in the mind of a shop stealer prior to, during and after the actual act of stealing. This involves an understanding of tension states, body language, personal space and escape routes:

- **Tension states.** The emotional surges that pass through the body of an opportunist or impulse thief before, during and after the act of theft.

- **Body language.** The use of body language that poses no threat or avoids indications of hostility. An open-handed approach showing your palms psychologically indicates that you bear no weapons and have friendly intentions.

- **Personal space.** Understanding and using personal body space and comfort zones to assist in directing and leading shop stealers on a desired course.

- **Escape routes.** Giving a shop stealer a 'way out' to overcome fear of detection and apprehension and particularly to avoid physical assault to employees and other customers.

Personal Body Space

When a shop stealer's emotions are out of balance, as shown in the Shoplifters Anonymous survey, retailers may use this knowledge to apply the use of controlled conduct to guide them to a desired result. That is, salespersons could use the shop stealer's emotional unrest to achieve loss-prevention aims. By approaching potential shop stealers using non-hostile body language and intruding into their personal body space, salespersons can consciously manoeuvre them towards the register. Hopefully, shop stealers will identify this as an escape route and pay for the goods, thereby removing the threat of apprehension for them.

Use body language that visibly portrays a friendly and passive stance which poses no threat. Pointing a finger, shaking a fist, or speaking through clenched teeth displays hostile body language and will only invite reciprocal hostility from the shop stealer.

Every individual has a personal zone or space that extends around the body. This zone has special significance for loss-prevention awareness strategies. In his book *Body Language* (Pease, 1981, p. 26), Pease suggests that personal space can be broken down into four distinct zone distances as shown in Figure 7.4.

INTIMATE ZONE (15–46 centimetres)	This is the most important zone because it guarded by the person as if it were his or her own property. Only those who are emotionally close to that person are permitted to enter it. This includes lovers, parents, spouse, children, close friends and relatives. There is a sub-zone that extends up to 15 cm from the body that can be entered only during physical contact. This is the close intimate zone.
PERSONAL ZONE (0.46–1.2 metres)	This is the distance that we stand from others at parties, social functions and friendly gatherings.
SOCIAL ZONE (1.2–3.6 metres)	We stand at this distance from strangers, the plumber or carpenter doing repairs around our home, the postman, the new employee at work and other people whom we do not know very well.
PUBLIC ZONE (> 3.6 metres)	Whenever we address a large group of people, this is the comfortable distance at which we choose to stand.

Figure 7.4. Zone distances of personal space

(Reprinted with courtesy and permission of the Pease Training Corporation.)

For a salesperson attempting to deal with a shop stealer, this knowledge on body language can be of great benefit. If an uninvited salesperson enters the personal body space of a shop stealer, the shop stealer will tend to step back to recreate the personal body-space safety zone. If salespersons are aware that moving into a shop stealer's personal body space generally tends to move them in the opposite direction, they can use this technique to subconsciously propel the shop stealer towards the cash register.

APPREHENSION OF SHOP STEALERS

A retailer's primary objective must always be to maximise profits. The case for preventing loss will always be greater than that for an apprehension policy. If simple prevention techniques are employed, theft cannot occur. Seeing a shop stealer acting suspiciously should immediately cause a salesperson to approach the thief and offer total unqualified customer service that will deny the shop stealer the opportunity to complete the act.

In everyday retailing, policy should be to prevent theft occurring in the first place. However, if policy includes apprehension, retailers must be aware that the law pertaining to the apprehension of shop stealers is extremely complex.

Apprehension of a suspect shop stealer is always a difficult situation. It can generate anxiety and confusion and therefore mistakes will be made. However, if observations are correct and all the necessary legal points of proof have been met, the law as it currently prevails offers apprehending staff certain degrees of security. At the same time, however, the following basic rules should be considered.

Basic Requirements

The following notes detail the observations and the legal requirements necessary to effect a lawful apprehension. An apprehension must only be made on what was actually seen. Observations by other salespersons or customers can never be used as a basis for apprehension.

Legal Requirements

Two vital elements must be present to prove that theft took place: selection and placement.

Selection means the actual taking of the goods. **Placement** means the actual place where the goods are deposited.

For example: 'I saw her select a red book from the rack marked 'History' with her left hand. I then saw her place this book into a black-coloured handbag and place a handkerchief over the book.'

Three questions must be asked:

- What was taken?
- Where was it concealed?
- Is it still there?

If the item can be identified, the place where it was concealed can be identified and its current location can be identified after the suspect has left the store, then an apprehension can be made. If any of the three basic questions cannot be answered, then continuity has been lost and an apprehension cannot take place.

Loss of Continuity

Although continuity may have been lost, the shop stealer should be followed at a discreet distance. Remember safety is paramount. In the majority of cases, a shop stealer will move the items from their concealed position at a time and place when the shop stealer feels it is safe to do so. If the goods are revealed, then continuity is continued, as long as the salesperson can prove the selection and the placement. Many apprehensions have been made in this manner. However it is imperative that salespersons have a backup or witness present to protect their own personal safety and to corroborate actions.

Apprehension Procedures

When making an apprehension there are several important steps to follow:

- ensure you have a witness present;
- always approach the suspect from the front;
- introduce yourself or produce a form of in-store identification card; and
- speak in a clear, calm and polite manner.

State:

Excuse me, my name is [give your name], I am [give your position], employed by [give the name of your company]. I have reason to believe that you have merchandise in your possession which may not have been paid for. Would you please accompany me back into the store to discuss the matter.

This particular moment can create an enormous emotional flow for both the person making the apprehension and the shop stealer. The resulting behaviour may be totally unpredictable. It is imperative that the salesperson maintains total control at this point and observes the suspect closely for signs of violence or flight. Take charge of the situation, be firm but assertive. Before the suspect can recover from the initial shock of detection and apprehension, say 'This way please'.

On the way back to the office, recall any conversation for inclusion in a statement. Any comment made by the suspect or facial expressions shown may help to prove intent. Avoid unnecessary conversation. Have a witness lead the way back into the store and walk slightly behind the suspect, watching them closely all the time and in particular their hands for signs of disposal of the merchandise. If the suspect places their hands into a pocket or handbag as you are walking, be firm and assertive and state: 'Please keep your hands in full view until we reach the office.' Maintain the upper hand and remain in control at all times.

Escape Routes

It is commonly accepted that if a wild animal is cornered and has no room to move away or to escape, it has no option other than to attack. Most animals would rather give flight than fight. The same applies to persons placed in a position where they must defend their own actions. If escape routes are not catered for in a shop-stealer prevention plan, then like some cornered animal, a shop stealer might react in a hostile manner, in some cases even violently. This could be verbally or physically and the last thing that a salesperson would want to generate is a potential adverse situation where a salesperson or another customer may be assaulted or otherwise injured.

Attempts to Flee

When apprehending, a small proportion of suspects become aggressive, attempt to flee or become violent. *Safety is always paramount* and at no time must salespersons place themselves, other salespersons or customers in any physical danger. Maintain control and be firm. Quite often, a salesperson's demeanour at this point will be seen by the suspect as one of complete control and this will usually overcome any aggression on the suspect's part. However, if attempts are made to flee, stand directly in front of the suspect, look them directly in the eye and state: 'I'm sorry but I must insist you return to the office.'

If this fails and the suspect does flee, the apprehending salesperson will have a number of options. First, pursuit and a formal citizen's arrest can be made to ensure the person's appearance before a court. The power to make a citizen's arrest only applies if the salesperson actually detected the person shop stealing. The legal rule of 'finds committing' is a vital element in this process and this option is not recommended unless the person in pursuit is a trained loss-prevention officer, store surveillance officer or similar. More passive options include:

- remain safe at all times;
- follow the suspect, watch for a drop, and retrieve the merchandise if possible;
- continue to follow the suspect, call for police assistance and attempt to obtain a car registration;
- avoid following alone, use two staff where possible; and
- if the situation becomes dangerous, walk away.

If a dangerous situation does develop, abort the actions. Responsible retailers would rather lose the goods than have a valued staff member risk injury.

If a suspect does escape apprehension, return to the store, look for merchandise that may have been discarded and report the matter immediately to police detailing descriptions of the suspect, the goods stolen and car details (make, model, colour and registration number). Complete an incident report form and report the matter to senior store management for their information.

Action on Return of Suspect to the Office

Once a suspect has been returned to an office, take control of the situation. If there is more than one offender, immediately separate them. This prevents fabrication of evidence. Always remain in front of a suspect. Turning a back on a suspect is not only dangerous, but the suspect may also attempt to hide stolen merchandise in the office or otherwise dispose of it. Have a witness present at all times. If the suspect is a female, then a female employee should remain with the suspect. If the suspect is a male, then a male employee should remain with the suspect at all times to prevent any allegations of impropriety.

In the office, make the following request: 'Please place all the merchandise in your possession which has not been paid for on the table.'

Take mental notes of what is removed from which pockets etc. Once the suspect has placed the goods on the table, other observations may have indicated other merchandise not yet revealed. For example, say, 'Please place the earrings in your top right-hand pocket on the table'. It is quite often possible for suspects to be in possession of more stolen items than apprehending staff may be aware of and this could prove to be further evidence in relation to 'intent and guilt'.

Salespersons may ask the following questions:

* Why did you take the items from the store without payment being made?
* When did you first intend not to pay for them?
* How much money do you have?
* For whom are these items for?
* Why did you come into this store?

A salesperson's control and firmness in these situations often produce the desired results. Once all stolen merchandise has been produced, give the suspect a pen, some paper and state: 'Please write your full name, address and date of birth.' At the same time, verify this information by requesting some form of identification. Once all the necessary information has been obtained, the information may make various options available.

Responses to Different Types of Offenders

Juvenile or Young Shop Stealers

If the suspect is aged between 8 to 14 years, it may be necessary to establish that the person knew the difference between right and wrong. This can be established by questions such as:

Q: Can you tell me what stealing is?
A: Taking something that doesn't belong to you.
Q: Would you like to tell me how you obtained these goods?
A: I stole them.   [Or]
   I took them.

Under-Age Children

If the suspect is under the age of eight years, in the eyes of the law, the suspect may not have committed a crime and cannot be prosecuted. In these cases, retailers will need to obtain the relevant details of the child and inform the parents. If parents or family are not contactable, retailers must call the police and advise them of the situation immediately.

Admission Forms

Some major retailers use admission forms as a means to administer corporate justice without the involvement of police. An admission form is simply a document that allows a person apprehended for shop stealing to walk away from the premises without further police action. Usually, an admission form lists the name, address, age and date of birth of the person apprehended. It describes the incident and requires that the suspect actually acknowledges the removal of merchandise without payment being made and the intention to retain possession of it. A signed admission form also absolves the retailer from accusations of false arrest and protects staff from future allegations.

An admission form usually involves young or aged persons where sufficient grounds exist not to call police. Major retailers employing store surveillance staff recognise the use of these forms as important and necessary for a number of reasons. However, their use should only be in exceptional circumstances and under strict guidelines as follows:

- for young children or the elderly, when it is their first offence and the merchandise retails for less than a specified amount;
- for those under medical or mental care where there is an obvious impact on their actions;
- for those where the merchandise is valued at less than a specified amount, it is their first offence and it is operationally expedient to keep staff on the floor.

Advising police of intention to use admission forms:

Determination of a first offence is usually through reference to in-store computer printouts on apprehensions or through the police. Obviously, the above guidelines cannot be adhered to on every occasion and retailers need to seek professional legal advice in the use of admission forms. They can be a contentious issue and if used at all, must be used with discretion and under strict guidance and supervision by senior management or senior loss-prevention staff.

If a decision has been made to use an admission form, retailers are still required to advise police of their intentions. This is for the protection of all retailers. A call to police, advising them of the suspect's name, address and date of birth, and that you intend to take in-house action will usually prompt police to check their records. If the suspect is not recorded, police will usually agree with your actions; however, if the person is on record, then police action will result. On some occasions, police records may indicate that the suspect is wanted on other matters, is listed as a missing person, has severe mental problems or for one reason or another may warrant the attendance of police.

Adult Offenders

Once an offender has been apprehended, and the situation does not fall into any of the categories listed above, then retailers have no real option other than to call the police. Call your local police number and provide full details of the offence, the name, address and date of birth of the suspect and answer all questions asked. Have someone remain with the suspect at all times. Always have a witness present. Once police have been called, the matter is out of your hands and there is no need for salespersons to discuss the situation further with the suspect. However, if the suspect wishes to talk, allow them to do so. It may provide you with further information or evidence about other criminal activity. Salespersons should avoid volunteering any information to the suspect. Note your observations. While waiting for police to attend, take notes of what was seen, what was said by the suspect and what was done. The person making the apprehension will need to relate these observations to police to enable them to establish in their minds that an offence has been committed.

Unless police are satisfied that an offence has been committed, they will not take action and it is therefore imperative that you have established the facts.

Procedures at Police Arrival

Once police arrive, they will ask the apprehending staff member to detail her or his observations to them in the presence and hearing of the suspect. This will enable police to determine whether an offence has been committed and, as a guide, the observations should be detailed as follows:

> At approximately 10.15 am this morning, I was on duty in the grocery section of this store, when I observed this person, who has since given her name as Julie SMITH, take four bottles of tomato sauce from a shelf and place them into a black leather bag she was carrying. I then continued my observations of her and followed her out of the store. During this time, she did not make payment for the goods. I approached her in the mall, and introduced myself to her and invited her back to the office. I then invited her to place on the table all the goods in her possession that had not been paid for. She then placed the four bottles of tomato sauce on the table together with two pairs of stockings and one video cassette. All these goods remain the property of our organisation and are valued at $32.45. No person has permission to remove goods from this store without first making payment.

Admissions

The police will then ask the suspect if what was said was true and correct. If the suspect agrees then police have a number of options:

- if certain criteria are met, issue the offender with a formal verbal or written warning in the form of a shop-stealing warning notice (check with your local police); or
- take the suspect back to a police station for further investigation and formal charges.

Denials

If a suspect denies the offence, the police will require formal statements to be prepared by all witnesses concerned to enable them to take further action. Police will usually take the suspect back to a police station for further interviews and will require all the facts and all the evidence. This will consist of all the statements by all those who saw the offence. The property involved may also be required as evidence.

Photographing Suspects

Some major retailers have loss-prevention departments that encourage the use of photo albums which display photographs of all suspects apprehended for theft in a particular store. This enables store management and oncoming loss-prevention officers and staff to become familiar with known suspects and to take positive action in the event they reappear. Although there is no law which prevents loss-prevention staff from taking photographs of suspects, the individual rights and civil liberties of any person must not be treated lightly. If a suspect refuses for any reason to be photographed, then the refusal must be accepted without further demand being made.

An alternative course of action is to request a photograph of the merchandise with the suspect. If the suspect asks why, the reply should be: 'I am required to take a photograph of all goods allegedly removed without payment, together with the person who removed them.'

This usually results in consent; however, if the suspect still refuses, photographs cannot be taken of the suspect, although photographs of the merchandise can still be taken.

Exhibits

In some States, police will require the merchandise to be taken away. In others, photographs will suffice. However, if police insist on taking merchandise as exhibits, ask police to provide you with a 'Property Receipt'. Retailers will still have to account for this property during the next stocktake. Police exhibits are still part of theoretical stock levels. If possible, take a photograph of the exhibit which shows the time, date, name of the police officer and his or her station. The name of the suspect should also appear on the photograph. Attach the photograph to the Property Receipt and record the information for your next stocktake or forward the documentation to head office with an in-store Incident Report Form.

Check List for the Apprehension of Shop Stealers

Always consider possible civil litigation when apprehending a shop stealer — if you are wrong, it may be a costly experience for you and your company. The following is a quick check list and guideline for the apprehension of shop stealers to prevent civil litigation.

BE SURE	The shop stealer possesses the merchandise
KNOW	Where the shop stealer has concealed the merchandise: 'I saw him put it into the right inside pocket of his jacket'
BE SURE	What the merchandise is: 'It was a yellow floral shirt with red buttons'
ENSURE	Continuity has been maintained
HAVE A WITNESS	The apprehension must always be carried out with a witness present to ensure your own safety and to provide corroborative evidence
AVOID ACCUSATIONS	Avoid accusing a person directly of shop stealing
AVOID CONTACT	Avoid touching the shop stealer. It may be construed as intimidation, roughness or even assault
LOCATION OF APPREHENSION	No apprehension should ever be made until the shop stealer has passed the last register and has left the store. (There are exceptions to this rule if other clear intentions are shown, but use the above guideline as a general practice.)

Figure 7.5. A check list for the apprehension of shop stealers

INCIDENT REPORT FORMS

On the completion of formalities, it is essential that Incident Report Forms are completed to enable ongoing data to be maintained. The data provide retail organisations with statistical information.

Incident Report Forms can be easily designed and should be short in length. They should contain information that describes the what, when, where, who, why and how. Incident Report Forms include:

- names;
- addresses;
- date of birth;
- ID produced;
- brief description of the incident;
- description of any suspects;
- resulting action;
- names of police officers; and
- police officers' location and contact phone number.

In short, an Incident Report Form is a summary of events that need to be recorded for later in-store action, and to provide a statistical basis for the analysis of future loss-prevention initiatives, insurance claims after burglary, compensation claims from suspects found guilty in court etc.

STATEMENTS TO POLICE

The laws of evidence consist of rules and principles which govern the proof of the facts in issue. It is concerned with that part of the law of procedures which determines:

- what facts may or may not be proved;
- what sort of evidence may be given of such facts; and
- by whom and in what manner the evidence may be proved.

The main general rule governing the whole law of evidence is that all evidence which is sufficiently relevant either directly or indirectly to a fact in issue is admissible, and all evidence that is not sufficiently relevant is inadmissible.

The provision of statements to police often depend upon the relevant experience of individual police officers. It is not necessarily the facts in issue that are questioned, rather the method of presentation. Individual preferences on what is admissible and what is not often means that a statement acceptable to one police officer may not acceptable to another. A statement may be changed on numerous occasions by police constables, sergeants and court prosecutors, as each may have different perceptions of how a statement should read. Unfortunately, retailers must learn to live with this situation. Yet if statements cover all the facts in issue and are complete in every detail in the first instance, then retailers can minimise requests from police to make statements more 'acceptable'.

Statement Guidelines

The sample statement shown is a guide only as no two statements can ever be the same. A statement regarding a shop stealing offence should contain facts relevant to the issue. In this case, the facts are certain observations, some physical exhibits and admissions made by the suspect. For the information to be valid, the statement should outline the offence, provide information about the offender and then connect the offence with the offender. The following information should be included in the preparation of a statement:

- reasons for suspicion;
- name and description of the offender;
- the observations of the witness;
- details of the apprehension of the suspect — time and place;
- conversations held;
- the call for the police;
- the police arrival;
- identification and value of the merchandise; and
- ownership of the merchandise and lack of consent to remove it without payment being made.

Sample Statement

The statement should be clear, concise and correct. It is best to have them typed on a word processor or typewriter. Failing that, obtain some standard police statement forms, and write the statement by hand — but set it out clearly. The following is a simple statement covering all of the points above.

SMITH, Sally Anne

BIG APPLE GROCERY STORES, Pineapple Shopping Centre

Maintown Road, MAINTOWN 3333

Contact phone: (03) 9123 4567

Assistant Manager

STATES:

My full name is Sally Anne SMITH and I am the Assistant Manager employed by Big Apple Grocery Stores. I have been employed with the organisation since 1991, and am authorised to speak for and on behalf of the company in relation to this matter. At about 10.40 am on Thursday the 2nd day of April, 1994, I was on duty in our Big Apple Grocery store located in Maintown Road, Maintown.

(Continues...)

(THE REASON FOR SUSPICION. This can be either your own observation or received information.)

As a result of something I was told.............................. or, I saw a male person constantly looking around.........................

(DESCRIPTION OF SUSPECT AND NAME) This person was aged about 35 years, was of solid build and was wearing................... I now know this person to be Alan David PURCELL.

(YOUR OBSERVATIONS) I saw this person looking at video tapes. I saw him take two blank video tapes and place them down the front of his trousers. While he was pushing the videos into his trousers, I observed him to be looking to his right and left. He then left the immediate area and walked to our freezer goods area. During this time I maintained by observations of him. While near the freezer goods area, I saw the male person remove the video tapes from his trousers and I watched as he peeled off the price tags and drop them to the floor. He then replaced the videos down the front of his pants and walked to the front of the store. I then watched him as he left the store past the check-out area where he turned right and commenced to walk east along Maintown Road.

(APPREHENDING THE SUSPECT: TIME & PLACE) At approximately 10.55 am, I approached this person about 40 metres from our store entrance where I held the following conversation with him:

(CONVERSATION)

I said: 'Excuse me, I'm Sally SMITH, and I'm the Assistant Manager employed by Big Apple Grocery stores. I have reason to believe that you have merchandise in your possession which has not been paid for. Would you please accompany me back into the store to discuss the matter.'

He said: 'Piss off, I don't know what you're talking about.'

I said: 'I'm sorry but I must insist.'

He said: 'Yeah OK, I guess you got me clean.'

He then accompanied me to the managers office where I held a further conversation with him. Also present at this time was the administration manager, David JONES.

I said: 'Please place all the merchandise in your possession which has not been paid for on the table.'

He said: 'Yeah, you got me this time, didn't you.'

PURCELL then produced two videos from the front of his trousers and placed it onto the table. I saw that the video bore the brand name 'SONY'.

I said: 'What is your reason for taking these items without payment being made?'

He said: 'I was bloody well, broke wasn't I?'

(Continues...)

I said: 'Is there any other merchandise in your possession which has not been paid for?'

He said: 'No that's it.'

I said: 'What is your full name and address?'

He said: 'Allan David PURCELL, I live at 21 Main Street, BOOMTOWN.'

I said: 'What is your age and date of birth?'

He said: 'I'm 33, I was born on the 23/11/1961.'

(CALL FOR POLICE) I then went to another office and at 11.10 am, telephoned the Maintown police and reported the matter.

(POLICE ARRIVAL) At about 11.30 am, Constables JOHNSTON and SHAW attended at the office, where in the presence and hearing of PURCELL, I detailed my observations to them.

SHAW then said: 'Is what this lady said true and correct?'

PURCELL said: 'Yep, she is spot on.'

Constables JOHNSTON and SHAW then conveyed PURCELL from the managers office and went to the freezer area. I was present when Constable SHAW said: 'Would you care to show me where you dropped the price tag?'

PURCELL then indicated a price tag lying on the floor and said: 'That's it there.'

Constable SHAW took possession of the price tag and both members then conveyed PURCELL from the store.

(IDENTIFICATION AND VALUE OF GOODS) The goods PURCELL had in his possession were two 'SONY' brand 180 VHS Video blank cassettes. The price tag was a BIG APPLE price tag and the goods were valued at $12.45 each.

(OWNERSHIP AND LACK OF CONSENT) The above mentioned goods are the property of Big Apple Grocery Stores and no person has permission to remove goods from the store without first making payment.

Statement taken and signature witnessed before me: (Police informants name, rank, time, date and place)

Signed..

(Sally Anne SMITH)

THE POWER OF ARREST FOR PRIVATE CITIZENS
Citizen's Arrest
All Australian States and Territories have their own versions of a citizen's power of arrest. A broad definition is:

> A private citizen may at any time arrest any person found committing any offence where the person believes on reasonable grounds that the arrest is necessary to ensure the offenders appearance before a court, to preserve the public order, to prevent a repetition of the offence or to ensure the safety of members of the public or of the offender.

The crucial element for a citizen's arrest is the element of 'found committing'. No person can arrest on behalf of another. A store manager cannot delegate this task to a subordinate, nor can the shopping-centre security guards arrest a suspect for shop stealing. The element of 'finds committing' is basic to a citizen's power of arrest. If a court dismisses evidence on the grounds that a citizen's arrest was made without this element, the person making the arrest could face charges of false imprisonment, false arrest, assault, or all of these.

Other secondary considerations may also apply. A private citizen may arrest any person found committing, but only for the following reasons:

- to ensure the appearance of the offender before a court of law;
- to preserve the public order;
- to prevent a repetition of the offence; and
- to ensure the safety of the public or the safety of the offender.

Although these conditions might not apply in all States, it would appear that only one might apply to the standard average shop stealing incident, that of being to ensure the appearance of an offender before a court of competent jurisdiction. But if the offender provides a name and an address which is verified by suitable identification, there may be no further grounds for the arrest.

The laws of arrest are complex and to provide an in-depth evaluation of those that apply is beyond the scope of this book. Because the issues involved in a citizen's arrest can be quite complicated, this formal type of arrest should be avoided at all costs.

Staff must be made clearly aware that most shop stealers should be invited back to the store. Shop stealers then voluntarily accompany staff back to an office or back room. In most cases, a shop stealer will follow staff back to the store and wait patiently until police arrive. Without inviting legal arguments: this is not a formal citizen's arrest. The person has been invited to accompany a member of staff back to the shop to further address the matter and has done so voluntarily. But it really does not matter whether the person came back voluntarily or not. *If that person believes that he or she would be prevented from leaving the premises — in a purely technical sense — then a formal arrest has been made.*

Search and Seizure

The law is quite clear on the powers of private citizens with regard to search and seizure. Private citizens cannot search persons or seize their property. Retailers have a right to retain their own property, but under no circumstances are persons to be searched or their personal property seized. In all cases, police are to be advised of the circumstances of each individual arrest and have clear observations outlined to them.

REVIEW QUESTIONS

1. How is shop stealing viewed in Australia today as compared with similar offences 200 years ago?

2. What are the common denominators of shop theft? Discuss.

3. What are the factors which make a retailer more susceptible to shop theft? Discuss.

4. List the five categories of shop stealing. From whom are retailers most at risk? Discuss.

5. Why is it important to understand the essential difference between buyers, browsers and shop stealers?

6. Explain the concept of deny, delay and deter. How do those strategies affect the actions of a determined shop stealer?

7. The three most effective pro-active measures for the reduction of shop theft are a combination of:

    a) customer service;

    b) anti-theft devices; and

    c) solid policies and procedures.

    Write a two-page report arguing your case either for or against this statement.

8. How can we use the common behaviour characteristics of shop stealers to prevent theft?

9. What is the essential difference between selection and placement in the apprehension of shop stealers?

10. What is the significance of the term 'Finds Committing'.

11. What are the essential elements in a statement to police regarding the apprehension of a shop stealer?

12. You have been instructed by your supervisor to prepare a 30-minute presentation to staff on shop stealing. Your supervisor emphasises a prevention rather than an apprehension policy.

13. Your manager instructs you to provide a new sales assistant with some apprehension tips. You have 10 minutes to write out what you believe are the key points.

8 Customer Dishonesty: Internal Controls

CHAPTER OBJECTIVES

1. To evaluate the need for a loss prevention and security budget.
2. To establish the need for administrative checks and balances.
3. To identify the control needs for:
   - fitting rooms;
   - customer bag inspections;
   - burglary;
   - aggressive, drunk and violent offenders;
   - emergency planning and response;
   - alcohol and drugs; and
   - security newsletters.

LOSS CONTROL BUDGETS

Setting the Loss Control Budget

The question of whether retailers invest enough in loss prevention and control strategies is a constant one. One senior retailing manager director was once asked how much should a retailer spend on loss prevention and security? His reply: 'Nothing!' This is certainly true. If retailers operated in a perfect world, there would be no need for loss controls. But as dreams of Utopia remain only as dreams, retailers are quickly brought back to reality to assess the costs of a loss prevention and security control program.

The cost of implementing loss prevention controls for retail operations needs to be weighed against the risks involved. Every retailing operation is different. What may be a good percentage loss figure to one retailer, may be a nightmare to another. Loss prevention measures must adapt to a changing retail environment. In the late 80s and early 90s, the introduction of passive dye-filled anti-theft tags became a popular and cost-effective means in deterring theft. Although still extremely useful, the initial impact of these tags has worn off and there is now a tendency to link passive dye-filled tags with active electronic article-surveillance tags.

The cost of implementing loss prevention and security controls is situational. But there is a suggestion that Australian retailers spend far less on loss prevention and security than other countries such as the United States, Canada and the United Kingdom. In 1994, The Australian Institute of Criminology released the results of the first Australian national survey of crimes against business. The report indicated that Australian retailers spend only 0.19% of gross annual sales on retail loss prevention and security (Walker, 1994, p. 111). This is in sharp contrast with other Western countries. Loss prevention expenditure for various countries is shown in Figure 8.1.

COUNTRY	SECURITY BUDGET	REFERENCE
United States	0.35%	Hollinger, 1993, p. 9
Canada	0.05% – 0.51%	Berlin, 1994, No. V, p. 7
United Kingdom	0.34% of average turnover	Braithwaite, 1992, p. 13
Australia	0.19%	Walker, 1994, p. 111

Figure 8.1. Loss prevention expenditure

The variations in the Canadian figure can be explained by the following:

...smaller retailers generally spend a lower percentage of their sales on security, the pattern of expenditures is not consistent as companies increase in size. What this suggests is that every retailer has different ideas about how much security is needed to help control shrinkage. [Berlin, 1994, p. 7]

The research indicates that budgets vary according to the needs of individual retailers. However, retail loss figures for these countries indicate a far lower percentage loss than those expressed for Australian retailers (see Figure 1.1. Overseas retail loss comparisons, p. 3). It naturally follows that if loss prevention expenditure increases to those levels generally accepted by overseas countries, Australian retail loss figures may fall accordingly.

As a simple guide, retailers may use the formula shown in Figure 8.2 to ascertain if their current loss prevention budgets are adequate. If current security budgets fall below 0.3% of gross sales and losses exceed 2%, then a case may exist to increase loss prevention expenditure.

	EXAMPLE	YOUR BUSINESS
GROSS SALES	$27,375,000	
CURRENT LOSSES	$734,625	
LOSS PERCENTAGE	2.68%	
SECURITY BUDGET	0.34% of sales	
DOLLAR VALUE	$93,075	

Figure 8.2. Loss prevention and security budget examples

Does Budgeting Work?

Case Study No. 30

Sales are over $200 million per year, the security budget runs at approximately 24% of gross sales or about $480,000. Losses average 0.85% or about $1.7 million annually. The total cost to the organisation is $2.18 million. If few or no strategies are in place and losses are allowed to increase to the national average of 2%, losses would inevitably rise to $4 million annually.

Planning a Security Budget

There are two major considerations in setting a loss prevention and security budget. In any control plan, retailers may be limited by what they themselves can do. Certainly the implementation of controls and guidelines may be introduced, but the supply of physical security requirements often are beyond the scope of many retailers. As part of the budget planning process, both internal and external elements of loss prevention and security need to be addressed. Internal controls are discussed in this chapter, while external controls are discussed in Chapter 9.

PROGRAMS FOR INTERNAL CONTROLS

These controls are cost-effective programs designed internally which become part of the retailer's policy and procedures. They should be contained in store operation manuals, and form part of standard operating procedures. Topics should also be integrated with all in-house training programs. Internal loss prevention controls are many and varied and each retailer will adopt different approaches. The following control measures need to be considered.

Verification Checks and Balances

This should include basic considerations such as separation of function that does not allow any one person to control a transaction from beginning to end (Office of Fair Trading and Business Affairs). This provides for:

- authorisation;
- accuracy confirmation;
- correct procedure; and
- verification.

These measures should apply to in-house documentation such as:
- gift vouchers
- credit notes;
- stock transfers;
- cash register discrepancies;
- lay-by control;
- stocktakes;
- receipt of stock; and
- cash handling procedures.

Simple methods can be employed and accounting documents designed that require two signatures, for example, for cash refunds.

The joint signing of a document which verifies a particular transaction, that is, a salesperson verifying a refund, the manger authorising it.

REFUNDS

Refunds and the Law

The most effective option to prevent fraud is to implement policy that states: 'no proof of purchase, no refund'.

But this general rule cannot be absolute, retailers have certain obligations under the law which deals specifically on issues such as faulty product, and product liability. There are seven circumstances where a trader may be obliged to give a customer a refund as shown in Figure 8.3.

REFUND ISSUE	CONDITIONS FOR POSSIBLE REFUND
NOT OF MERCHANTABLE QUALITY	If the goods are shown not to be of a standard reasonably expected in the market place by the 'reasonable man' test.
INHERENT FAULT	If the goods suffer from a fault which is either apparent or latent. An inherent fault may not be detected for some time after the purchase.
FIT FOR THE PURPOSE	Where, at the time of sale, the consumer makes it known to the trader the purpose for which the goods are being acquired, there is an implied condition that the goods will be suitable for the purpose. The consumer should also reasonably be able to rely on the skill or judgement of the salesperson or the trader in providing goods that will be suitable for the purpose.
MISREPRESENTED IN ADVERT OR AT TIME OF SALE	If it can be shown that the goods do not fit the description or sample, have been inaccurately represented by the salesperson as being suitable for a particular purpose, having certain features, made of a particular material etc.
CONTRACT PROBLEM	Where there is a basic mistake or flaw in the contract, the consumer may be entitled to withdraw and expect to get back any money they have paid.
CONTRACT OR STATUTORY CONDITIONS	If at any time of contracting, the parties agree to certain conditions being built into the contract e.g. 'Subject to finance', 'Subject to spouse approval', the consumer, upon implementing the escape clause, must be released from the contract and all money refunded. Statutory conditions relate to things like cooling off periods, court orders, etc. (cooling off periods in Victoria apply to door-to-door sales, insurance sales, some real estate purchases and the purchase of second-hand motor vehicles for licensed dealers).
CONSENT	Where both parties agree to cancel the contract and walk away from the deal.

Figure 8.3. Circumstances where refunds are required
(Source: Office of Fair Trading and Business Affairs.)

Exchanges, Issues of Credit Notes and Cash Refund Controls

There is one basic factor involved in refund issues and that is that the consumer has to provide 'proof of purchase'. The Fair Trading Office acknowledges that larger retailers often dispense with this requirement and refund regardless of how the goods were obtained. This certainly places pressure on smaller retailers. In determining individual refund policies where an open refund policy has been decided upon, retailers should consider the sample guidelines in Figure 8.4 that set out to retain a good customer relationship but, at the same time, deny or minimise the opportunity for fraudulent activity to take place.

CUSTOMERS WITH DOCKETS, RECEIPTS OR PROOF OF PURCHASE

- **EXCHANGE, CREDIT NOTE OR CASH REFUND**

If customer returns an item and provides the retailer with proof of purchase which verifies the original purchase, then the transaction should take place, unless the salesperson has reasonable grounds to suspect a fraudulent transaction. All exchanges, and the issuing of credit notes must be authorised by a store manager.

CUSTOMERS WITHOUT DOCKETS, RECEIPTS OR PROOF OF PURCHASE

- **EXCHANGES**

No documentation required apart from point of sale update on product codes, stock keeping units to accurately amend theoretical stocktake data. Authorisation required.

- **CREDIT NOTES**

If no exchange is possible, then a Credit Note should be issued and ID noted as per instruction below.

- **CASH REFUND**

A Cash Refund Advice slip should be completed. Customer must produce identification which shows customer's signature. Details of the identification must be endorsed on the Cash Refund Advice slip and customer must then sign the docket. If signatures match, refund should be given. Manager must authorise.

Figure 8.4. Guidelines for exchanges, issues of credit notes and cash refunds

Refund Warning Programs

All instances where customers have obtained cash refunds without producing proof of purchase should be collated on a cash-refund advice slip, and forwarded to a central location for data collection and analysis. Currently, retail refund warning programs are available as self-contained computer software packages to detect frequent refunders.

Forged and Counterfeit Receipts

Although not a major problem in Australia or New Zealand as yet, the availability of home computer systems with assorted fonts, printing styles and printer capabilities has assisted offenders to replicate any register receipt produced by retailers today. Duplicated receipts have already been found in some Queensland stores. Some of the measures now recommended to prevent the duplication of receipts is the use of multicoloured ribbons that allow register printers to hit two colours at once. The receipt produced becomes difficult to duplicate. Other measures include printing a retailer's logo on the reverse of all receipts and the use of non-reproducible ink.

Forged and counterfeit receipts have not been identified as a major concern. The reason for this may be twofold. First, instances of forged receipts in Australia and New Zealand may be rare and therefore carry a low profile. Second, retailers may be unaware that forged or counterfeit receipts are currently being used, thereby not providing staff with the necessary awareness training to examine refunded receipts. Retailers should be aware of the potential damage these receipts can do and should include the topic in all loss prevention training programs, security bulletins etc. to enable staff to report receipts that may be suspect.

CHEQUE FRAUD

Case Study No. 31

A Tasmanian construction company had a clean out of documents no longer applicable to their operations. They threw out a considerable amount of paperwork, including a book of cheques no longer used by the company. The cheque book contained in excess of 70 blank cheques and was dumped in a local paper recycling plant where it was found by an employee. The employee then used 20 of the cheques to purchase goods from retailers to the value of $2,500 before being apprehended.

Case Study No. 32

An offender walked into a Melbourne eastern suburbs bank and opened a cheque account for $1.00. He received a cheque book containing 25 cheques. The teller, being suspicious, took a bank photo of him, but still handed over the cheque book.

Over the next six months, the offender passed nearly all of the cheques on to retailers and purchased merchandise valued more than $25,000. The ID he used was a driver's licence he had found. To cover his tracks, he had false number plates on his vehicle. The only constant clue was the use of a particular late model sedan with an unusual colour. A lengthy process of elimination at eastern suburbs car-yards finally identified the offender. He was convicted and released on a 12-month good behaviour bond. His family mortgaged their homes to help repay restitution ordered against the offender.

Case Study No. 33

Two career criminals registered a number of companies with the Corporate Affairs Office. They opened business accounts for all of the businesses and cross-referenced each as a credit reference. Over a six-month period, they proceeded to purchase goods from retailers with valueless cheques to the value of $120,000. These goods were all re-sold. The company was then sold off to a third party who admitted purchasing the businesses, but denied purchasing the debts of the companies bought. All involved were charged with many offences including 'conspiracy', but all were found not guilty due to technical legal problems in establishing who was actually liable. Unfortunately the 42 retailers who lost the $120,000 were the ultimate victims.

Types of Cheques

A cheque is an unconditional order in writing that:

- is addressed by a person to another person (being a bank);
- is signed by the person giving it; and
- requires the bank to pay on demand a certain sum of money.

Banks and other financial institutions may issue several types of cheques and the more common types are:

- **Counter cheques.** These are cheques, normally about five, which are given to customers, whilst customers are waiting for normal cheque books to be printed. As they are open to a high degree of manipulation and fraudulent misuse, many retailers will not accept counter cheques.

- **Bank cheques.** Bank cheques are those which are drawn on the bank itself after having being purchased from the bank. They offer a higher degree of security than other forms of cheques, but can still be fraudulently manipulated. Offenders use home computers, cheque-creating programs and special magnetic ink cartridges to make what appears to be legitimate bank cheques. Modern scanning techniques allows genuine bank cheques to be scanned which, after a few details such as cheque numbers and dates are changed, can be used to defraud retailers (Hurst, 1994, p. 15a).

- **Personal cheque accounts.** These are the everyday cheque accounts opened by individuals or in joint names, such as husband and wife. These are easy to open, require little identification and virtually no funds. Abuse from personal accounts would account for the majority of cheque fraud in Australia.

- **Business cheque accounts.** These accounts are opened by businesses for normal day-to-day business operations and generally cause few problems; however, some businesses refuse to accept proprietary limited company cheques unless prior arrangements have been made. If a proprietary limited company liquidates, the debt dies with the company and, unlike personal cheques, restitution cannot be sought from the company's directors.

Obligations with Cheques

When accepting cheques, retailers do so in good faith, and for value.

A bank is obliged to honour all cheques provided that:

- there are sufficient funds available in the account;
- there is no countermand of instruction to pay;
- there is no legal reason to justify a refusal to pay; and
- that the cheque is drawn in a proper form.

If any of the above provisions are not present, then the bank can dishonour the cheque and endorse it either:

- **No account.** The account does not exist, or more usually it has been closed. Cheques drawn when there is 'No Account' are probably dishonestly drawn and intended to deceive the receiver. 'Account Closed' cheques may be dishonestly drawn; however, there have been many cases where the customer has moved address and changed banks with no dishonest intent.

- **Refer to drawer.** An account exists, however the bank will not pay the cheque and is advising the receiver of the cheque to directly approach the drawer of the cheque to negotiate payment or to make alternative arrangements. This usually means that the bank may regard the account as a problem and could be a prelude to the bank closing the account due to its operating conditions.

- **Insufficient funds or present again.** These markings usually indicate that funds are currently inadequate, but this may be corrected. It is possible that there are insufficient funds because of a miscalculation by the drawer who expected funds to be paid in but they did not arrive, consequently the drawer will not be deliberately dishonest. It is also possible that the drawer may be reckless or has dishonestly calculated to have the cheque marked 'Present Again' to enable his cash flow to continue.

- **Stop payment.** These could merely be as a result of a civil dispute regarding goods or services purchased. It does not necessarily mean dishonesty. However, stopping payment is a common ploy used by dishonest customers to obtain cash refunds, that is, purchasing goods with a cheque to the value of $200, stopping payment on the cheque but immediately cash refunding the goods. When approached, they justify the actions by saying, 'But I've sent the goods back'.

- **Payment deferred, effects not cleared, drawer deceased.** These are more unusual markings and are fairly self-explanatory. These markings indicate that there are funds in the account, however for one reason or another, further inquiries are necessary before funds will be cleared.

Cheque Offences

The main offences likely to be committed in relation to cheques include:

- theft of the cheque;
- obtaining property by deception;
- obtaining a financial advantage by deception;
- false pretences;
- forging;
- uttering; and
- passing valueless cheques.

Australia's largest cheque verification agency, Telecheck, advises that 2% of all cheques presented to banks for payment are dishonoured (see Figure 8.5).

CHEQUE DISHONOUR TYPE	RECOVERY PROBABILITY
FINANCIAL MISCALCULATIONS These are simply dishonoured cheques that result from individual error and financial miscalculations and are normally recoverable through simple request letters.	30%
PROFESSIONAL DEBTORS These are cheques presented by dishonest customers who delay and deter payment until the very last moment. They presume that eventually the retailer will give up trying to collect the debt and write it off. These dishonours are usually recoverable but through vigorous recovery action.	30%
FRAUDULENT ACTIVITY These are deliberate and intentional acts of criminality. In most cases, there is little or no hope of recovering the value of the cheque. In some cases, goods purchased may be recovered but are of little resale value. Restitution from convicted offenders may be sought, but the recovery process is complex.	40%

Figure 8.5. Recovery probabilities for cheque dishonours (Source: Telecheck Australia.)

Cheque Controls

Proactive measures taken in reducing instances of cheque fraud are becoming more prevalent. Retailers need to adopt policies an procedures which aim to eliminate or minimise cheque abuse. Proactive measures are those aimed to prevent fraud in the first place. These may include:

- verifying all cheques through a central cheque verification agency before accepting any cheque; and
- formalising and enforcing cheque and ID acceptance policies.

Reactive measures are those actions taken after a dishonoured cheque has been identified and these should include:

- assigning responsibility to one person at a central location to ensure that the administration function for bad or fraudulent cheques are performed immediately a cheque is returned;
- providing prompt feedback to salespersons who have accepted bad cheques;
- following up action with store managers who approved cheques that should not have been accepted; and finally
- immediately reporting all instances of fraudulent cheques to police.

Proactive Measures

The principle causes of cheque loss are:

- lack of cheque control procedures;
- failure to examine every cheque; and
- failure to record issuer's details.

Cheques should only be accepted by retailers if:

- they are written out and signed at the time of purchase;
- the amount is the value of the goods purchased;
- the date of the actual day of sale is written on each cheque;
- the cheque is made out correctly and crossed 'not negotiable' (see Figure 8.6);
- suitable identification is obtained to identify the cheque with the customer, including:
  - drivers licence,
  - police and armed forces ID or similar,
  - Australian passport,
  - credit card,
  - transaction card,
  - current utilities account,

  provided that:
  - the signature on the cheque matches the signature on the ID produced, and
  - the customer's name address and phone number are recorded on the back of the cheque together with details of the ID (see Figure 8.7).

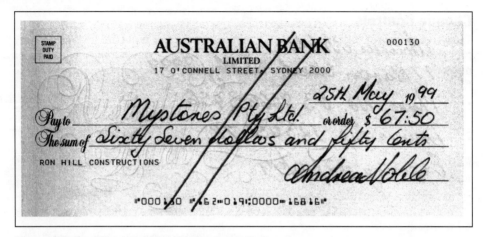

Figure 8.6. Sample requirements for face of cheques

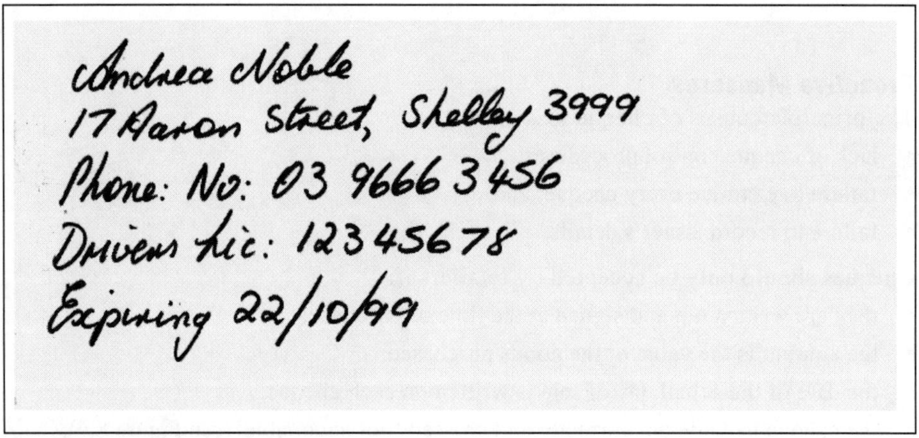

Figure 8.7. Sample requirements for reverse of cheques

Verification Agencies

Verification agencies such as Telecheck and Transax provide advisory information to help retailers evaluate the risk of accepting a cheque. In basic terms, if the cheque meets certain specified criteria, the agency warrants the information so that if the cheque is returned unpaid for any other reason than one-off stopped payment (such as a customer–retailer dispute), the agency will pay the client the face value of the dishonoured cheque.

These agencies also provide a 'negative data base'. This data is provided by retailers from the information recorded on all dishonoured cheques. When a cheque is used for the payment of goods, a retailer will verify the cheque with the agency. If the cheque is recorded, the retailer will be advised to decline the cheque. The customer issuing the cheque is then advised to contact the agency for further details.

The costs for guaranteeing cheques usually runs at approximately 2% of the face value of total cheques insured. For example, if a retailer has an annual turnover in cheques of $1 million, then the cost of insuring the cheques would amount to $20,000. However, if the retailer's losses from cheques are only $15,000, then the costs of guarantee are not justified. In this case, the retailer would need to compare in-house costs for recovery of bad debts with the cost of using a reputable external debt collection agency.

Travellers Cheques

Because travellers cheques are so readily available and the only requirement being a signature match, instances of counterfeit travellers cheques are now more prevalent, particularly with the introduction of advanced technology in colour copiers. Travellers cheques are usually purchased from a host of different financial or travel institutions. At the time of purchase, the purchaser signs the cheque. When it is transacted, the purchaser countersigns the cheque and if the two signatures match, the travellers cheque is accepted.

Good policies for retailers accepting travellers cheques should include:

- Salespersons checking all travellers cheques to ensure they contain a water mark.

- Only accepting Australian currency travellers cheques unless registers are capable of converting up-to-date international currency. In some cases, when travellers cheques are in a foreign currency, depending on that currency, retailers may lose on the exchange rate — this is particularly the case when foreign currency is expressed in 'dollars', that is, Australian dollars, US dollars, Canadian dollars or NZ dollars.

- If the signatures are in any way different, or the travellers cheque is in any way suspect, a call should be made to the issuing agency direct and a request for an authorisation made.

CREDIT CARDS, EFTPOS AND ATMS

Credit cards can be obtained fraudulently by various means as shown in Figure 8.8.

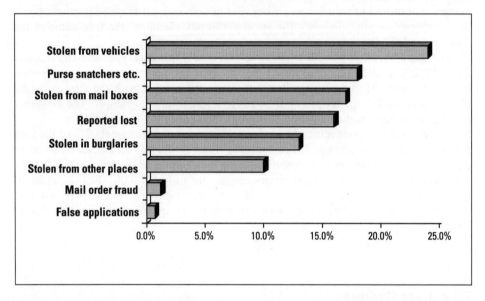

Figure 8.8. Common methods of obtaining credit cards for fraudulent use

(Source: Cardlink Services Ltd.)

Case Study No. 34

Julie was an 18-year-old shop assistant working for a reputable shoe chain in Melbourne. A customer had just purchased two pairs of shoes and had used her credit card. As the customer left, Julie noticed that she had left her card behind. Without thinking, she picked it up and put it into her pocket. A few days later she found the card. She went into a department store and used it to purchase some merchandise. She found that the card was accepted, and no questions were asked. Over the next three weeks, she used the card on 49 occasions and obtained goods valued at more than $5,000. One of the surprising aspects of this case study was that Julie was a Caucasian with long blond hair, yet the name on the card was Lee Yin CHONG. Nobody bothered to question this obvious discrepancy.

Credit Card Controls

For credit card and EFTPOS transactions, there are four simple rules to follow to ensure that credit cards are accepted correctly to enable retailers to receive payment from the bank for goods purchased by customers:

RULE 1   Ensure that any purchase over the floor limit is authorised by the appropriate authorisation centre.

RULE 2   Ensure that the signature on the card matches the signature on the voucher.

RULE 3   Ensure that the validity date is current.

RULE 4   Ensure that the card is not on the current warning bulletin.

Suspect Warning Signs

Fraudulent card users usually show some warning signs. These translate into nervous or suspicious characteristics and may include:

- nervousness or too talkative;
- attempting to upset sales staff;
- making numerous single purchases to stay under floor limits;
- declining to have purchases wrapped;
- appearing to be agitated or in a hurry, forcing sales staff to hurry the sale;
- producing the card from a pocket instead of wallet or purse; and/or
- using a name on the card with does not correspond with the gender or ethnic features of the card holder, for example, a young male with a card in the name of Martha Smith, or a heavily accented European with a card bearing the name Harry Johnson.

Case Study No. 35

Two young males working together made multiple applications to various financial institutions to open both cheque and credit card accounts. Through a subsequent 'round robin' of deposits at automatic telling machines (ATMs) of valueless cheques, the pair were able to draw the nonexistent funds from ATMs on 409 occasions and obtained cash to the value of $55,000.

COUNTERFEIT CURRENCY

Case Study No. 36

One busy Saturday morning in Wellington, a young man entered a jeans shop in Lampton Quay and purchased a pair of Levi 501's. He paid for the jeans with two $50 dollar notes. The salesperson was suspicious, the notes were waxy and did not feel right, and the customer was very nervous. 'Everything OK?' he asked. The salesperson replied, 'Where did you get these, they feel a bit odd? I'll have to check them'. Our suspect then walked out of the store leaving the notes and the 501's on the counter. A quick phone call to the police with the suspect's description had police apprehending him a few blocks away. In his possession, police found $5,000 worth of counterfeit bills.

Counterfeit Currency Controls

Figure 8.9 depicts signs to look for when checking notes.

PAPER NOTES: $10, $20, $50 & $100

- Look at the differences between the suspect note and a genuine note. Hold the note up to the light and look for the watermark and the metal thread. The watermark is a profile of Captain James Cook in the white area of the note. On the $50 and $100 notes, positive and negative images alternate one above the other. The metal thread is located between the watermark and the centre of the note and is only visible when the note is held up to the light.

- Check the feel of the special paper and feel for the raised printing. A genuine note is printed on special paper made from cotton fibres. You can feel the raised printing (black ink) by running your fingernail across the main design elements such as portraits.

- Compare the raised printing between the genuine and suspect notes. Look for any print defects in the suspect note such as fuzzy broken or missing lines. Compare the background printing (multi coloured inks) of the genuine and suspect notes. Check for anomalies such as less clearly defined patterns, thicker or thinner lines, colour distortion.

- Check that the suspect note is not excessively thick compared to the genuine note.

- Check whether the suspect note fluoresces under UV light. Genuine banknote paper (unless treated eg with detergent) does not fluoresce under UV light (Note: ALL counterfeits will fluoresce).

- A genuine $100 has one black serial number and one blue serial number.

(Continued...)

POLYMER NOTES: $5, $10 & $20

- Look for differences between a suspect note and a genuine note. Check that the note has a transparent area. There is a stylised gum flower ($5) or windmill ($10) compass embossed with numerals '20' ($20) printed within the transparent zone

- Look for the seven-pointed star. Hold the note up to the light. Diamond-shaped patterns printed on each side of the note should combine perfectly to form a seven-pointed star. Check that you feel the slightly raised printing (black ink) by running your fingernail across the main design elements, such as the portrait,

- Look for micro-printing:
  $5 — words 'FIVE DOLLARS' in top left corner;
  $10 — words 'TEN DOLLARS' between each line of the poem 'Man from Snowy River' around portrait of Banjo Paterson;
  $20 — words 'TWENTY DOLLARS' right side of forehead of Mary Reibey.

- With the aid of a magnifying glass, words should be clearly and sharply defined.

- Compare the background printing (multi-coloured inks). Check for anomalies such as less clearly defined patterns, thicker or thinner lines, and colour distortion.

- Look at the note under UV light: in a genuine note, the serial number fluoresces; on the back of the $5 note, a checkerboard can also be seen.

- $10 — serial number fluoresces green;

- $20 — serial number fluoresces green.

- On the $5 note look for the Australian Coat of Arms. Hold the $5 note up to the light. The Coat of Arms can be seen under other printing to the left of the word 'Australia' when looking at the front of the note (Queen side).

Figure 8.9. A guide for cash handlers looking for counterfeit Australian notes

(Source: Currency Squad Australian Federal Police, 1995.)

INTERNAL EXCEPTION REPORTING

These reports are usually conducted by larger organisations with on-line computer services that monitor 'exceptions in reports', for example, a daily report detailing all cash register discrepancies over a certain amount. Exception reports can determine store averages on refunds and then indicate which stores have unusually high or unusually low refund returns.

Exception reporting identifies potential problem areas. These may indicate high levels of staff discount sales and major stock delivery discrepancies. Once identified, suspect offenders can then be verified and confirmed through further investigation which may include covert mystery, honesty and integrity shopping operations.

Case Study No. 37

One deficiency report prompted a retailer to install a hidden closed-circuit television camera above a cash register which then identified massive thefts, where staff were providing family and friends with free stock, pocketing cash and providing customers with falsified receipts. $40,000 was written off due to the malpractice of these employees.

FITTING ROOMS

Fitting rooms are one of the most vulnerable areas of store operations which can create potential for massive abuse by dishonest customers if not controlled. There cannot be enough emphasis placed on this fact.

In very general terms, retail fitting room controls are dependent on the type of operation. Larger retailers have specially located fitting rooms controlled by specially trained fitting room staff. Controls include the use of numbered tags that correspond with the number of garments going into a fitting room.

For smaller retailers, this style of control is obviously not economically viable. Other controls are more conducive to proper fitting room management in a smaller style of operation.

Fitting room controls are vitally important for two basic reasons:

- fitting room controls provide staff with policies, objectives and procedures that deny, delay or deter potential loss; and
- fitting rooms offer salespersons a prime opportunity to develop their suggestive selling, add-ons or multiple sale techniques.

A customer in a fitting room trying on a garment may be keen to add to this garment. As salespersons may already have a psychological advantage over the customer being in the fitting room in the first place, salespersons might bring in a colour coordinated scarf, tie, socks, belt or anything that may be considered useful to the customer. By providing this additional service, salespersons not only provide positive customer service, but may add to the daily sales figure, and once again, deny any opportunities for dishonest customers to steal.

Fitting Room Controls

The following guidelines are for commonsense fitting room controls:

- Provide a total fitting room service.

- Escort customers and avoid pointing and saying, 'They're over there' — not only is this bad manners, it is likely to put the customer off, and may well instil a sense of mild frustration that the customer relieves by ultimately stealing the garment.

- Take the garments from the customer. En route to the fitting room, count the garments and shake them out — this will reveal any garment that may have been rolled up inside another. Explain to the customer that you are shaking out the garment to loosen it up. Advise that new garments are often a little stiff. By shaking out the garment you do two things:
  - provide greater customer service to genuine customers; and
  - deny the opportunity to steal.

Customers with Bags

If a customer has a large bag, or a considerable number of other shopping bags, these could be used to conceal stolen merchandise. These situations can be overcome by:

- offering to consolidate all the other shopping bags into one large bag; or

- offering to secure the bags behind the counter until the customer is finished.

This type of assistance provides customer service for which genuine customers will be grateful. For customers with a dishonest intent, it will quickly shows intolerance of would-be shop stealers and actively denies them opportunities to steal.

General Fitting Room Procedures

Store managers and staff should ensure that:

- customers are aware that staff are present and are constantly available for assistance;
- that only four garments are allowed into fittings at any one time;
- that customers in fitting rooms are constantly monitored and provided with service that limits the opportunity for theft;
- staff not performing selling floor duties ensure that customers in fitting rooms are not left unattended;
- all fitting rooms are to be checked immediately after they are vacated by a customer for:
  - personal property left by the customer,
  - empty hangers left by the customer,
  - garments left in the fitting room by the customer;
- that only one customer is in any one fitting room.

While customers are in the fitting rooms, frequent visits should be made to the customer. This limits the potential for theft. It also provides opportunities to check sizes: 'Is that size right. Can I get you one up (or one down)?' Once again, the customer may see this as a genuine attempt by the retailer to provide assistance.

Fitting Room Signage

A further passive control that could be employed is the use of signage. Signs inside fitting rooms which shout, 'Shop stealers will be prosecuted' could be viewed as aggressive and hostile and may have a negative effect. On the other hand, passive signage appeals to the consciousness of customers. Passive signage could simple state: 'A Store without shop stealers is a nice place to shop. Mystore — caring for our customers.'

In a shop stealers' manual published overseas, the following advice was offered: 'The most important thing to remember in working in fitting rooms is to make sure no-one can tell how many pieces you have taken in.' Remove the motivating factors for theft, and shop stealers will go elsewhere.

CUSTOMER BAG CHECKS

The issue of bag checks is often an emotional one and few retail staff, or members of the general public for that matter, really understand the rights of both parties. It is fundamental to retailing to maintain good customer relations, without this interaction, service and sales will suffer. All the same, there are many customers who view good courteous service as a weakness and may take these opportunities to exploit circumstances to steal from retailers. In these instances, a staff member may believe that a customer has stolen an item and placed it inside a bag. What are the guidelines then, that allow retailers and staff to check customers bags or to search the customer in an effort to retain property?

Condition of Entry Signs

In the majority of cases, retail premises are classified as private property. When instances of theft are high, a retailer may decide to erect condition of entry or bag control signage that warns customers that a condition of entry exists. If a customer then chooses to enter the store, the customer enters into an 'implied contract' which suggests that they can enter the store provided that they allow their bags to be checked and inspected if requested to do so. If a customer refuses a request, then technically speaking and provided that a condition of entry signs exists, the customer has breached the implied contract, and is liable.

The remedy at law and other options are:

- a retailer may sue for breach of contract (highly unlikely as costs involved outweigh the principles involved);
- a retailer may refuse to sell;
- a retailer can terminate the customer's authority to be in the store, and ask the customer to leave immediately — failure to do so, may make the customer liable to the laws of trespass; or
- retailers could simply withdraw the request and let the matter lapse.

Frequently Asked Questions

Q: Must customers show the contents of their bags?

A: Most retailers would prefer them to, but the answer is 'No'.

Q: What happens when customers say 'No'?

A: Call your manager, who can explain the legal rights, if the customer still refuses, a number of options exist:

- you can refuse a sale;
- you could ask the customer to leave;
- you can refuse future entry; or
- you could call the police if there are reasonable grounds to believe that an offence has been committed.

Q: Are customers free to leave the store if staff wish to keep them there?

A: Retailers have no right to detain any person unless a citizen's arrest has been made.

Q: Can I grab them and physically force them to stay?

A: Absolutely not.

Q: Is it true that I'm not allowed to touch anyone or hit back if I am threatened in any way?

A: Legal advice suggests that to avoid any possible claims of assault, no attempt should be made to make physical contact with any suspect person. If you are assaulted, you have the legal right to defend yourself. However, your defence must be in accordance with the threat offered.

Q: What are customer's rights?

A: If a wrongful arrest is made, the customer can sue for damages, possible assault and even false arrest.

Q: It would appear that most retailers are disadvantaged whatever course of action is taken. If nothing is done, stock may be lost; if bag inspections are attempted, we risk being sued. What is the answer?

A: Managers and store staff should always remember that the prime objective of retail is sales and service. Most retailers place great importance on customer relations and strive to maintain those relationships at high levels. However, if a person blatantly abuses goodwill and uses apparent weaknesses for dishonest purposes, then quick positive and affirmative action must be taken to prevent further occurrences

BURGLARY

Case Study No. 38

This particular incident occurred in a small regional shopping centre in Sydney which contained approximately 80 retail outlets. The stocktake loss for the casual fashion retailer was inconsistent with past results. Previous stocktake figures indicated good control by the manager and staff. There had been no change in staffing for some years, and there was no change in their circumstances that might suggest an internal theft. All the same, the stock loss was unacceptable. Convinced that it was an outside job, the local security manager installed a time-lapse video and low light closed-circuit television camera in the store.

Unfortunately, there was insufficient ambient lighting to obtain good imaging results, but the tapes showed unusual shadowy movement. Spot checks revealed that the thefts were continuing, but how remained a mystery. The security manager tried a different track, he sprinkled talcum powder lightly on the floor. He did this for a week. Every morning staff would vacuum the floor, but before locking the shop at the end of the day, would repeat the process. Finally, on one Saturday morning, they had success. Staff found footprints in the talcum powder and the pattern indicated that the thief had come down through the roof, removed the overhead tiles in the ceiling and had climbed down onto the fitting room supports and then into the shop. The security manager now had sufficient evidence to show police.

The following Friday night, two detectives sat in the small shop and waited. At 4.12 am on Saturday morning, the detectives heard the overhead tiles being removed and saw two feet protrude from the ceiling. As the thief climbed down onto the floor, he was greeted with a friendly, 'Good morning, sir. You're under arrest!' The investigation revealed that the thief was a casual baker employed at the local bakery. Once his bread was in the oven baking, he would climb into the centre's ceiling space and go shopping. The items he stole were sold to friends and relatives.

Burglary Controls

Burglars will often strike at retail premises after closing time, when unoccupied during the night, weekends or holidays. Restricting the opportunities for burglary is again the key element. Burglary prevention guidelines are explained in Figure 8.10.

Work Arrival Procedures

Armed robbery and burglary are never likely, however both are possible. As part of any loss prevention control procedures, retailers should apply simple precautions that can be built in to daily routines. The last thing sales staff need when opening stores is to walk into a burglary while the burglars are still on the premises, or to walk into a robbery situation, where robbers have broken into the premises and are waiting for staff to arrive. The following procedures should be followed when arriving at work:

- **Check whether conditions are normal.** Are all the windows intact? Are doors still locked? Look through windows if possible — is everything normal? If the premises are large, have only one person enter. Once the 'all clear' is given, the remaining staff can enter the premises. If first the person does not give the 'all clear' within a predetermined time, call the police.

- **Take note of any suspicious behaviour.** Make a note of anything that arouses your suspicion. Notes may come in handy for future events. Strange behaviour of people loitering around the entrance, or evidence that suggests that suspects may be watching the store from parked cars.

Enter premises only when you are satisfied that everything is normal.

AGGRESSIVE, DRUNK AND VIOLENT OFFENDERS

These types of offenders can cause severe emotional trauma to both staff and customers. The key issues here are to remain safe and to remove the potential threat. The following are guidelines:

- ensure the safety and wellbeing of all staff and customers;
- attempt to diffuse the situation;
- take a description of the offender;
- take a note of the offender's car registration;
- note vehicle description and direction of travel;
- note and record any threat made to you;
- telephone the police;
- compile a short report and hand it to the police on their arrival; and
- note and record any property damage caused by the offender.

LIGHTING	Use effective interior/exterior lights. Burglars wish to go unseen.
DEADLOCKS	Use quality deadlocks on solid doors. Have good key-control procedures.
WINDOWS	Use toughened glass, bars or grills over windows to restrict access.
MONITOR PREMISES WITH 24-HOUR ALARM SYSTEM	A good quality internal and external audible alarm will scare off even the most determined burglar before he can steal or further damage property. Use a voice driver in your alarms that provides a digital voice message that states: 'Warning! You have entered a restricted area — police and guard patrols are now en route to this location!' Alarm systems can be monitored by either Direct Line, Securitel or through high speed Digital Diallers. **Direct Line** monitoring involves direct line communication between the site and a monitoring station. Used for high profile and vulnerable premises such as banks, building societies, retailers with large amounts of cash in concentrated areas such as cash offices. **Securitel Network** monitoring is similar to direct line monitoring. However, where direct line monitoring uses an exclusive line for user clients, the Securitel Network involves a shared line which is a less expensive option. **Digital Dialler** monitoring is a system whereby a high speed dialler actually dials up the monitoring station when a reportable incident occurs. This can only occur if the telephone line is intact. Digital diallers need to be backed up with an on-site satellite siren that activates if telephone lines are cut.
MOBILE PATROL GUARDS	Have premises patrolled after hours by reputable guard patrols at random intervals.
ALARM & PATROL STICKERS	Let potential burglars know by using signs/stickers that premises are alarmed, monitored and being patrolled.
CASH REGISTERS	Implement register controls that leave register drawers, containing only small amounts of cash, open. This may satisfy the impulse burglar without causing damage to empty and locked cash drawers.
CASH	Make arrangements for daily deposits through night wallets, or install an effective floor safe.
FIRE CABINET	Leave valuable and accountable documents such as gift vouchers, credit notes and other important paperwork in a fireproof cabinet or safe at the end of each day.
DAILY INSPECTIONS	Develop a closing policy that requires the physical checking of doors, windows, lights and alarm systems prior to staff leaving premises at the end of day. Ensure that all operate effectively.

Figure 8.10. Burglary prevention guidelines

IDENTIFICATION OF OFFENDERS

In some instances, the shop stealer or other type of offender will leave your premises before police arrive. Offenders may plead not guilty and you may not see them until the Court hearing, which could be some months away. It is vital to be able to correctly identify all offenders to:

- assist the police in proving the identity of the offender; and
- successfully prosecute the offender in a court of law.

Points to be considered when observing and describing the offender:

- To avoid confusion, keep the description as simple as possible.
- When observing the offender, do so by glancing every second or so. Avoid direct eye contact in violent situations which can arouse aggression from the offender.
- To gather the information, start from the offender's head and work down the offender's side nearest you.
- Once the base has been completed you will be able to start gathering additional information about the offender. In disguises, specific points about clothing should be noted etc.

EMERGENCY PLANNING AND RESPONSE

The need for emergency planning is vital to ensure that operational efficiency is maintained during an emergency event. Emergencies may include:

- bomb threats;
- arson threats;
- major burglary;
- armed hold-up;
- fire, flood and earthquake;
- extortion demands;
- executive kidnapping; and
- product contamination.

Case Study No. 39

In the busy pre-Christmas rush of 1980, NSW shoppers were keen and eager to complete their final shopping sprees, when the Woolworths chain was suddenly and without warning subjected to a series of bombings that rocked the retail industry. In the early hours of 17 December, an explosion occurred in premises occupied by Woolworths in the Warilla shopping complex some 100 kilometres south of Sydney. Two days later, a second explosion occurred at Woolworths' Maitland store, 200 kilometres north of Sydney. Damage was estimated at nearly $400,000. A week later, at 3.10 pm on Christmas eve, a caller to Woolworths announced that a third explosion would occur in Woolworths' George and Park

Streets store in downtown Sydney. The store was evacuated within 10 minutes and at 3.25 pm, a loud explosion occurred on the ground floor which blew out plate-glass windows for two streets.

These bombings were part of an elaborate extortion demand on Woolworths for $500,000 in cash, $250,000 in gold bullion and $250,000 in diamonds. After an intensive and dedicated effort on the part of investigative teams, the extortionists were arrested attempting to retrieve their ransom from the bottom of Sydney Harbour (Anderson, 1985, pp. 52–75).

In concluding his article on the Woolworths extortion, Detective Inspector Anderson wrote: 'The extortion attempt in December–January, 1980–1981, created a great deal of terror, not only for the executives of Woolworths Limited, but also for the general public.'

The incidence of hoax calls throughout Australia increased immensely. In one period of approximately five weeks in the Sydney Metropolitan area, there were 514 bomb hoaxes resulting in 256 evacuations. The disruption to business houses and traffic was such that the Police Department had to address senior executives from these firms in addition to enlisting support from the shop assistants unions. Many calls were frivolous and obviously instigated by children. The commonsense of management and employees had to prevail (Anderson, 1985, p. 75).

Emergency Planning to Counter Disaster

For retailers, education and research is required to convince senior management that disaster planning is necessary. Research needs to be undertaken by individual organisations to assess local and overseas retail industry threats that have had both disastrous consequences for retailers and their customers.

Retailers that sell potentially dangerous products such as petroleum, gas, oil, lubricants, chemicals and other hazardous substances need to be aware of potential hazards in terms of storage, displaying and selling these products. Relevant legislation would need to be researched to ensure that all safety standards and safety requirements are being met.

Additionally, some retailers are being targeted by animal liberation and environmental groups. More often than not, these groups act on moral grounds and the majority seek passive ways in which to achieve change. These pose no major threat. However, there is a radical element that will exploit the well-meaning intentions of these groups by conducting dangerous and often violent activities against targeted retailers. This may be in the form of product contamination, mass product destruction, arson, and assaults on staff.

A survey of employees and premises should be undertaken to ascertain levels of preparedness and readiness in the event of a disaster contingency.

Additional research should be undertaken that shows the cost-effectiveness of counter disaster planning in terms of the retailer's responsibility on matters relating to both moral and legal obligations.

The subsequent financial savings in work care or work cover claims, insurance losses, stock losses, loss of corporate image in the community and loss of potential earnings, all suggest that counter disaster planning is an effective proactive tool.

Planning a Program

In planning counter emergency responses, retailers might consider the use of a 'Counter Disaster Responses Committee'. This committee could have two roles. First, the committee may analyse, design, develop, implement and validate the disaster response plan. Second, it may act as a ready reaction team in the event of an emergency or disaster. This may involve:

- activity coordination between family and friends of any employees involved;

- attendance on site for liaison with appropriate authorities; and

- maintaining a 'Counter Disaster Control Room'.

The 'Counter Disaster Response Committee' or 'Emergency Ready Reaction Team' would need to have senior management decision-making skills to implement action plans and approve expenditure.

The development of a management team would require the full and unqualified support of senior management. A commitment is required to fund the project with an annual budget set aside to manage and maintain its effectiveness. Senior management would need to demonstrate full support by showing active participation and involvement in the analysis, design, development, implementation and validation stages.

ALCOHOL AND SUBSTANCE ABUSE

Over recent years the use of drugs, especially by young adults, has dramatically increased. The problems that arise from alcohol and drug abuse are not socially unacceptable but can threaten the safe working environment and efficient operation of any organisation. Dependency on drugs or alcohol is a serious health problem and management should be concerned about the welfare of all company employees.

Alcohol and drug habits are expensive to maintain, and the purchase of drugs is usually beyond the earning capacity of most employees. This factor may lead to employee malpractice. The alcohol or drug-dependent employee can be helped through Employee Awareness Programs and counselling if the problem is identified and the correct agencies notified. Any staff member who believes that an employee may be involved in the illicit use of drugs or have alcohol-related problems should promptly raise the matter with management.

SECURITY NEWSLETTERS

Security newsletters can be extremely serious publications or be used for a whole range of motivational and fun activities. Some of the content should be devoted to exception reporting and deficiency analysis capabilities. Information which highlights the number of dismissals due to acts of dishonesty should also be disclosed.

Staff like security newsletters. If a number of well-written stories about prevention and apprehensions are included, it adds an air of excitement, especially if names are mentioned. For example, 'Sally at Maintown saved the loss of 22 vases, when she…'.

Other uses include 'hot' items such as a persistent refunder 'doing the rounds' of stores. For example, the drawing below was put together by the display department staff of one retailer, using descriptions staff had provided and then placed in the newsletter. The drawing is animated and has a sense of urgency in it. It had the desired effect, within three days of the newsletter going to stores, staff instantly recognised the offender and he was apprehended and charged.

The newsletter should also report instances where staff have prevented major loss to the company. This may be the simple prevention of theft by a staff member applying customer service, or a staff member identifying and reporting a major internal refund scam.

Newsletters such as these are motivators for honest staff and de-motivators for potential thieves.

REVIEW QUESTIONS

1. Why set a budget for loss control? Discuss.

2. Evaluate the rationale of checks and balances for retail operations. In what way will they benefit the retail loss cause? Discuss

3. You are instructed to prepare a two-page report for a new manager explaining your 'No receipt, no refund' policy. Prepare a refund plan of action and discuss any exceptions to your policy.

4. Your sales are $3 million per year. You accept cheques and your annual report indicates that you accepted $278,000 in cheque value. Of these, 8% or $22,240 worth of cheques were returned dishonoured last year. You conduct a review and discover that:

    a) the $22,240 have never been recovered; and

    b) no cheque procedures are in place.

5. Last week, you were hired for the position of assistant manager in a large casual fashion outlet. The owners of the shop would like you to prepare a no-nonsense fitting room control plan. They believe that all their retail loss is as a result of fitting room theft. Develop a plan to evaluate the situation. What are your options?

6. What are the implications for retailers if 'condition of entry' signs were not allowed? What are alternative control measures regarding customers bags?

7. Review your own workplace. Conduct a review of the premises and evaluate current control measures for the safety and security of:

    a) staff employed at the site;

    b) security of assets, including both stock and information.

    Did you discover any major discrepancies in your internal controls? If so, what were they? How would you report these matters to your superiors?

8. You are the proprietor of a small grocery store in the suburbs. You employ six staff. The premises has one front entrance and a back dock with a roller shutter and side door. You are worried about evacuations in the case of fire. Seek help from your local fire authority and prepare an emergency counter-disaster plan for your store.

9 External Services and Equipment Controls

CHAPTER OBJECTIVES

1. To provide guidelines of external services and equipment available to assist in loss reduction.

INTRODUCTION

The development of loss prevention control plans utilises both in-house and external services. For many smaller retailers, the development of a total in-house approach is beyond their limited resources. This chapter provides those retailers with the necessary information to seek out effective solutions from external sources.

External programs include the use of:

- access control keys, locks and other products;
- after-hours monitoring;
- anti-theft dye tag devices;
- anti-theft mirrors;
- barrier systems;
- cable lock systems;
- cash collection agencies;
- cardboard cut-outs of police;
- covert surveillance officers;
- closed-circuit television (CCTV);
- customer service officers;
- electronic article surveillance (EAS) systems;
- safes;
- signage; and
- training programs.

ACCESS CONTROL KEYS AND LOCKS

Access control is a fundamental tool in securing the safety and protection of staff, customers, company assets and information. The range of security product available is vast, due to the many applications involved. General access control product includes:

- keying systems;
- fire-door hardware;
- padlocks;
- display cabinet locks;
- deadbolts;
- digital access control locks;
- hydraulic door closers;
- mortice-lock furniture; and
- cylinder rim and knob lock sets.

Retailers with multiple sites might consider the use of special keying systems that utilise individual keyed systems, keyed alike systems or a master key system. In seeking assistance and advice, only locksmiths who are members of industry organisations such as the Master Locksmiths Association of Australia should be used.

Reputable locksmiths can provide retailers with a wide range of services. They can also provide advice on manual or computerised key controls which provide for a three-way monitoring system on:

- the key itself;
- the person to whom it is issued; and
- the lock to which the key and the person has access.

AFTER-HOURS MONITORING

The very fact that most retail premises carry varying amounts of cash and contain valuable and resaleable stock items makes retailers vulnerable to attack from both professional and amateur thieves. This problem is not only limited to external thieves but also applies to the unauthorised entry of staff who have keys to premises and may be tempted to return to stores after hours.

The most cost-effective solution to safeguard against these possibilities is the installation of an alarm-monitoring system which provides valuable data for retailer owners and occupiers to monitor their premises after hours. There are various types of alarm-monitoring systems, but most provide information on:

- unauthorised entry — burglary;
- out-of-hours openings;
- duress alarms (hold-up alarms);
- late-to-close services;
- smash-and-grabs through display windows; and
- alarm response teams.

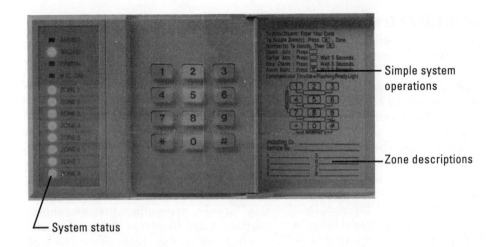

Simple system operations

Zone descriptions

System status

Figure 9.1. An Australian-designed alarm-monitoring system: the DAS Series DL250

(Illustration is reprinted here by permission and courtesy of DAS Direct Alarm Supplies Sydney.)

Modern 'off-the-shelf' alarm systems are sophisticated and can be programmed to perform most required functions. Alarm systems can be designed to reflect the individual operating needs of the client which provide for a higher degree of access controls, remote key pads, swipe-card reader access, proximity card access and many other features to further protect retail premises.

Reporting functions can also be tailored to suit most needs to provide information on 'who, when, how long and where' of retail operations.

The criteria for selecting an alarm installer and an alarm monitoring station should be based on the ability of a supplier to provide a cost-effective and efficient service which meets clients needs and which is carried out in accordance with recognised industry standards.

All potential security providers need to be carefully scrutinised for their capability to competently install systems using qualified personnel, providing a complete back-up service and a 24-hour monitoring service that meets all current industry and government standards.

Independent retail loss prevention and security consultants can provide a service which can independently assess clients' needs for alarm monitoring and recommend a number of suitable organisations to meet those specific needs.

ANTI-THEFT DYE TAG DEVICES

The concept of anti-theft dye tag devices was introduced in the early 1980s by a Scandinavian inventor who used the principle that if a targeted item is rendered worthless, it will not be stolen. This principle is used by banking institutions to dye-bomb cash in cash containers and drawers in the event of a hold-up. Once activated, the dye stains the cash, rendering it useless. The same principle is used to protect garments. The unauthorised act of attempting to remove a dye filled tag from a garment causes the dye capsule to break, thereby staining merchandise and making it worthless. If potential thieves see a dye tag on a garment and are aware that unauthorised removal will make the item useless, the motivation for theft is gone.

Dye tagging has become a highly successful means of passively protecting merchandise. The leader in passive anti-theft dye tag devices is Colortag™. Since the introduction of the popular Colortag™ range, many other loss prevention organisations have entered the market with passive dye-filled tags. The passive anti-theft dye tag device industry now provides a huge range of dye tags that meet most of the requirements of the industry.

Figure 9.2. The Dymark® passive anti-theft dye tag

(Illustration is reprinted here by permission and courtesy of Colortag Australia Pty Ltd.)

The greatest advantage of dye tagging is that tags are completely transportable from one site to another and do not require expensive electronic surveillance. Colortag™ use a light weight and portable air compression system to release tags. Other release systems use special hand-operated detachers or special magnetic detachers. The only expenses involved in passive dye tags are:

- the cost of the tags (between $2.00 to $4.00 per tag, depending on quantity purchased); and
- the need to install a special tag removal device.

The major disadvantage with dye tags is the total loss of any stained garments. However, the tags themselves create the demotivating factor for theft. It also de-motivates the thief from returning to the store, as the thief is now aware that to do so is an uneconomical exercise. Tag-accounting control mechanisms put in place that provide for the before and after counts of tags, test the effectiveness of the system.

ANTI-THEFT MIRRORS

The uses of anti-theft mirrors in a retailing environment are many and varied. Anti-theft mirrors can enhance security and reduce instances of shop-theft provided that they are used judiciously. Strategically placed mirrors allow retail staff to see customers in otherwise remote or unobservable locations. Their major disadvantage is that shop stealers can also use the mirrors to locate the whereabouts of staff.

Anti-theft mirrors can take the form of:

- see-through ceiling domes;
- convex mirrors to provide broad or expansive views; and
- see-through observation stations.

See-through observation stations can be utilised by covert surveillance officers to monitor customers in large areas. Often, one officer might direct the movement of another working the floor through portable radio transmission.

Other uses for see-through one-way mirrors may be in cash offices or in offices where administrative staff are able to see store operations.

BARRIER CONTROL SYSTEMS

Barrier control systems tend to control the flow of movement in busy environments. Barrier control systems are usually seen in supermarkets, large discount stores such as Target, Big W, K-Mart, Toys-R-Us and other retail shops where the high levels of customer traffic warrant special measures to safeguard against customer theft. Barrier systems tend to deny random exit by forcing customers to pass through control aisles where cash register operators can check bags, prams and shopping trolleys for unpaid items. These aisles may also incorporate electronic scanning devices through which customers pass.

In some stores, bag-checking functions are performed by store greeters, who provide dual roles as customer service officers in welcoming customers into the shop and directing them to desired products, as well as security officers in checking bags on exit.

CABLE LOCK SYSTEMS

Cable lock systems provide retailers with a wide range of physical security that locks merchandise to a control point. In most cases, the merchandise can still be handled, tried on and tested, but a salesperson is required to release the product from its anchor.
Cabling can take the form of:

- mechanical ball and loop steel cables linked through garments to a lock box;

- lanyards linked with anti-theft tags that can protect smaller and inexpensive items such as sporting goods, handbags, belts, leather goods and shoes; and

- electronic cables that set off an alarm device if removed from items such as expensive leather clothing, stereo equipment, televisions, computers and power tools.

CASH COLLECTION AGENCIES

The use of a cash collection agency to clear cash from premises has two basic effects:

- a cash collection service provides for the additional safety of staff; and
- the reduction of cash on the premises reduces the risk profile for the retailer.

CARDBOARD CUT-OUTS OF POLICE

Cardboard cut-outs of police were first used in Scandinavia with great success. The idea was taken up by some British retailers who also found that full-size cardboard cut-outs of police placed strategically in shops had a beneficial effect in reducing retail loss. The concept is now a loss prevention strategy employed by retailers in both Australia and New Zealand.

Cardboard cut-outs can be either full-size or chest-high profiles of male or female police officers. Some police forces are reluctant to allow the use of images of their officers for this purpose, forcing some retailers to use the cardboard images of other State police officers. The most effective results of their use has been when cardboard cut-outs are used seasonally to address special theft problems. When used constantly, their effectiveness diminishes with time.

COVERT SURVEILLANCE OFFICERS

Covert surveillance operations utilise the services of either in-house or externally sourced staff to provide a plainclothes reactive patrol of retailers' premises specifically to detect customer dishonesty and, to a lessor degree, report on weaknesses in loss prevention controls.

Many retailers now use these personnel in a variety of ways. They operate in teams, or are used in conjunction with control room operations where control room staff identify possible suspects on closed-circuit television monitors. Once identified, the suspect is then followed by a covert operative who then observes the suspect's behaviour in the hope of making an apprehension.

Some retailers prefer to use these operatives purely as a means to deter theft. That is, if a suspect is seen to be in the act of a theft, the operative assumes the role of a salesperson to offer assistance, thereby denying the suspect the opportunity to commit a crime. Other retailers require their operatives to detect, then follow the suspect out of the store before introducing themselves and apprehending the suspect for further police action.

Only in some States are covert surveillance officers required to be licensed.

Covert surveillance staff require special qualities. Although most candidates for these positions can be trained to detect and apprehend dishonest customers, many fail in this task. A good covert surveillance officer develops an instinct — one which cannot be taught.

Covert surveillance operations provide support to salespersons through allowing staff to concentrate their own expertise to selling products. This, of course, does not negate the need for salespersons to remain diligent, but the mere fact that a covert support mechanism is in place, often increases morale for staff who feel safer and better equipped to get on with making sales.

CLOSED-CIRCUIT TELEVISION (CCTV)

Closed-circuit television is by far the most effective means by which to deter shop stealing offences (see Figure 9.3). Peter Jones, in his book *Retail Loss Control*, suggests that retailers can achieve a 40% reduction in loss rates if CCTV is well managed and put to its full use (Jones, 1990, p. 226).

When considering the use of any CCTV system, retailers should determine: first, the objectives for the use of CCTV; and second, how these objectives can be achieved.

The objectives may include, for example, a total in-house surveillance system monitored through a central control room with closed-circuit cameras installed in pendant domes or drop-ceiling domes that pan, tilt and zoom into all areas of the retailer's premises. This capability may be further enhanced with sequential switching devices to enable control room operators to manually or automatically switch to any camera on the premises. This can be an excellent control device that enables control room staff to monitor suspect customers or employees. Incidents can be video-recorded through real-time or time-lapse video recorders to provide positive evidence.

In addition, video motion detectors can be set for after-hours monitoring of vulnerable areas to provide audible or visual flashing LED signals to an off-site operator or activate relay switches that automatically turn on time-lapse video recorders.

For some retailers, of course, the sophistication of this type of installation is far beyond both their means and their requirements.

For a small retailer who prefers a simpler approach, the use of highly visible television cameras placed strategically around the store may provide sufficient deterrent to shop stealers who do not know whether the cameras are in use or not. The object here is to demotivate the desire to steal. In some cases, placement of television monitors around the store that show store scenes often achieve the demotivating effect. Staff can also be utilised to view the monitors and, where necessary, provide assistance to those who appear to need help.

The use of smoked, tinted or metallic-coloured pendant or drop-ceiling domes that may or may not contain cameras will add to the illusion that the premises are being monitored. Once again, this will add to the demotivational factors to deny theft.

Figure 9.3. A variety of closed-circuit television equipment

(Illustration is reprinted here by permission and courtesy of Vicam CCTV Systems Pty Ltd Port Melbourne.)

Dummy Cameras

These cameras are also becoming a popular inexpensive means by which retailers can continue the illusion. However, the range of plastic dummy cameras on the market look cheap and are easily recognisable for what they are. Dummy cameras need to be seen to be operating as effectively as real cameras. The extra few dollars spent on dummy cameras that appear to pan, zoom and tilt will be ultimately more effective than the one that is motionless.

CCTV Applications

The applications for CCTV are numerous. Cameras are now available that provide a remote monitoring capability. A miniature camera the size of a credit card can be set up in a clock, a fire sprinkler system, air condition duct — in fact, virtually anywhere — and remotely monitored by radio frequency transmitted to a TV monitor. Coordinated dual camera systems that provide for point-of-sale register transactions are available that reveal images of cashpoint information as well the person conducting the transaction. CCTV cameras can be linked to alarm detection devices that when activated, will dial up a pre-designated telephone number and transmit video images over the lines to a TV monitor in a retailer's home, office or other site. Cameras can also be linked to electronic article surveillance systems that when activated, will video record the action of the person moving through the EAS system. In the same manner, unauthorised after-hour entry to shops can also be video taped.

For retailers, CCTV technology has enormous potential, but the many varied applications can create some confusion resulting in the wrong equipment being utilised. For retailers considering the use of CCTV technology, specific achievement objectives need to be set. Once those objectives are known, retailers can source professional suppliers of CCTV services and equipment to achieve the most cost-effective solution to meet those objectives.

CUSTOMER SERVICE OFFICERS

Customer service officers, unlike covert surveillance officers, provide a highly visible customer service profile that also provides a secondary role for loss prevention initiatives. Customer service officers are usually immaculately groomed and dressed in the retailer's corporate colours. This uniform usually stands out from uniforms worn by other staff. Customer service officers may be in bright jackets bearing the words, for example, 'Customer Service Host' or 'Your Store Host'. These personnel have a primary function to provide maximum service to all customers appearing to be in need of assistance. Their secondary role is to act on all instances of potential theft and offer assistance. Their role is not to apprehend shop stealers, but to provide a high profile preventative measure with an emphasis on service.

ELECTRONIC ARTICLE SURVEILLANCE (EAS) SYSTEMS

Electronic article surveillance systems are perhaps the most innovative physical loss prevention initiative available. Australian and New Zealand retailers have had the availability of EAS systems for some 20 years, and recent technological advances have resulted in a vast array of technologies, tag design and activation systems (see Figure 9.4).

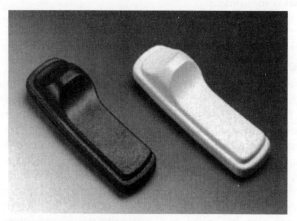

Figure 9.4. Active EAS tags

(Illustration is reprinted here by permission and courtesy of Sensormatic Australia Pty Ltd.)

Claims about the effectiveness of EAS systems differ. Some claims suggest that shop stealing can be reduced by 70–90% (Neil, 1981, p. 66). Other claims are more conservative and suggest that a well-managed system can reduce previous loss rates by about 30% (Jones, 1990, p. 224). Sensormatic, who claim to be the world leader in loss prevention technology, suggest that their Ultra-Max™ system reduces shrinkage by an average of 60%.

The basic EAS system utilises one of four technologies:

- electromagnetic;
- magnetic;
- microwave; or
- radiofrequency.

All EAS systems involve two processes. First, merchandise is tagged by a variety of active tags or labels. Active tags and labels contain magnetic fields, radiofrequency fields or circuits that activate alarm devices positioned at exit points. These alarm activation devices can be positioned:

- as single post systems;
- at exit gates;
- as dual pedestal systems (Figure 9.5);
- as overhead and hidden systems;
- in manikins or display dummies; or
- in floor-mat systems.

Figure 9.5. Dual pedestal EAS system

(Illustration is reprinted here by permission and courtesy of Sensormatic Australia Pty Ltd.)

An EAS system will activate if either of the two following events occurs:

- If a shops stealer steals merchandise which has an active tag and walks past one of the alarm activation devices, the system will generate an audible or visual alarm or both.
- If a salesperson fails to remove or deactivate the tag, the result will be the same.

Some manufacturers have also incorporated a camera into their systems. Esselte Meto retail their 'Photo-Larm EAS system', which takes a snapshot of the person activating the alarm panels.

Primarily, EAS systems are designed to achieve the demotivation of shop theft from two directions.

- First, the physical presence of alarm activation devices placed at exit points is a constant reminder to all potential shop stealers that merchandise is being protected through the use of EAS.
- Second, physical tags placed in full view of the customer on the merchandise itself also acts as a major deterrent.

One consideration for most retailers is to use a combination of:

- passive tags;
- active tag; or
- smart tags.

Used with appropriate signage throughout stores and fitting rooms, the use of EAS systems will certainly provide retailers with cost-effective returns on their investments.

Dual Tagging Techniques

Retailers may combine different strategies to improve their loss rate by using dual tagging techniques where two tags or labels are placed on one garment: one which is visible to the customer, one which is not (Figure 9.6). A second consideration for garment control is the use of both an active tag combined with a passive anti-theft tag such as an ink-tag or other dye-filled capsule. This further demotivates the thief as the thief must overcome two obstacles:

- to successfully pass through the alarm activation device undetected; and
- to then remove the tag from the garments without breaking the ink capsule.

This may overcome situations where shop stealers might consider placing stolen merchandise in foil or metal-lined bags aimed at defeating alarm activation systems.

Some EAS manufacturers employ the use of interchangeable passive and active tags that can be used with another manufacturer's releaser or detacher.

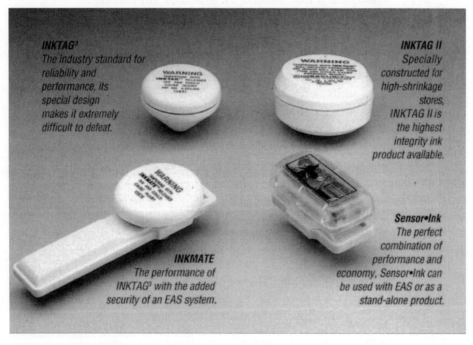

Figure 9.6. Dual tagging techniques using both active and passive tags

(Illustration is reprinted here by permission and courtesy of Sensormatic Australia Pty Ltd.)

Smart Tags

A further and more recent innovation is the use of 'smart tags' (Figure 9.7). These tags themselves have an inbuilt audible alarm system that stays with the merchandise. For a thief who has just stolen merchandise that has a smart tag attached, the tag and the highly audible alarm goes wherever the thief goes. The immediate response for the thief is to separate from the alarm and dump the merchandise and the offending noise.

Figure 9.7. An EAS 'smart tag'

(Illustration is reprinted here by permission and courtesy of Sensormatic Australia Pty Ltd.)

Source Tagging

Another EAS initiative is source tagging where merchandise is actually fitted with active labels at the point of manufacture. This negates the need for staff to tag or label stock when it arrives in store. Source tagging or labelling is usually invisible to customers and therefore may not provide the degree of deterrent as with other more visible tags. Source tagging is also dependent on mass quantity where the retailer has alarm activation devices installed at each of its outlets.

EAS Training

While EAS technology provides a high degree of protection, EAS systems cannot be successfully employed without the thorough training of staff to manage the systems. Training must be conducted to ensure that all targeted merchandise is tagged or labelled correctly. Training should include the correct placement of tags or labels to avoid damage to the merchandise. It is pointless to place a heavy duty electronic tag on a flimsy garment. Placement must also ensure that a customer can still see, feel and try on the garment without tags interfering with this process.

Procedures should also be implemented on alarm activation incidents. As stated, alarms may be activated for two reasons: when a shop stealer attempts to steal tagged merchandise; and when staff fail to remove or deactivate tags. Response procedures should include an apology to customers when an active tag in their possession has not been removed or deactivated. This approach avoids embarrassment for all parties. Customers who are confronted with this approach usually offer up the garment and the process can then be completed. If the alarm is as a result of a theft, the shop stealer may sheepishly offer up the merchandise or flee with or without the goods. In this event, salespersons should not pursue the offender, rather an incident report form should be completed and circulated to warn against further thefts from the offender.

SAFES

The protection of cash and other valuables held by retailers overnight poses many problems. The risks associated with holding cash takings, change and register floats will always be there. The threats retailers are exposed to from burglary and armed hold-ups depend on the levels of retail operations. The range of commercial safes available equals the many needs of end users to safeguard valuable assets. The construction of safes takes into account the many varied forms of attack and are usually graded upon the time it takes to successfully access the contents. Safes are vulnerable to:

- theft of the safe itself;
- key and combination manipulations;
- manually operated tools that rip or cut open older safes;
- flame cutting with oxyacetylene equipment or plasma arc; and
- explosive attack and acid attack.

There are four factors that retailers need to consider when reviewing safe requirements:

- the testing standards applied and how they were achieved;
- the resistance of the contents to fire;
- insurance requirements — insurance cover may only be provided if retailers conform to certain cash limits; and
- the cost-effectiveness of the safe.

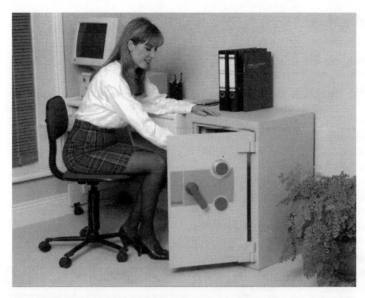

Figure 9.8. An example of a general purpose safe

(Illustration is reprinted by permission and courtesy of Chubb Safes, Chubb Australia Pty Ltd.)

Classification and Standards

Safes can be classified or graded by the levels of importance a retailer might place on its potential contents. For example, a Class 1 safe is for vital and irreplaceable records and documents; Class 2, for important records; Class 3, for useful records; and Class 4, for nonessential records.

Most safes claim some form of fire resistance time frame, and conformity to various international test standards. The US 'UL' standard uses testing methods related to construction standards; whereas the Swedish Bankers Association testing requirement suggests a performance standard.

The UL standard involves predetermined testing based on the time it takes, using specified tools, to overcome the safe. These testing procedures have come under question, because it has been established that, in some cases, safes have been successfully attacked in half the time stated on the UL label.

The Swedish tests, rather than being predetermined tests of safes, actually attack a given sample by any of the known forms used by criminals. The testing agency then allocates a point system based on the timed results. The points are totalled and are placed into one of four categories. The higher the total figure, the better the safe.

Types of Safes

For retailers, safes include:

- in-ground vaults;
- heavy duty strong rooms;
- safe deposit boxes;
- lightweight home safes;
- banking night safes;
- in-floor safes (Figure 9.9);
- wall safes;
- two-key drop safes;
- key and combination safes;
- low, medium to high security stand-alone safes;
- hotel room safes;
- key cabinet, wall or drawer safes;
- security drug cabinet safes for pharmacies;
- computer disk data cabinet safes; and
- fire-rated cabinets for document protection.

Figure 9.9. An in-floor safe

(Illustration is reprinted here by permission and courtesy of Chubb Safes, Chubb Australia Ltd.)

Safes range in price from $350 for the supply and installation of a low-cost drop-slot floor strong box, to in excess of $10,000 for speciality safes. A mid-price range for a good general purpose safe is approximately $1,500–$3,000.

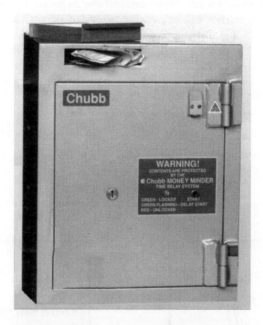

Figure 9.10. Mid-range, general purpose safe.

(Illustration is reprinted here by permission and courtesy of Chubb Safes, Chubb Australia Ltd.)

SIGNAGE

The primary objective for retailers is to maximise profits. To this purpose, retailers entice customers into their stores with bright coloured signage offering discounts and revealing special bargains. Signage in this form motivates the desire in customers to buy. In promoting this desire to purchase, signage is scattered throughout stores in bold and bright colours that are pleasing to the eye and set shopping moods. A large amount of money goes into achieving this selling objective. On the other hand, signage that is aimed to de-motive theft is often of a standard that shows a 'couldn't care less attitude' about whether the retailer lost stock or not.

For anti-theft signage to be effective, it must also reflect the same level of zeal as that of sales signage. Photocopied and tacky A4-sized signs stuck on pillars and fixtures that state 'Warning shop stealers will be prosecuted' are a waste of time. Loss prevention and security signage must be designed to achieve certain objectives. For example, the trend to use 'Condition of Entry' signage is now common place.

Some retailers suggest that any loss prevention or security signage in shops is a de-motivator for sales and refuse to have any loss prevention signage at all. That philosophy is fine as long as the retailer is content with retail loss figures. In some cases, however, retailers have been reluctant to put up loss prevention signage because it may be considered as too aggressive. This is certainly true: many loss prevention signs in stores in Australia and New Zealand *are* aggressive. Signage needs to be designed as both a passive and aggressive means of demotivating theft while still reflecting the culture and image a retailer wishes to portray.

In Chapter 7, it was suggested that the majority of shop theft results from opportunity or impulse thieves. Many of these thieves enter shops without the intention of stealing but, for one reason or another, succumb to temptation due to opportunities offered. It has been suggested that an impulse shop stealer will usually make up his or her mind to steal, or not to steal, within a 3 to 4-second time frame. If retailers can provide passive signage that demotivates that desire in that time, then theft will not occur.

Loss prevention signage is usually either passive or aggressive. Look at the two examples below. Both signs relate the same message, but the tones used are entirely different.

A passive sign is one that appeals to the consciousness of impulse and opportunity thieves.	An aggressive sign, on the other hand, may be more confrontist.

Signage for retailers is an individual choice. The trading culture and philosophy will largely dictate the choice of either a passive or aggressive approach. However, if signage is to be used, it must be at least commensurate with the level and professionalism of other signage used. Retailers will need to analyse the most effective locations. For example, in identified areas such as hidden spots in stores where empty packaging is usually found, subtle signage can be utilised that suggests: 'Our sales staff make a point of frequenting this area to meet your needs.' Fitting rooms are also a high theft-prone area, and each fitting room should contain professional signage that provides the demotivation for theft: 'All garments in this store are protected by anti-theft devices. Our staff are only too happy to deactivate devices at your request.'

LOSS PREVENTION TRAINING PROGRAMS

Retail loss prevention training often falls into the area of specialised training and unless retailers are large enough to develop their own training needs, usually it is far more cost-effective to enlist the training services offered by specialist training providers. Training programs designed, developed and conducted by these agencies are usually offered through employer organisations such as the various employers' chambers of commerce and industry and retail traders associations throughout Australia. In New Zealand, similar training organisations also exist. These agencies offer in-depth courses which cover:

- basic induction loss prevention awareness programs;
- manager and supervisor loss prevention courses;
- employee malpractice awareness programs;
- covert surveillance officer courses;
- armed robbery and violent incident prevention courses;
- shop stealer prevention courses; and
- reduction of human and administration error presentations.

Usually, these loss prevention training providers can tailor training to the individual needs of the retailer and can offer validation services through the conduct of mystery shopping operations in training needs analysis surveys.

REVIEW QUESTIONS

You have just been appointed area sales manager for a small chain of six stores in South Australia. The chain sells clothing, camping gear, sports equipment and other general outdoor merchandise There are some 5,000 units of stock in each of the six stores. The company has an annual turnover of $2.4 million. The annual retail loss amounts to some $84,700, or more than 3.5% of annual turnover.

Your managing director (MD) provides you with the following break-up:

STORE	ANNUAL SALES	DOLLAR LOSS	RETAIL % LOSS
MODBURY	$287,800	$3,222	1.12%
ELIZABETH	$432,000	$26,320	6.1%
KILKENNY	$587,000	$19,220	3.3%
NOARLUNGA	$356,200	$11,160	3.13
BURNSIDE	$472,000	$21,076	4.5%
GLENELG	$265,000	$3,702	1.4%

The MD has already brought in some consultants who have prepared new operational controls which have provided for internal checks and balances. Although all stores are currently alarmed and monitored, each of the six stores is monitored independently. The MD is also worried that some ex-staff members she sacked some months ago still have the shop keys. She says to you: 'I hate shop stealers and I want to give them the message that they're not welcome in my stores. But, I don't want my honest customers feeling intimidated — get the idea!' You of course, say that you do. Your MD then tells you that you have an authorised budget of $15,000 to spend during the next 12 months on any external program, services or equipment you think may be necessary. She says that if you want more than that, you will have to justify it.

The MD also states that she has covered both human and administrative errors, and she does not believe that any staff are now stealing from her. You have no reason to doubt this statement. She believes that she is being hit by professional thieves from Victoria.

She tells you that your objective is to provide her with a full operational shop-stealing prioritised control plan that provides for maximum efficiency, cost-effectiveness, and low staff input which enhances, rather than detracts, from sales.

Prepare your plan and be prepared to justify it.

10 Retail Violence: OHS Considerations

CHAPTER OBJECTIVES

1. To examine the application of occupational health and safety for retail employees.

THE ISSUE OF SAFETY

Case Study No. 40

In Campbelltown, NSW, a staff member believed that a customer had placed some items into his bag and requested a bag inspection. As she bent over to look into the bag, she was 'king hit' by the customer. She suffered a depressed fracture of her cheek bone.

Case Study No. 41

At closing time, a lone sales person was cashing up in a shop near Forest Hill shopping centre in Melbourne, when a male offender entered the shop and without a word, knocked the staff member to the ground and began kicking her. She managed to grasp a fixture attachment and hit the offender with it. The offender then ran out of the shop.

Case Study No. 42

A pizza shop employee in Coburg, Victoria, was punched in the face when he tried to reason with an irate customer. The employee went outside the shop to speak with the customer, who verbally abused then punched him.

Case Study No. 43

A more tragic incident involved a pizza shop employee in New South Wales who was shot dead after he refused to hand over the day's takings from the register.

Case Study No. 44

In Queensland, a service station console operator was seriously injured after an armed offender shot her after she refused to comply with his demands.

There is now a far greater emphasis on workplace safety than ever before. Employers are responsible for the health and safety of all persons employed in their head offices, warehouses, distributions centres, shops and any other workplace used in the course of retail operations. Retailers must also take reasonable steps to ensure that customers remain safe while they are in their shop.

Practices governing workplace safety are governed by common law provisions, State and Federal Acts of Parliament and, in some cases, Local Government Acts.

Occupational health and safety legislation throughout Australia and New Zealand places special emphasis on any employer for the safety and welfare of their employees. The issue of safe work practices also extends to the training of employees in safety issues. It naturally follows that any employer who fails to provide training in safety may render themselves liable to prosecution for occupational health and safety offences under common law, Local Government, State or Federal Acts.

Duty of Care: Common Law

Common law considerations on duty of care are shown in Figure 10.1.

FORESEEABILITY:	Could the incident have been one which the employer should have foreseen?
PROBABILITY:	Was the incident one which could reasonably be expected to occur?
PREVENTABILITY:	Could the incident have been prevented through training awareness or its effects minimised?
CONSEQUENCES:	Were sufficient procedures in place to adequately address all consequences such as post-trauma counselling?

Figure 10.1. Common law provisions of duty of care

Under common law provisions of duty of care, an employer's liability extends to:
- providing a safe place of work;
- laying down a safe system of work;
- providing safe and adequate tools and equipment;
- providing employees with competent fellow employees; and
- providing adequate instruction and supervision of the performance of work.

Applicable Legislation

Figure 10.2 shows the statutory requirements that place specific legal obligations on retailers to ensure the safety and wellbeing of their employees.

FEDERAL

Occupational Health and Safety (Commonwealth Employment) Act 1991 (Cwlth)

The objects of this Act (in part) are:

a) to secure the health, safety and welfare at work of employees of the Commonwealth and of Commonwealth Authorities; and

b) to protect persons at or near workplaces from risks to health and safety arising out of the activities of such employees at work.

NEW SOUTH WALES

Occupational Health and Safety Act 1983 (NSW)

Section 15 (1) states: 'Every employer shall ensure the health, safety and welfare at work of all his employees.'

VICTORIA

Occupational Health and Safety Act 1985 (Vic)

Section 21 provides for the Duties of Employers. Section 21 (c) – (e) requires employers:

c) 'to maintain any workplace under the control and management of the employer in a condition that is safe and without risks to health';

d) 'to provide adequate facilities for the welfare of employees at the workplace';

e) 'to provide such information, instruction, training and supervision to employees to enable them to perform their work in a manner that is safe and without risks to health'.

QUEENSLAND

Workplace Health and Safety Act 1989 (Qld)

Objectives of the Act (in part) are to:

a) Promote and secure health and safety of persons performing work.

b) Protect persons from risks to health and safety.

c) Protect persons from danger to health and safety due to the undertakings conducted at the workplace.

Section 9 (2) (e) provides for:

'Information, instruction, training and supervision.'

(continued...)

WESTERN AUSTRALIA

Occupational Health, Safety and Welfare Act 1984 (WA)

Legal requirements include:

Employers must, as far as practicable, provide and maintain working environments in which their employees are not exposed to hazards. This duty includes:

a) provision and maintenance of a safe system of work;
b) provision of necessary information, training to and supervision of employees to enable them to perform their work safely; and
c) consultation and cooperation with health and safety representatives, if any, and other employees at the workplace, regarding occupational health, safety and welfare at the workplace.

SOUTH AUSTRALIA

Occupational Health, Safety and Welfare Act, 1986 (SA)

Duties of employers:

Section 19 (1) An employer shall, in respect of each employee employed or engaged by the employer, ensure so far as is reasonable practicable that the employee is, whilst at work, safe from injury and risks to health and, in particular:

a) shall provide and maintain so far as is reasonably practicable:
   i) a safe working environment;
   ii) safe systems of work;
   iii) plant and substances in a safe condition;
b) shall provide adequate facilities of a prescribed kind for the welfare of employees at any workplace that is under the control and management of the employer; and
c) shall provide such information, instruction, training and supervision as are reasonably necessary to ensure that each employee is safe from injury and risks to health.

TASMANIA

Industrial Safety, Health and Welfare Act 1977 (Tas.)

Part IV, Duties and Obligations, Section 32 states: 'Every occupier of a work place and every person carrying on an industry shall take reasonable precautions to ensure the health and safety of persons employed or engaged at that work place or in that industry.'

NEW ZEALAND

The Health and Safety in Employment Act 1992 (New Zealand)

Part II, Section 6 states: 'Employers to ensure the safety of employees'.

Figure 10.2. Applicable Federal, State and New Zealand OHS legislation

It appears that the risks that may be associated with failing to provide employees with adequate training to equip them in the event of violent situations could leave retailers vulnerable to prosecution. The case studies provided at the opening of this chapter revealed death and injuries as a direct result of violence. Could those employees have been trained to handle the situations? Could these events have been foreseeable? Were they probable? Could they have been prevented? In nearly all of these cases, the answer must be 'yes'.

Implications for Retailers

The implications of occupational health and safety legislation for retailers are numerous. From a violence point of view, they are twofold: first, salespersons have a legal right to work in a safe environment; second, salespersons have a legal right to be trained in safe work practices. This philosophy is not just for factory plant or equipment application, but also includes areas in which it is foreseeable and probable that employee safety may be at risk. This applies to public areas such as retail shops. If an offender suddenly becomes violent in a shop, the safety and welfare of both staff and customers are at risk. Failing to provide appropriate skills and knowledge training to minimise the risks of injury to both staff and customers in situations such as these may well invite prosecution if it could proved that the retailer failed 'duty of care' obligations.

Protecting Retail Employees

The remainder of this chapter is presented as an instructional plan which retail trainers or loss prevention personnel can utilise to present information that will provide skills, knowledge and expertise required for retail employees to handle the many contingencies that they may confront. The information can either be used as a general resource for readers or be duplicated as overhead transparencies for a classroom environment. Accompanying trainer notes are also included to facilitate the process of learning.

Violent-Incident Prevention (VIP) Training Program

PRELIMINARY INSTRUCTIONS

Preparation

Materials
As a session leader, you will require the following materials:
- overhead projector;
- TV monitor and VHS tape player;
- white board and white board markers;
- participants' reference notes;
- participants' note paper and pens; and
- overhead transparencies covering this session.

Preparation Tasks
Session leaders should arrive approximately 30 minutes prior to commencement of scheduled starting time to:
- set up training facilities;
- test TV monitor, OHP and VHS monitor;
- place sufficient paper and pens for participants;
- place participants' reference notes; and
- review training material.

Delivery Methodology
Group participation through session leader and group discussion:
- maximum number of participants: 30;
- seating formation: semi-circle preferred.

INTRODUCTION

Preliminary Welcome
- welcome each person personally on his or her arrival;
- hand out name tags;
- offer tea and coffee if available;
- maintain program schedule: start on time (no delays longer five minutes); and
- check that everyone is present

Conduct of Program
- welcome all participants as a group;
- introduce yourself (and any other session leaders);
- introduce the session;
- introduce the program;
- give the reasons for learning; and
- state the objectives of the program.

Key Teaching Points
1. Staff are vital to retail operations and, therefore, their safety is paramount.
2. Those staff employed in areas where public interaction is prevalent are the most likely to be exposed to all the variables of human behaviour.
3. Therefore, staff employed in high exposure areas should have highly developed interpersonal skills.
4. This identifies the need for these staff to develop knowledge, skills and techniques to handle those variables.

Session Leader's Work Notes
Persons engaged in roles as either shop owners, store managers, potential managers, supervisors or just working as an employee in the general industry where you might find customers, you are engaged in the world's largest industry. In serving customers, you are expected to:

- acquire the patience of a saint;
- acquire the logic and rationality of a philosopher;
- be a skilled negotiator to handle the many facets of human behaviour; and, at the same time,
- be able to make sales and provide for a first class result.

To be able to perform all these tasks, it is vital that you are acquainted with all the knowledge, skills and techniques available to enable you to handle the many contingencies that occur in the normal course of everyday business.

Reasons for Learning

1. Emphasis on greater accountability.
2. Occupation, health and safety legislation requiring not only the development of safe and secure work environments, but also development of skills, knowledge and techniques for staff to handle contingencies.
3. Other law emphasising training for staff members.

Session Leader's Work Notes

In today's trading world, there is a greater emphasis on accountability. Employers are accountable, business managers are accountable and employees are accountable. It would appear that where ever we look we see greater focus on:

*   management by objectives;
*   total customer service;
*   best industry practice; and
*   total quality management;

These may seem to be industry buzz words or phrases, but the underlying theme is an ever increasing emphasis on accountability. We have to acknowledge that we live in a turbulent world and that our exposures to risk are greater than ever before. There is greater emphasis on businesses to provide an environment where both customers and staff can go about their business feeling safe and secure. Accountability is not just another business requirement.

Accountability is enshrined in common law in both Federal and State occupational health and safety legislation and under local government acts. Formal accountability is now demanded, and employers are required to provide staff employed in the industry with *skills, knowledge and techniques training* necessary to handle the many contingencies that may occur to enable staff to remain safe.

STATEMENT OF OBJECTIVES

Session leader to state:

At the conclusion of today's program, each participant will have gained the skills, knowledge and the techniques necessary to implement safe and secure practices that will minimise your exposure to the risks involved. In particular, you will be able to:

[Show OHT]

[Provide a short explanation of each objective.
Limit each explanation to 15 seconds or less.]

VIP PROGRAM'S OBJECTIVES

- Develop an awareness of current commercial and financial crime prevalence.

- Develop a greater value of security work standards and a preparedness for potential violence.

- Prepare a workplace to minimise opportunities for violent incidents

- Implement action plans during incidents of violent confrontation.

- Implement actions plans after incidents of violence.

- Utilise a systems approach for describing violent offenders, their weapons and their vehicles.

- Maximise the use of incident report forms by recording vital information for subsequent police action.

- Take control of crime scenes to :

  a) ensure the wellbeing and safety of all staff and witnesses; and

  b) protect the crime scene from any contamination.

- Understand the value of utilising post-trauma counselling services, assistance programs and other applicable agencies for victims of crime.

- Describe employer obligations under both common law and relevant legislation.

Figure 10.3. VIP program statement of objectives

[Remove OHT]

Session Leader to ask:

Q. I'd like to ask the following question: In what field do you work?
1. Invite participant discussion.
2. Note main points on whiteboard.
3. Lead to:
    *   retail industry;
    *   service industry;
    *   restaurants;
    *   pharmacists;
    *   supermarkets;
    *   convenience stores;
    *   video libraries;
    *   other areas?

Q. What is the common denominator here?
1. Invite participant discussion.
2. Note main points on whiteboard.
3. Lead to:
    *   access open to general public.

Q. We have established the fact that the very nature of our respective businesses involves a great deal of public interaction. After all, without that interaction, we would not have any customers, therefore no sales and no business. But are we in fact at risk? If we are, from what?
1. Invite participant discussion.
2. Note main points on whiteboard.
3. Lead to:
    *   armed robbery or robbery situations;
    *   abnormal customers;
    *   violent customers assault;
    *   person adversely affected by alcohol or drugs;
    *   violent or abusive persons;
    *   persons who indecently expose themselves;
    *   persons who use fitting rooms and rest rooms for deviant behaviour;
    *   other examples?

Q. Are we overemphasising these problems? Are we being too cautious? What is the reality of the situation?

1. Invite participant discussion — refer to:
    *   newspapers cuttings on display; and
    *   current police statistical data.
2. Hand out statistical data — emphasise the fact that the figures shown in the handout represent only what is actually reported.

[Show OHP with current published police statistics]

3. Further evidence:

    In early 1994, The Australian Institute of Criminology in Canberra released its first Australian National Survey of Crimes against Business. In the report, the author John Walker revealed that:

[Show OHT]

CRIMES AGAINST BUSINESS

*   1 in 40 of the businesses surveyed had experienced an armed robbery.

*   1 in 10 of the businesses surveyed had reported an assault on one of their staff members.

    (Although the survey indicated it was extremely rare for an armed robbery to occur, we can make an assumption that, although an armed robbery may be unlikely for the majority of organisations, the chances of some form of violence occurring is still relatively high.)

Figure 10.4. Crimes Against Business Survey — Australian Institute of Criminology

[Remove OHT]

Q. Can it happen to me?

1. The crimes against business survey revealed that the larger the organisation, the greater the likelihood of an assault (ratio of 1 : 20) The smaller the business, the smaller the likelihood of an assault (ratio of 1 : 60). These figures show that assaults can still take place anywhere.

2. Invite participants to provide case studies.

We have now established that the very nature of our business exposes us to risk.

Q. What else makes us targets?

1. Invite participant discussion.

2. Note main points on whiteboard.

3. Lead to:
   - levels of cash are usually high;
   - merchandise is on open display;
   - premises are open to the general public.

Q. If we are exposed to the risks involved in a possible violent incident, do we have a legal responsibility to our employees to equip them with necessary knowledge and skills to minimise the danger involved?

1. The answer to this question is simply 'yes'.

   Let us look at the possibility of a male employee being seriously injured after he tries to prevent an armed robbery by attacking the offenders.

   If he had never received any structured training regarding safety and protection, could he have a case against his employer? Once again, the answer is 'yes'.

Q. What does the law say?

1. In very basic terms, there appears to be two courses of action open. First, the employee could sue the employer under common law provisions of duty of care. Considerations include:

[Show OHT]

COMMON LAW PROVISIONS OF DUTY OF CARE

FORESEEABILITY

- Could the incident have been one which the employer should have foreseen?

PROBABILITY

- Was the incident one which could reasonably be expected to occur?

PREVENTABILITY

- Could the incident have been prevented through training awareness or its effects minimised?

CONSEQUENCES

- Were sufficient procedures in place to adequately address all consequences such as post trauma counselling etc.?

Figure 10.5. Common law provisions of duty of care

[Remove OHT]

2. Under common law provisions of duty of care, an employer's liability extends to:

[Show OHT]

EMPLOYER'S LIABILITY UNDER COMMON LAW

- To provide a safe place to work.

- To lay down a safe system of work.

- To provide safe and adequate tools and equipment.

- To provide employees with competent fellow employees.

- To provide adequate instruction and supervision of the performance of work.

Figure 10.6. Employers liability under common law

[Remove OHT]

3. Relevant State authorities could take action against the employer under applicable State or Federal occupational health and safety legislation. In Victoria, Section 21(1) of the *Occupational Health & Safety Act* states:

[Show OHT]

OCCUPATIONAL HEALTH & SAFETY ACT STATES:

Responsibilities of Employers, Section 21(1):

- 'An employer shall provide and maintain so far as is practicable for employees a working environment that is safe and without risks to health.'

Duties of Employers, Section 21(2):

- 'An employer shall provide and maintain:

  a. SAFE PLANT AND SYSTEMS OF WORK

  b. SAFE USE, HANDLING, STORAGE AND TRANSPORT OF PLANT AND SUBSTANCES

  c. SAFE WORKPLACES*

  d. ADEQUATE FACILITIES FOR EMPLOYEES WELFARE

  e. INFORMATION

   INSTRUCTION

   TRAINING*

   SUPERVISION

  to enable employees to perform their work safely.'

Figure 10.7. OHS Statutory requirements in Victoria

[*Emphasise these points]

[Remove OHT]

4. Session leader to cite other examples where necessary.

It would appear then, that the risks associated with failing to provide employees with adequate training to equip them in the event of violent situations could leave employers wide open to legal prosecution. For the general business community at large, this could be a very real concern.

Q. What can I do to protect myself and my staff?
1. Actions must be a combination of both proactive measures and reactive measures.

Q. What can we do that may constitute proactive measures?
1. By proactive we mean simply being prepared. We already conduct security operations without really thinking about it. For example, when we left our homes today, we didn't leave the front and back doors open. We didn't leave the windows open. We automatically went around our homes and conducted a basic security check to ensure we minimised our exposures to the risks of burglary.

    The same occurred when we parked the car. We instinctively locked it — once again to minimise the risk of a break in.

    Now, we need to think 'security', not only for our business lives but also for our personal lives. We need to think 'safety and protection' about small things that we take for granted, such as:
    *   leaving doors open that should be closed or locked;
    *   leaving cash registers unattended or open;
    *   leaving handbags in open and unlocked backrooms;
    *   counting end-of-day takings in full view of the general public; and
    *   telling all and sundry how much money you took today.

These are the sorts of things we tend to forget about. Let's take a few minutes to discuss all the positives and the negatives involved.

SYNDICATE EXERCISE 1

Form participants into four syndicates. Have each syndicate appoint a syndicate leader.

Discussion Topics

Syndicate A and Syndicate C to list all the positive proactive measures that businesses can take to minimise exposure to risks of violence.

Syndicate B and D to list all the negative things that some businesses might have a habit of doing that may expose their staff to the risk of violence.

Maximum discussion time should be five minutes. After five minutes, have the participants resume their normal seating and have each syndicate leader present their findings as follows:

1. Syndicate A
2. Syndicate B
3. Syndicate C
4. Syndicate D

1. Write headings of 'POSITIVES' and 'NEGATIVES' on the whiteboard.
2. List findings under each heading.

Session Leader to Explain

Under the heading of 'POSITIVES', we have listed a considerable number of proactive measures we can take to maximise safety and protection. Generally, these measures are referred to as 'target hardening'. Target hardening refers to the processes which aim to reduce the target potential of a business, making it more difficult for a profitable attack to be conducted. Target hardening is a proactive measure and is one undertaken prior to an event occurring. This includes the development of policy and procedures with regard to:

[Show OHT]

TARGET-HARDENING PREVENTATIVE STRATEGIES

- Cash-handling procedures

- Opening and closing procedures

- Key controls

- Alarm systems

- Cash refund policies

- Shop stealing

- Customer complaints

- Customer injuries etc.

- Incidents of violence

- Incident Report Forms

Figure 10.8. Target-hardening preventative strategies

[Remove OHT]

A good business has a set of proactive guidelines that enable staff to react to any given situation. Banks, for example, may use pop-up screens, bullet-proof glass, closed-circuit television cameras an uniformed guards. All these proactive measures 'hardens' targets against the possibility of an armed robbery.

However, one of the more negative side-products of target hardening is that, while the more traditional targets of banks, building societies, service stations and convenience stores continue to implement proactive target hardening policies, robbers may focus on softer targets such as retail stores, restaurants and similar targets. This is known throughout the industry as 'displacement'.

Displacement is the transfer of the attention of robbers to softer targets that do not appear to have rigorous proactive policies.

Q. What's the answer?

[Show OHT]

STRATEGIES TO CONTROL EFFECTS OF DISPLACEMENT

- Analyse your security needs.

- Design appropriate proactive security systems and precautions into your operating philosophy.

- Develop and implement appropriate policies and procedures.

- Conduct training programs that give staff the skills, knowledge and techniques necessary to meet your operational needs.

- Constantly review and validate your security and security training needs.

Figure 10.9. Prevention strategies to control effects of displacement

[Remove OHT]

Once policy and procedures have been set to maximise the operational efficiency of your business, staff members need to be trained in the use of them. Training sessions could be conducted through in-house training, induction sessions or through external agencies. But training must be done and records maintained on employee files that detail the level of training each employee has undertaken. The VIP training program you are now undertaking is a proactive measure. As part of your training philosophy, training must take place on three aspects of violent incident prevention:

[Show OHT]

VIOLENT-INCIDENT PREVENTION

THE BEFORE

- **Proactive measures:** Primarily designed to deny /delay or to deter the incidents occurring in the first place.

THE DURING

- **Action plans:** Designed to provide staff with the necessary skills to provide safety and protection for themselves and their customers.

THE AFTER

- **Reactive measures:** Designed to ensure the emotional and physical wellbeing of all involved and to provide police with as much accurate information about the offenders as possible.

Figure 10.10. The three elements of violent incident prevention

[Remove OHT]

We can well understand the rationale for developing proactive policies. Let's now look at what we can do in the event of an armed robbery utilising the principles of the before, the during and the after.

ARMED ROBBERY PROCEDURE

Armed robbery is a traumatic and emotional event which, in many cases, results in totally unpredictable behaviour. The likelihood of emotional and physical injury is high and therefore we must ensure that any proactive action we undertake is designed to minimise the risk of injuries. The preservation of life and the prevention of injury are paramount, and no amount of money supports the taking of risks that might invite serious injury or even death.

CARE

An attitude must be developed that highlights the need for safety. We need to care about what happens. We need to care about ourselves, care about our workmates and care about our customers. In any armed robbery situation, I want you to actively think of the word care. Why? — because we are going to use the word care to instil into our minds a formula for remaining safe in any violent situation. By utilising the word care, we will trigger action plans during violent incidents that highlight four key factors:

[Show OHT]

C A R E

C — (Remain) **calm** and in **control**

A — **Act** on all instructions

R — **Remember** features of the offender

E — **Ensure evidence** is retained

Figure 10.11. The four key factors of CARE

In this OHT, we introduce the word 'CARE'. CARE is a mnemonic where each letter prompts your memory. We have chosen the word 'CARE', as it means to feel concern or display an interest. When confronted with a potentially violent incident, we should immediately think of the word 'CARE' because it will reduce immediate feelings of anxiety and assist you to focus on emotions that express concern and interest for the safety of yourself and others around you.

[Remove OHT]

Let's look at CARE, more closely. We have dealt with proactive measures that are designed to deter/delay and deny opportunities from occurring. CARE deals primarily with action plans during the event and reaction plans after the event.

Action Plans
Action plans are designed to provide staff with the necessary skills to provide safety and protection for themselves and their customers.

[Show OHT]

CARE — C: REMAIN CALM & IN CONTROL	
STAY CALM AND REMAIN IN CONTROL	Most robberies take less than a minute. The longer robbers are on premises, the more nervous they will be.
STAND SIDE ON TO THE ROBBER	This reduces your profile, and is also less threatening to the robber.
AVOID SUDDEN MOVEMENTS	Robbers are often extremely nervous and unstable. Avoiding sudden movements prevents robbers from over- reacting. If you have to move, tell the offender what you have to do: 'The money is in the register, I have to open it.'
RAISE YOUR HANDS	This is a sign that you are submitting. If robbers can see your hands, they will be less likely to be nervous.
IF SAFE, CREATE A PHYSICAL BARRIER	Wherever possible, create a physical barrier between yourself and the offenders. This might mean moving behind a fixture, or other solid object. However, sudden movements must be avoided.

Figure 10.12. The 'C' of CARE

[Remove OHT and show next OHT]

CARE — A: ACT ON ALL OFFENDER'S INSTRUCTIONS

TELL THE TRUTH

Answer all questions truthfully. If robbers discover you have lied, they may react unexpectedly.

DO EXACTLY AS YOU ARE TOLD AND OBEY ALL INSTRUCTIONS

Robbers may be under the influence of drugs or alcohol. Therefore they are prone to being unstable and may react unexpectedly if they don't get want they want.

Figure 10.13. The 'A' of CARE

[Remove OHT and show next OHT]

CARE — R: REMEMBER FEATURES OF THE OFFENDER(S)

OCCASIONALLY GLANCE AT THE ROBBERS

Remembering features of the robbers may assist police in apprehending the robbers. Look for physical characteristics.

AVOID STARING

This may cause an over reaction by the robbers.

REMEMBER WHAT THE ROBBERS TOUCHED & WHERE THEY WALKED

This information is invaluable to police. They may be able to take fingerprints from counters, or identify robbers through patterns left by footwear.

Figure 10.14. The 'R' of CARE

[Remove OHT]

Incident Report Forms

To remember all the features of offenders, their action, their weapons and their vehicles, we need some form of documentation to record this information. This document needs to be clear, concise and correct to enable police to act on the information. The information that may assist the police in apprehending the offenders includes:

[Show OHT]

Remembering features of the robbers may assist police in apprehending them.

Look for physical characteristic such as:

HEIGHT	Use your door height markers.
HEAD	Headgear colour, shape, type.
HAIR	Length, colour, style.
AGE	Estimate age.
COMPLEXION	Light, olive or dark skinned.
NATIONALITY	Australian, European, Asian etc.
ACCENTS USED	Distinctive speech mannerisms.
CLOTHING	Shirts, jackets, trousers, footwear.
WEIGHT	Skinny, medium or heavy build, fat.
EYES	Bloodshot, blue, green.
UNUSUAL FEATURES	Scars, tattoos, unusual rings or jewellery.
NAMES USED	Did they use names? Tom, Simon.

Figure 10.15. Physical characteristics checklist

[Remove OHT]

SYNDICATE EXERCISE 2

Prior to session, enlist the service of a person not involved with the program. Complete a blank OHT Incident Report Form and insert the person's full description. At a prearranged signal:

• have the person walk into the session with a fictional message;
• ask the person to remain while you write out a fictional reply;
• give the person your fictional response;
• thank the person; and
• apologise to the group for the interruption.

[Show OHT — Figure 10.16. Incident Report Form]

1. Explain the use of the form. Highlight direction of travel, weapons used, vehicles used.

2. While OHT is being displayed, hand out pads of Incident Report Forms to all participants. Advise that:

    • the person who recently entered and produced a note was an offender;

    • the note was actually a demand note; and

    • police have requested that we complete an Incident Report Form while they are en route to the scene.

    Have all participants complete an Incident Report Form — allow approximately five minutes for this task.

[Remove OHT]

3. Show the OHT with the full description of the 'offender' (the person who brought in the note).

    • Compare this with participants' reports.

    • Highlight anomalies between the two.

    • Emphasise the need for reports to be as:

      clear, correct and concise as they possible

INCIDENT REPORT FORM IRF NO: 123456

Location:	Date:	Time:

Address:		

City:	P/Code:	Phone:

Type of incident:	Person reporting:

WHAT HAPPENED?

_____

_____

_____

HOW DID IT HAPPEN?

_____

_____

_____

WHY DID IT HAPPEN?

_____

_____

_____

WITNESS DETAILS (Use more than one page if necessary)

Name:		

Address:		

City:	P/code:	Phone:

Figure 10.16. Incident Report Form (continues...)

DESCRIPTION OF OFFENDER (Use more than page if necessary)						
height	hair	eyes	age	build	race	accent
compl'n	headgear	upper body	lower body	footwear	any unusual features	

Police notified: YES NO	Police Station:	Officer attending:	When:

Describe any weapons that may have been used — knife, revolver, automatic pistol, rifle, shotgun, single or double barrel, under or over, sawn offs, other weapons used:

_____

Other relevant information:

_____

_____

_____

_____

Figure 10.16. Incident Report Form

Reactive Measures

So far, we have looked at CAR of CARE. The 'E' of CARE is part of the reactive measures we take.

Reactive measures are designed to ensure the emotional and physical wellbeing of all those involved and to provide police with as much accurate information as possible about the offenders.

[Show OHT — Figure 10.17. The 'E' of CARE]

[Remove OHT]

Session leader to reiterate:
- Armed robbery is a violent and traumatic event.
- Safety and protection are the key issues.
- Remember **C A R E**.

During this part of the program, we have developed skills, knowledge and techniques that will assist us to minimise exposure to physical and emotional injury during a potentially violent armed robbery. However, armed robberies or hold-ups are not the only incidents that have the potential to cause us injury. Let's look at other potential violent incidents.

CARE — E: ENSURE EVIDENCE IS RETAINED

SAFEGUARD THE SCENE

Your shop is now a CRIME SCENE. You must leave everything intact. Leave everything untouched to avoid contamination. You may unwittingly destroy vital forensic evidence. If demand notes were used, leave them were they are. Keep everyone away from areas that robbers were in. Delegate this responsibility to a staff member if necessary.

AFTER THE ROBBERY:

WHEN THE ROBBERS HAVE LEFT

Take charge and stay in control.

WALK TO THE DOOR, CLOSE AND LOCK IT

This prevents robbers from re-entering your store. It also ensures the safety and protection of those present. Check the direction and mode of travel of the offenders if you can. Obtain a registration number if possible, but stay on the site, avoid the temptation to follow.

REASSURE ALL PRESENT

Feelings of anger, cowardice, guilt and paranoia may result after any traumatic incident. Reassure everyone that they have done nothing wrong.

Remain calm and stay in control

RENDER FIRST AID IF NECESSARY

If anyone is injured, render immediate first aid. Use your store first aider if present. People may react by going into shock.

Figure 10.17. The 'E' of CARE (continues...)

CALL 000 AND ASK FOR POLICE	The operator will ask you several questions such as your name, where you are, if anybody has been injured. They will ask questions on the number of offenders, their descriptions, their direction and mode of travel. Remain calm and speak slowly and clearly. Keep the line open at all times.
ASK ALL WITNESSES TO REMAIN ON SITE	This ensures that police will be able to obtain all the available evidence. If a witness refuses to stay, let them go, but get their names, addresses and phone numbers and hand to police on their arrival.
COMPLETE YOUR INCIDENT REPORT FORMS INDIVIDUALLY	Give an Incident Report Form to everyone present and ask them to commence filling them out. Avoid discussing the robbery with others and avoid the temptation to copy someone else's form. This will prevent distortion of the facts. Police need to have your information, not information influenced by others.
CALL HEAD OFFICE	Tell Head Office what has happened. Keep it short and simple. Request the services of your Trauma Counselling Service. Robberies are a traumatic event: symptoms may not show up immediately. The attendance of a trauma counselling team may well reduce the effects of post-trauma shock.

Figure 10.17. The 'E' of CARE (continues...)

ON POLICE ARRIVAL	Allow uniform police to enter. If plain clothes police arrive, ask for their police ID. Follow all their instructions. Cooperate fully. Your information is vital in the follow-up investigation and may result in the detection and apprehension of the robbers.
MEDIA REPORTERS	Refer all media inquiries to the senior police member present. Advise all employees present that policy forbids any communication with the media. Police have experience with the media and will provide the media with the necessary facts.
POLICE GO AHEAD TO RECOMMENCE OPERATIONS	Once you have been given the go ahead to clear up, delegate responsibility to clean up any damage etc. Balance the till and ascertain levels of cash missing. Document all results and advise Head Office.
TRAUMA COUNSELLING	On arrival of the trauma counselling team, be guided by their instructions. These may include: • contacting relatives or friends; • sending employees home with an escort; • using a taxi if necessary; • ensuring that somebody will be home for them; • calling replacement staff if necessary.

Figure 10.17. The 'E' of CARE

ABNORMAL CUSTOMERS

1. As we have stated earlier today, abnormal customers are those customers who are:

[Show OHT]

ABNORMAL CUSTOMERS

- Persons adversely affected by alcohol or drugs.

- Violent or abusive persons.

- Persons who indecently expose themselves.

- Persons who use fitting rooms and rest rooms for deviant behaviour.

Figure 10.18. Abnormal customers

[Remove OHT]

2. Although these incidents are rare, they have all in turn occurred to staff at one time or another. Behaviour such as this is unnatural, deviant and totally unacceptable.

[Show OHT]

ACTIONS PLANS IN DEALING WITH ABNORMAL CUSTOMERS

REMAIN CALM   Stay in control and remember: you have
                             done nothing wrong.

REASSURE STAFF

DEFUSE THE   Depending on the circumstances:
SITUATION
                             • Attempt to calm the person.

                             • Take down a complaint if warranted.

                             • Politely request the person to leave
                               your shop.

REQUEST ASSISTANCE   Quietly call the police immediately if
                             the behaviour has resulted in an
                             offence being committed. Also seek
                             assistance from shopping centre
                             security personnel where applicable.

NOTIFY MANAGEMENT   Report the incident to management on
                             an incident report form.

Figure 10.19. Action plans in dealing with abnormal customers

[Remove OHT]

3. The important thing to remember here is your safety and the safety of your staff
    and your customers. If you believe that the safety of any person is threatened
    by the actions of an abnormal customer, then leave the area immediately and call
    the police.

TRAUMA COUNSELLING

Author's Note. In conducting this phase of the Violent Incident Prevention Program, trainers are strongly advised to enlist the services of trained and qualified consulting or clinical psychologists.

During the course of today's program, we have constantly referred to trauma, stress and emotional injury.

Q.   Just what is post-traumatic stress?
1.   Symptoms or reactions that follow a stressful or traumatic incident, and may include:

[Show OHT]

REACTIONS FOLLOWING A TRAUMATIC INCIDENT

- Mental replays of the incident

- Avoidance of situations or thoughts which remind you of the incidents

- Increased anxiety

- General lack of interest

- Physical symptoms

- Behavioural changes

Figure 10.20. Reactions following a traumatic incident

[Remove OHT]

Q.   Who is affected?
1.   Everyone, not only the person traumatised, but all those around the person, family friends loved ones etc.

Q. What can cause it?

1. Although not exhaustive, this list describes some of the incidents likely to create post traumatic stress.

[Show OHT]

INCIDENTS WHICH CAN CAUSE POST-TRAUMATIC STRESS

- Armed hold-ups

- Shootings

- Work-related accidents

- Sexual assaults

- Serious assaults or threats of harm to your life or to your family, friends and workmates

- Disasters such as road, plane, train or ship disasters

- Accidents or disasters resulting from natural causes such as bushfires, earthquakes or floods

---

Figure 10.21. Incidents likely to cause post-traumatic stress

[Remove OHT]

2. Post-traumatic trauma will affect everyone. Symptoms may appear immediately or not for some time, even for several months. Each person's response is unique and personal. Common reactions are:

[Show OHT]

COMMON REACTIONS IN POST-TRAUMATIC STRESS

SHOCK   Disbelief at what has happened, event may seem unreal. Feeling numb.

FEAR   Fear of damage to yourself or death. Panicky feelings. Strong irrational feelings or phobias.

ANGER   General irritability and angry outbursts, feeling' of injustice and senselessness. Anger at what caused this to happen. 'Why me?' is often asked.

NUMBNESS   Diminished feelings. Feelings of detachment. Feeling estranged or isolated from others.

GUILT   Guilt for feeling and acting helpless. Not reacting as you would have liked. For having survived while others did not. Feeling 'responsible' for another's death.

SADNESS   Feelings of loss.

LONELINESS   Feelings of being alone.

Figure 10.22. Common reactions in post-traumatic stress

3. These feelings are not uncommon for most people who have experienced a traumatic event.

[Remove OHT]

4.   As an example, lets look at some of the emotions experienced for an armed robbery or other violent incident. The immediate reactions may be:

[Show OHT]

POST-TRAUMATIC STRESS RESPONSES

- Panic

- Helplessness

- Tearfulness

- Anger

- Confusion

Figure 10.23. Emotional reactions to post-traumatic stress

[Remove OHT]

5.   But these reactions may be through the application of the basics of CARE philosophy. If we understand the rational of normal reactions and behaviour to trauma then it follows that we are better equipped to handle the reactions.

[Show OHT]

POST-INCIDENT REACTIONS

- Fear of being along

- Startled by noises

- Suspicion of new or unusual customers

- Fear of the dark

- Difficulty in leaving home

- Distress over media reports of similar incidents

- Desire to change jobs

- Lowered self-esteem (I should have done more)

- Thoughts of the offender finding you

Figure 10.24. Post-incident reactions

The common denominator here is that most people experience these feelings one way or another.

[Remove OHT]

Q. When do you know that you are suffering post incident reactions?
1. If you have experienced a trauma-related incident, you will have experienced some of the symptoms expressed. These are normal. Your symptoms have also extended to your family. Family reactions may include a sense of loss, or feelings of helplessness. There may even be some family disintegration. It is imperative that families work together as a unit. Sometimes it is the family unit who becomes the best judge as to when to seek outside help.

Q. How can people help?
1. Invite participant discussion.
2. Write responses on white board.
3. Lead to:
   * by making understanding comments;
   * by offering support;
   * by developing an employee assistance program which includes the provision of post trauma counselling;
   * by enlisting the services of a professional organisation such as:
     - The National Trauma Clinic.

SESSION SUMMARY

Over the past few hours, you have covered relatively new ground. The VIP program has provided you with new skills and new techniques. During the course you have:

[Show OHT]

SESSION SUMMARY

- Developed an awareness of current commercial and financial crime prevalence.

- Described employer obligations under both common law and relevant legislation.

- Developed a greater value of security work standards and preparedness for potential violence.

- Prepared a workplace to minimise opportunities for violent incidents.

- Implemented action plans during incidents of violent confrontation.

- Implemented action plans after incidents of violence.

- Utilised a systems approach for describing violent offenders, their weapons and their vehicles.

- Maximised the use of incident report forms by recording vital information for subsequent police action

- Taken control of a crime scene to ensure:

  - the wellbeing and safety of all staff and witnesses; and

  - the protection of the crime scene from any contamination.

- Understood the value of utilising post-trauma counselling services, assistance programs, and other applicable agencies for victims of crime.

Figure 10.25. Outcomes of the VIP program

[Remove OHT]

Over the past few hours, you have undertaken an intensive proactive program designed to minimise the risks of physical or emotion injuries caused through violent confrontation.

VALIDATION PROCESS

We are keen to learn if the training you have received today is relevant to your job and has, in fact, met the training objectives we have just reviewed. We believe that training needs should be constantly validated or critiqued. We ask that you take a few moments to complete our program validation sheet which will enable trainers to constantly meet your needs. The report can be totally anonymous.

Finally, we encourage you to:

*   pass on your new skills, knowledge and expertise;
*   encourage the use of CARE;
*   encourage others to undertake the VIP program; and
*   seek specialist advice to develop proactive policies and procedures.

End of Session Tasks

*   gather up unused paper and pens;
*   clean the white board;
*   turn off all TV monitors, VHS players and OHP (unless otherwise directed);
*   check training room for any property left by participants;
*   turn off lights;
*   lock up facilities;
*   return keys; and
*   collate validation data and amend program as required.

REVIEW QUESTIONS

1.   Take a group of retail employees and conduct the lesson as previously described.

2.   Validate your actions.

Bibliography

ABS, *Retail Trade —Australia,* Cat. No. 8501.0, AGPS, March 1995.

Albrecht, W. Steve and Wernz, Gerald, W. 'The Three Factors of Fraud', *Security Management,* Vol. 37, No. 7, July 1993, pp. 95–96.

Anderson, J.T. 'The Woolworths' Extortion', *Australian Police Journal,* Vol. 39, No. 2, 1985, pp. 52–75.

Australian Federal Police, 'Looking for counterfeit Australian notes — A guide for cash handlers', *Information Bulletin,* Currency Squad, Southern Region Australian Federal Police, May 1995.

Barefoot, J. Kirk and Maxwell, David. A. *Corporate Security Administration and Management.* Stoneham, Butterworths, 1987.

Baumgartner, Albert. *Industry Strategies to Reduce Retail Theft.* Paper presented at the Inaugural Retail Loss Prevention Symposium, Sydney, March 1994.

Berlin, P. 'Does Employee Theft Exceed Shoplifting?', *The Peter Berlin Report on Shrinkage Control,* April 1993, p. 5.

Berlin, P. *Key Controls for Retail Systems and Procedures.* Jericho, The Peter Berlin Retail Consulting Group Inc., 1990.

Berlin, P. 'Highlights of 1994: Shrinkage Survey of Canadian Retailers', *The Peter Berlin Report on Shrinkage Control,* No. V, 1994, p. 7.

Berlin, P. 'Shrinkage Survey of Canadian Retailers', *The Peter Berlin Report on Shrinkage Control,* Nov/Dec 1993, p. 1.

Berlin, P. 'Shoplifters Walk an Emotional Tightrope in Your Store', *The Peter Berlin Report on Shrinkage Control,* Feb 1990, pp. 6–7.

Berlin, P. '1993 Shrinkage Survey sponsored by Price Waterhouse', *The Peter Berlin Report on Shrinkage Control,* Sep 1993, p. 1.

Berman, Barry and Evans, Joel. R. *Retail Management: A Strategic Approach.* New York, Macmillan Publishing Company, 1986.

Bologna, G. Jack and Lindquist, Robert. *Fraud Auditing and Forensic Accounting.* Toronto, Wiley, 1987.

Braithwaite, M. and Fuller, P. *Retail Shrinkage and Other Stock Losses —Results of the 2nd UK Retail Survey January 1992,* London, Touche Ross & Company, 1992.

Bullen, Stephen. *Internal Audit in the Retail Industry —A Pro-active Approach to Reduce Shrinkage.* Paper presented at the Crimes Against Business Conference, conducted by the Australian Institute of Criminology, Melbourne, March 1994, p. 10.

Byrne, Denis E. and Jones, Peter H. *Retail Security: A Management Function.* Surrey, 20th Century Security Education Ltd, 1977.

Carson, Charles R. *Managing Employee Honesty.* Los Angeles, Security World Publishing Company Inc., 1977.

Cave, Michael and Botten, Christobel. 'Looters were choosing sunglasses that suited them'. *The Age,* 24 Nov, 1986.

Challinger, Dennis. *Stop Stealing from our Shops: Retail Theft in Australia*. Canberra, National Retail Crime Prevention Council, 1988.

The Chicago Tribune. 'Cop Between Rocks and a Hard Head', 10 Nov, 1994, p. 3.

Clarke, John. P. and Hollinger, Richard. C. *Theft by Employees*. Lexington, DC Heath & Company, 1983.

Criminal Justice Commission (Queensland). *Corruption Prevention Manual*. Toowong, Criminal Justice Commission, 1993.

Cropp, Allen. *Shrinkage Control*. Paper presented at the Retail Loss Prevention Symposium, Sydney, March 1994.

Crowley, Francis. *Documentary History of Australia*, Vol. 1, West Melbourne, Thomas Nelson Australia Pty Ltd, 1980.

Curtis, Bob. *Retail Security —Controlling Loss for Profit*. Woburn, Butterworths, 1983.

Davis, Ron D. 'Dodging the Fickle Finger of Fraud', *Security Management*, Vol. 39, No. 3, March 1995, p. 47.

Duffee, D. and Fitch, R. *An Introduction to Correction: A Policy and Systems Approach*. Pacific Palisades, Goodyear Publishing Company Inc., 1976.

Flew, A. (Editorial Consultant). *A Dictionary of Philosophy*. London, Pan Books Ltd, 1979.

Fraud Policy and Prevention Branch – Federal Justice Office. *Best Practice Guide —Fraud Control in Commonwealth Departments and Agencies*. Canberra: Attorney-General's Department, 1993.

Geason, Susan and Wilson, Paul R. *Preventing Retail Crime*. Canberra, Australian Institute of Criminology, 1992.

Gordon, Harry. 'The World of 1788 — A Nation is Born', Special Issue, *Time Australia*, No. 1788–1792, 1987, p. 91.

Grover, Kenneth R. *Retail Security Policy Manual*. Stoneham, Butterworth–Heinemann, 1992.

Haldane, Robert. *The Peoples Force – A History of the Victoria Police*. Carlton, Melbourne University Press, 1986.

Hall, T. *Tobruk 1941 – The Desert Siege*. Sydney, Methuen Australia Pty Ltd, 1984.

Harris, Barry. *Fraud and Theft in Supermarkets*. Paper presented at the Retail Loss Prevention Symposium, Sydney, March 1994,.

Hayes, Read. *Retail Security and Loss Prevention*. Stoneham: Butterworth–Heinemann, 1991.

Heath, Ian W. and Hassett, John T. *Indictable Offences in Victoria*. Melbourne, F.D. Atkinson, Government Printer, 1983.

Hollinger, Richard C. *1993 National Retail Security Survey —Final Report*. Gainesville, University of Florida, 1993.

Hurst, Barbara E. 'Technology Challenges the Trade', *Security Management*, Vol. 38, No. 3, March 1994, p. 15a.

Iannacci, Jerry. 'Leading the Charge against Credit Card Crime', *Security Management*, Vol. 38, No. 8, August 1994, pp. 83–87.

Jones, Peter H. *Retail Loss Control*. London, Butterworths & Co. (Publishers) Ltd, 1990.

Krupka, W.M. 'Retail Crime: The Problems, the Parameters, the Realities', *Police Chief*, No. 51, 1984, pp. 146–148.

Lawrence, Jeanette and Hore, Phillippa. 'Greedy, Needy, or Troubled? High School and University Students' Views of Shopstealers', *Technical Report*, Department of Psychology, The University of Melbourne, undated, p. 2.

Lawrence, Jeanette and Toh, Catherina. 'Professionals' and Non-Professionals' Views about Shop Stealing', *Technical Report*, Department of Psychology, The University of Melbourne, Jan 1989, p. 3.

Little, Norman. *Australia's Foundations*. Sydney, Reed Education, 1972.

5 O'Clock News (video recording) 4 Sep 1994, Channel 10 Television, Australia.

Madden, M. *Retailing in Australia, 1991–1992,* Cat. No. 8613.0, ABS, Aug 1–2, 1993.

Neill, W. Jock. *Modern Retail Risk Management*. Sydney, Butterworths Pty Ltd, 1981.

Paul, William. *The Victoria Police Guide*, 5th edn, rev. Kevin Anderson. Melbourne, Government Printer, 1969.

Pease, Allan. *Body Language: How to Read Others' Thoughts by their Gestures*. Sydney, Pease Training Corporation, 1981.

Rabey, Gordon P. *The Training Handbook — A Do It Yourself Guide For Managers*. Melbourne, The Business Library Information Australia, 1990.

Riell, Howard. 'Crime Prevention in the Commissary', *Security Management*, Vol. 38, No. 10, Oct 1994, pp. 36–38.

Ross, Stephen David. *Moral Decision: An Introduction to Ethics*. San Francisco, Freeman, Cooper and Company, 1972.

Schaub, James L. and Biery, Ken D. *The Ultimate Security Survey*. Newton, Butterworth–Heinemann, 1994.

Sennewald, Charles A. *The Process of Investigation*. Stoneham, Butterworth–Heinemann, 1981.

Stenning, P.C. and Shearing, C.D. 'Corporate Justice: Some Preliminary Thoughts', *Australian and New Zealand Journal of Criminology*, Vol. 17, No. 2, June 1984, pp. 79–86.

Sutherland, E.H. and Cressy, D.R. *Criminology,* 10th edn, Santa Barbara, J.B. Lippincott Company, 1978.

Taylor, Peter. *Australia, The First Twelve Years*. Sydney, George Allen & Unwin Australia Pty Ltd, 1982.

Turner, Cecil J.W. *Kenny's Outline of Criminal Law*, 16th edn, Cambridge, Cambridge University Press, 1952.

Victoria Police. 'Evidence'. Student handout. Detective Training School, Victoria Police, 1983.

Victoria Police. 'The Investigator'. Student handout. Detective Training, Victoria Police, 1983.

Walker, John. *The First Australian National Survey of Crimes against Business*. Canberra, Australian Institute of Criminology, 1994.

Walsh, Timothy J. and Healey, Richard J. *Protection of Assets*. Santa Monica, Merrit, 1982.

Wilson, Paul R. (Ed). *Issues in Crime, Morality and Justice*. Canberra, Australian Institute of Criminology, 1992.

Index